Just War and Jihad

Recent Titles in
Contributions to the Study of Religion

Just War and Jihad

HISTORICAL AND THEORETICAL PERSPECTIVES ON WAR AND PEACE IN WESTERN AND ISLAMIC TRADITIONS

Edited by
JOHN KELSAY and
JAMES TURNER JOHNSON

CONTRIBUTIONS TO THE STUDY OF RELIGION, NUMBER 28
Henry Warner Bowden, *Series Editor*

Greenwood Press
NEW YORK • WESTPORT, CONNECTICUT • LONDON

Library of Congress Cataloging-in-Publication Data

Just war and jihad : historical and theoretical perspectives on war
and peace in Western and Islamic traditions / edited by John Kelsay
and James Turner Johnson.
  p.   cm. — (Contributions to the study of religion, ISSN
0196–7053 ; no. 28)
  Papers presented at four conferences held at Rutgers University in
the winter and spring of 1988–1989.
  Includes bibliographical references and index.
  ISBN 0–313–27347–2 (alk. paper)
  1. War—Religious aspects—Christianity—Congresses.   2. War—
Religious aspects—Islam—Congresses.   3. Just war doctrine—
Congresses.   4. Jihad—Congresses.   5. War (International law)—
Congresses.   I. Kelsay, John.   II. Johnson, James Turner.   III. Series.
BT736.2.J87   1991
297'.72—dc20   90–19914

British Library Cataloguing in Publication Data is available.

Copyright © 1991 by John Kelsay and James Turner Johnson

Library of Congress Catalog Card Number: 90–19914
ISBN: 0–313–27347–2
ISSN: 0196–7053

First published in 1991

Greenwood Press, 88 Post Road West, Westport, CT 06881
An imprint of Greenwood Publishing Group, Inc.

Printed in the United States of America

The paper used in this book complies with the
Permanent Paper Standard issued by the National
Information Standards Organization (Z39.48–1984).

10 9 8 7 6 5 4 3 2 1

Copyright Acknowledgments

The author and publisher gratefully acknowledge permission to use the following:

Loeffler, Reinhold, *Islam in Practice: Religious Beliefs in a Persian Village*. Reprinted by
permission of the State University of New York Press. Copyright © 1988 State
University of New York.

Contents

Foreword

As one of the three most significant religious traditions with Western origins, Islam has developed a following that stretches around the globe. Because of political and economic crises in recent years, this faith and its peoples have become more highly visible. But Europeans and Americans still know very little about Muslims, their culture, or their ideology. This book tries, as does its companion volume, *Cross, Crescent, and Sword,* to change that lamentable state of affairs by supplying pertinent information drawn from a wealth of sources. It pulls together chapters by eight specialists in Islam and other aspects of Western culture. The result instructs readers about the religious contexts that nurtured ideas regarding statecraft, international law, and the aims and limits of peace and warfare.

These chapters are accessible to general readers, affording a much better understanding of Muslim ways of life and the manner in which they intermesh with other cultural traditions. At the same time, this book's collaborators explore issues at the cutting edge of new scholarship, testing the possibilities of correlating heretofore disparate fields of study into a better cognitive synthesis. As the introduction points out, the following chapters develop a balanced approach, grounded equally well in both analytical and historical perspectives. They are not doctrinaire about either Christian or Muslim ideology; and they pay special attention to the practical situations from which ideas emerged and to the concrete experiences that made such thoughts workable. Without becoming mired in too much detail or remaining entirely abstract, they probe difficult questions where love and faith inform ethical situations in which law, public policy, and limited force must be brought to bear.

As is often the case in specialized studies, these chapters concentrate on discrete amounts of material within somewhat narrowly defined topics. But they are judiciously chosen subjects, selected because they shed light on a great many ancillary areas. There are still untold riches to be discovered in relation to Muslim life, with its different cultural expressions and varying emphases. These chapters open new avenues for English-speaking readers to learn about Islam and its place as a partner in Western thought. It is hoped that, in addition to contributing new knowledge about a relatively unknown field, this book will stimulate others to extend the horizons of learning and understanding even further.

Introduction

John Kelsay

In the winter and spring of 1988–89, a group of scholars met four times for discussions of Western and Islamic approaches to war, peace, and statecraft. The present work and a companion volume[1] constitute one result of these conferences, which were held at Rutgers University and sponsored largely by a grant from the United States Institute of Peace.

One major purpose of the conference series was to encourage dialogue between scholars in two highly diverse and, up to this point, disengaged fields. The first of these, represented in this volume by James Turner Johnson, John Langan, David Little, and William V. O'Brien, focuses on the study of Western responses to issues of war, peace, and statecraft. Historians, theologians, ethicists, and international lawyers have all made contributions to this study. Over time they have produced a substantial body of literature focusing on the just war tradition—perhaps the most significant and certainly the most influential form of discourse about war, peace, and statecraft developed by Western culture.

The second field is that of Islamic studies. The chapters here by Fred Donner, Richard C. Martin, Bruce Lawrence, and Ann Mayer show that the study of Islamic religion and culture has up to now been underrepresented in discussions of war and peace. While there have been some noteworthy exceptions to this rule, for example in the work of Majid Khadduri,[2] much remains to be done. The Islamic tradition, in both its classical and contemporary forms, presents a rich variety of materials for discussions of statecraft, including issues connected with the justification, conduct, and ultimate aims of war. It was the hope of James Turner Johnson and myself, as codirectors of the conference series, that an organized conversation with scholars focusing on the history and development of the just war tradition might provide an opportunity for Islamicists to probe more deeply into this rich variety. At the same time, we hoped that an ongoing conversation with Islamicists might deepen and enrich the perspectives of scholars working on the just war tradition.

The format of the conference series, and also of this book, was established to facilitate such conversation. Scholars of the just war tradition and Islamicists examine a number of important issues from their differing perspectives. Four chapters deal with "foundational" issues, that is, the identification of the sources and basic themes of religious thought that influence the two traditions. Two other groups of chapters address the more specialized issue of "holy war," or war fought for religious reasons, and the relationship of the two traditions to international law. In every case the chapters are broadly historical and comparative in nature. Together they set forth a great deal of information about Western and Islamic approaches to war and peace.

From the essays in this volume we may extract two of the major themes that preoccupied participants in the conference series. These are indicated in the subtitle of this volume: "historical" and "theoretical" perspectives on war and peace in Western and Islamic traditions. Each of these terms deserves elaboration.

First, the chapters stress historical perspective. Fred Donner provides the most succinct indication of this tendency when he writes that "what really matters in human terms is how the Muslims of a particular time and place dealt with the vital questions of war and peace." We are not to focus, then, on a select canon of theological and juridical texts as the key to understanding the "official" Islamic attitude toward war—at least, not purely and simply. Even studies that do focus on such texts must locate them historically, geographically, and culturally. As Donner indicates, such an approach forces consideration of the impact of "non-Islamic" factors on Muslim approaches to war, peace, and statecraft. While one cannot deny the intrinsic and crucial influence of such canonical sources as the Qur'an and the example of Muhammad, there can be no doubt that other factors—such as the traditions of Byzantine or Sassanian cultures in the lands conquered by the early Muslims, or the needs of statecraft created by imperial rule during the high period of the Abbasid or Ottoman influence—also figure in the development of Muslim attitudes and thus must be counted as sources of Islamic conceptions of war.

On this point, Donner's chapter parallels the contributions of Johnson and O'Brien. Here, as in a number of his publications, Johnson stresses that the just war tradition is a cultural product. By this he means to indicate the way that a variety of ideas and institutions have played a role in shaping the approach of Western culture to the issues posed by the phenomenon of war. Just war tradition is never simply a religious or theological tradition; it draws its material from legal, military, and historical sources. At the same time, the tradition of just war thinking cannot be reduced to its sources or to the interests of particular institutions or social classes. It represents the attempt of Western culture as a whole to respond to the moral issues posed by war—or better, to respond to the variety and complexity of its own beliefs over time.

Similarly, O'Brien stresses the interaction between the just war tradition and international law. Historically the just war tradition incorporated large aspects of the "law of nations," conceived in terms of the practice of nations and the agreements between them. This was particularly true of the *jus in bello*. O'Brien concludes with a call for contemporary just war theorists to learn from this history and to incorporate the considerations of international law into their discussions of contemporary warfare.

The importance of history is also stressed, albeit in different ways, in the chapters by Bruce Lawrence and Ann Mayer. Lawrence focuses his attention on the place of *jihad*, or effort in the path of God, in the context of the struggles of Muslims with Western colonial and imperial power. He thereby highlights the crucial role of power in discussions of Islam and war. There are important differences between the rhetoric of *jihad* as used by resisters to European power in Morocco or Algeria and the formally similar rhetoric of Sunni jurists working in the context of Islamic imperial power during the period of the high caliphate. Similarly, there are important differences between the appeal to *jihad* of minority, Shi'i jurists and those of the Sunni majority. Considerations of power, which affect and are affected by changing historical realities, help to qualify our understanding of religious discourse about war and statecraft.

With respect to international law, Mayer's chapter suggests a similar focus on the power relations between Western and Islamic cultures. Yet the overall impression of her chapter is different from that of Lawrence's. In particular, the relationship between the Islamic tradition and international law is multivalent, and contemporary Muslims show a good deal of ambivalence about it. On the one hand, international law appears to be a product of Western culture, a judgment that is clearly suggested in William V. O'Brien's chapter. Mayer's evidence indicates that many Muslims recognize this, and it is (for some) a troubling fact. Is international law, after all, simply another tool of Western imperialism? On the other hand, Muslim governments recognize the authority of international law, and for good reasons. International law and the Islamic tradition are in agreement on a number of issues. Beyond this, international law itself is a developing phenomenon to which Muslims are contributing as they participate in a variety of international organizations, particularly the United Nations. With respect to judgments about the standing of national liberation movements and the determination of legal personality, for example, Muslim groups have been able to exercise influence. The relationship between the Islamic tradition and international law is not one-directional; the two traditions are at present interacting and thus affect one another's development. Thus a focus on history can lead to discussions of the interaction of Western and Islamic approaches to war, peace, and statecraft even as it tries to draw out their particular, contextual character.

The second direction of conversation suggested by the chapters collected here is theoretical. Johnson's chapter points to this, even with its historical focus. According to Johnson, the just war tradition cannot be reduced to its component parts: "Understood as a totality, it encompasses and represents attitudes, beliefs, and patterns of behavior from across the breadth of that culture over time." Just war thinking is an attempt by various persons and groups to respond to religious and moral beliefs they hold to be justified or true. Similarly, Donner's concern with "how the Muslims of a particular time and place dealt with the vital questions of war and peace" does not rule out consideration of the place of Muslim beliefs. Claims about the normative value of the Qur'an or the example of Muhammad are crucial to Muslim views about war and peace, as about the world in general. How should the theoretical claims of particular traditions inform a conversation about the justification and conduct of war?

John Langan and David Little address this question. Both focus on the role of Christian beliefs in the development of the just war tradition. For Langan, such factors as the value placed by the Christian tradition on love and on the example of Jesus suggest that Christian justification of war is problematic. The key to such justification has been the development of a "historical theodicy" in which beliefs about God's providence and the duty of love are related to beliefs about the fallen nature of humanity. The diversity of Christian beliefs creates the possibility of Christian just war thinking even as it creates the possibility of Christian pacifism or "crusade" thinking.

David Little elaborates on the relationship between these various possibilities. Taking his cue from Roland Bainton's discussion in *Christian Attitudes toward War and Peace*, Little argues that the "Christian story is a story of shifting combinations among . . . three essentially irreconcilable attitudes": just war, pacifism, and the crusade. Some of Bainton's historical analyses, in particular his unqualified attribution of a crusade mentality to the Puritan movement, are in need of refinement. Little notes that Puritan discourse not only reflected the kind of discourse characteristic of a crusading approach to war but also contributed to the "emergence of a secular just war theory of force . . . whereby the legitimation of force is completely disconnected from religious belief and practice."

From Little's perspective, then, the key issue is not so much the development of a historical theodicy as the shifting relationship between religious and moral justifications for war. One sees a demonstrable shift in Western/Christian thinking about war at the beginning of the modern period, a shift away from the notion that religion is a just cause of war and toward an emphasis on moral justifications for war.

Whether we follow Langan or Little on these matters, the suggestion is that discussions of war, peace, and statecraft will attend to the explicit beliefs advocated by persons and groups and to the relationships between them. By contrast, Richard Martin's chapter suggests that some aspects of the problem of war remain hidden from view so long as our attention is focused on explicit beliefs. Those who wish to learn about religious approaches to the question of war must attend to the multiple levels of meaning present in any act of human speech or writing. Martin maintains that while one such level is comprehended in the analysis of "moral traditions in terms of what texts qua texts say propositionally," another "level or dimension of meaning . . . is what the speaker, writer, or reciter of a text wanted to do by offering the text—perhaps something barely alluded to, or even suppressed, in the text but indicated in the context in which it is produced or recited or interpreted." An examination of Islamic discourse indicates that judgments about war and peace, or about politics in general, are at some deep level an attempt to deal with the more basic problem of violence. They are thus related to aspects of Islamic tradition that are usually ignored in discussions of warfare: the phenomenon of religious argumentation, for example, or rituals of blood sacrifice. Martin concludes with a proposal and challenge for discussions of religion and war: "The symbolism and semantics of violence in religion . . . require a much greater and more complex interpretation of the religious experience than the issues of *jus ad bellum* and *jus in bello* comprehend."

What shall we make of these various perspectives? In the closing paragraphs of chapter 1, Johnson notes that it is possible to argue that just war tradition has expanded beyond its Western borders. Insofar as there is an international community that acknowledges the authority of international law, "just war tradition has become global." Following this line of reasoning, Johnson argues that the "present theoretical task [in discussions of war and peace] is to reach beyond such de facto acceptance of the international law of war to discover whether it is possible to identify underlying this phenomenon a global consensus as to justice in war." One could certainly argue that the conference series of which the contributions collected here were a part is one way—a very preliminary one, to be sure—to address this theoretical task.

Given the diverse perspectives illustrated in this volume, however, it seems requisite to ask: what chance does such a proposal have? Consider

Martin's challenge, for example. If the fundamental problems are more complex than the criteria of the just war tradition comprehend, there seems to be little point in addressing the issues connected with the "universality" of the just war tradition. Again, to come at the issue from a slightly different perspective, Lawrence's chapter makes the point that the distinctive religious and cultural experiences of Western Christians and Muslims make conversation difficult. For Lawrence, this fact is underscored by the predominance—in international law and in our conference series—of Western just war categories. The "universal" claims made for such categories build upon the "preformed biases" of Western culture—actually, of a particular gender, class, and race that dominate that culture. The development of just war thinking is intimately connected with the triumph of Christianity, the phenomenon of patriarchy, and the world hegemony of nation-states in which Caucasians hold power.

This issue of the universal possibilities of just war categories ran throughout the conference discussions and exists as an undercurrent throughout this volume. Faced with the fact that Muslims also claim universal validity for the judgments of their tradition on war, peace, and statecraft, some participants reflected on how the discussion might look if it began by assuming the predominance of Islamic categories. In the end, however, it seems one must agree with Bruce Lawrence's comment:

Even though preformed biases of gender, class, and race are inscribed into the "universal" theory of just war, they do not negate our task; rather, they complicate its performance by underscoring just how necessary it is. . . . While we cannot erase our own ideological formation, we can at least stretch its parameters by conversing with ourselves as well as about those others whom we are endeavoring to understand.

It is a commonplace that comparative inquiry should avoid the danger of ethnocentrism. In the context of these studies, that danger would take the form of assuming the normative superiority of just war tradition to the claims of Islamic thought. Whether they succeeded completely or not, the contributors to this volume worked hard to avoid this danger. Lawrence's comment reminds us of another commonplace, less often acknowledged but equally important: comparative study must have a starting point. In the mode suggested by Max Weber, our conversation (and thus, the present chapters) began with the categories of a tradition that has value "for us"; that is, the just war tradition. Discussions of Islamic categories are necessarily developed in response to this tradition.

There is no a priori reason, however, that discussion must keep to the form of (just war) proposition and (Islamic) response. Granted the

starting point, comparative inquiry becomes a conversation that can
proceed in many directions. For example, we might note that the Islamic
tradition is consistent in construing just wars as those fought for religious
reasons. As Ann Mayer points out, even those Muslims who understand
jihad as limited to defense nevertheless think of defending Islamic territory or the interests of the Islamic community. This stands in contrast
to the judgment of modern just war theory (following the sixteenth-
century Spaniard Victoria) that "difference in religion is not a just cause
of war." It also reminds us that this modern judgment builds on the
enormous shift in Western approaches to war that took place at the
beginning of the modern period. David Little describes this as the development of a "secular just war theory"; William O'Brien speaks of an
emphasis on "humanity" in war. The different conceptions of just cause
implied in the contrasting traditions of just war and *jihad* point to a more
fundamental difference in cultural experience and identity. Whatever
has occurred by way of secularization in the traditionally Islamic lands,
it is still appropriate to speak of Islamic culture. By contrast, the role of
Christianity in the societies associated with "the West" is rather different
and in some ways less direct. That is one justification for adopting the
terminology "Western" (rather than "Christian") and "Islamic" in the
subtitle of this volume.

The differing roles of religion in Western and Islamic cultures may be
evaluated in a number of ways. It is often assumed, for example, that
the exclusion of religion as a cause of war is the characteristic contribution
of just war tradition, one that saves Western civilization from "holy
wars," in which religious motivations lead to the use of indiscriminate
and disproportionate tactics. Yet, as examination of Islamic materials
shows, this typical judgment about religion and war is open to question.
The judgments of Islamic law and the practice of Muslims over time
bear witness to a notion of war as a rule-governed activity. To fight "in
the path of God" does not necessarily lead to total war, any more than
fighting according to the interests of humanity ensures that wars will
be conducted with discrimination. In this connection it is much more
interesting to compare the different content given to discrimination and
proportionality by the two traditions, and to ask about the role of an
emphasis on religion or on "humanity" in establishing this content, than
to assume the a priori superiority of the latter.

In any event, comparative study and the conversations that develop
out of it do not deny the validity of the just war tradition. They extend
and transform it. At least, that seems a likely hypothesis, based on the
chapters in this volume. It may be true, as Martin argues, that there is
more to the relation of religion and war than the *jus ad bellum* and *jus
in bello* comprehend. It is certainly true, as Lawrence suggests, that there
are important historical and theoretical asymmetries between Western

and Islamic approaches to war, peace, and statecraft. At the same time, it is difficult to deny the persistence of certain concerns across the boundaries of particular cultures: that violence not be gratuitous; that wars be justified; and that conflicts be governed by a concern to distinguish the innocent from the guilty. These, I submit, are human concerns, tied to the necessities of ordering social life. They are, in turn, deeply entrenched in the traditions of just war and of Islamic thought. That they are formal considerations that particular cultures specify in a variety of ways is obvious. That they provide a starting point for further conversation—a conversation that will indicate both agreement and disagreement between Western and Islamic approaches to war and peace—is equally so.

Expressions of gratitude are due to many who contributed to this project. First, James Turner Johnson and I wish to express our thanks to the participants in the conference series on Western and Islamic traditions. Besides those who contributed to the present volume, these include Charles Butterworth of the University of Maryland; Courtney Campbell, formerly of the Hastings Center but now an assistant professor at Oregon State University; Khaled Abou El Fadl of Princeton University; Stephen Lammers of Lafayette College; Robert Phillips of the University of Connecticut, Hartford; Abdulaziz Sachedina of the University of Virginia; Jeffrey Stout of Princeton University; and Tamara Sonn of St. John Fisher College. Our thanks are also due to many others without whose tireless and able assistance the project could not have been carried out: at Rutgers, Henriette Cohen, who meticulously arranged travel and accommodations for the four seminars; Connie Burke, who assisted in these arrangements; at Florida State, Joel Elliott, who prepared the composite Select Bibliography that appears in this volume; and Maureen Jackson, who provided invaluable help with that awesome terror of the modern scholar, the computer. Finally, we wish to thank the United States Institute of Peace for the grant that made this project possible, Rutgers University for hosting the conference series, and both Rutgers and Florida State University for various types of support for the work illustrated in this volume.

NOTES

1. See James Turner Johnson and John Kelsay, eds., *Cross, Crescent, and Sword: The Justification and Limitation of War in Western and Islamic Tradition* (Westport, Conn.: Greenwood Press, 1990).

2. See, for example, Majid Khadduri, *War and Peace in the Law of Islam* (Baltimore: Johns Hopkins Press, 1955), and his translation of the very important treatise of al-Shaybani (d. 804), *The Islamic Law of Nations: Shaybani's Siyar* (Baltimore: Johns Hopkins Press, 1966).

I

Foundational Issues

1

Historical Roots and Sources of the Just War Tradition in Western Culture

James Turner Johnson

INTRODUCTION: AN OVERVIEW OF THE CULTURAL CONTEXT

The just war tradition of Western culture is a product of the influence of a broad variety of cultural sources over a centuries-long history of development. While strong religious sources and manifestations of this tradition can be identified, it is not a purely or uniquely religious phenomenon. While at times the development and continuity of this tradition have depended heavily on the influence of secular forces, it is not properly reducible to them. Rather, just war tradition is a major moral tradition of Western culture, shaped by both religious and nonreligious forces and taking shape in both religious and nonreligious forms within that culture. Understood as a totality, it encompasses and represents attitudes, beliefs, and patterns of behavior from across the breadth of that culture over time. Identifying its historical roots and sources and sorting out their relationship and their particular contribution to the development of just war tradition is thus a complex task.

Historical and anthropological evidence suggests that every human culture has generated some analogue of just war tradition: a consensus of beliefs, attitudes, and behavior that defines the terms of justification for resort to violence and the limits, if any, to be set on the use of violence by members of that culture.[1] Sometimes these have taken the form of elaborate and broadly approved rules for the practice of war, as in China during the period of the warring states, when warfare was carried on as a highly stylized game by the belligerents. Similar gamelike aspects of the justification and limitation of conflict can be observed in medieval chivalry in Western Europe and among the American Plains Indians prior to the coming of white people.[2]

Making armed conflict more gamelike tends to increase its frequency as the price for restraining its destructiveness. The sheer frequency of the resort to armed force for whatever purposes are deemed justified may lead to efforts to impose cultural restraints on such resort, as by controls on who may bear arms, restrictions on who may authorize resort to arms, and more tightly circumscribed circumstances in which use of armed force is held to be justified. When this happens within a culture, the pendulum may swing the other way, and the gamelike aspects of armed conflict may diminish: such conflict becomes no longer a game, but something far more serious.[3] Thus, ironically, restraints on the resort to violence seem historically to have an inverse relationship to restraints on the use of violence within a culture.

The breakdown of a consensus on the proper limits to be observed on the destructiveness of armed conflicts does not come only from a reaction aimed at limiting the frequency of resort to violence. More severe strains on cultural efforts to restrain the destructiveness of such conflicts come from two other factors.

First, the end of war as a game comes when enemies do not play by the same rules. Thus, in practice, cultural restraints on violence are observably difficult to maintain in violent conflicts that cross important cultural boundaries.[4] Then the enemy may be represented as subhuman or otherwise not worthy of the same respect shown adversaries in intracultural combat, or he may be represented as an embodiment of evil forces or values that must be combated at all costs. In either case a more ruthless style of fighting may be justified against him. Even when both belligerents attempt to observe their own conventions of restraint, where these do not match, the conventions are placed under great stress, and their power to mitigate the destructiveness of the conflict in question diminishes. One important expression of this kind of challenge to the effort to restrain the destructiveness of conflicts is the idea of holy war, an armed struggle on behalf of the constellation of values associated with religion and the concept of the divine, or, more broadly, ideological war, armed struggle against threats to the highest values accepted in the culture and against the values represented by the enemy.[5]

Second, the introduction of new technology unanticipated by the older conventions or otherwise not included in them loosens the effect of those conventions on the actual character of combat. Western medieval attempts to outlaw certain weapons correlate with the fact that these were not weapons used by the knightly class; rather, the weapons in question—crossbows, siege weapons, bows and arrows—were those employed by commoners or by mercenary bands. In the American West the introduction of firearms radically disrupted and reshaped the code and practice of warfare of the Plains Indians, replacing the custom of counting coup by touching an enemy or stealing something of his as a sign of manhood with the much more deadly practice of using the rifle to wound or kill.

Reciprocally, when restraints are loosened for other reasons, the effect may be to heighten the ideological character of the conflict (as occurred in Iran during the recent war with Iraq) or to encourage the introduction of more destructive means into the conflict (as in Iraq's repeated use of poison gas in the same conflict). In short, cultural restraints on war are universal but somewhat fragile, and they are difficult to extend across cultural boundaries. Thus cross-cultural conflicts tend to undercut the effect of existing traditions of restraint, and such conflicts may also introduce the element of ideological justification for one's own cause and with it the justification of more ruthless, unrestrained forms of conflict.

All these general characteristics of cultural efforts to justify and limit war can be observed, at one point or another, in the just war tradition of Western culture. This tradition has developed around the two foci of justification and limitation, denominated within the tradition by the Latin terms *jus ad bellum*, which defines when it is justified to resort to armed force, and *jus in bello*, which sets the boundaries or limits for the use of justified force. The latter has gamelike aspects, determining who are the proper "players" and who not (the combatant-noncombatant distinction) and establishing the rules to be observed in the conflict: defining the proper proportionality between means and proximate ends, sometimes attempting to outlaw certain weapons or classes of weapons, and establishing sanctions aimed at protecting from harm in war the rights, persons, and property of noncombatants and individuals rendered hors de combat. If the *jus ad bellum* can be said to have gamelike aspects, then its rules have to do with the game of statecraft. In its broadest form it defines what causes justify resort to armed force, who may rightly authorize such resort, what the context must be before it is right for such resort to take place, and what sort of ends may properly be sought by it. In just war tradition taken as a whole, the *jus ad bellum* and *jus in bello* exist as two aspects of the same body of doctrine and practice. Yet between them there are important differences as to source, purpose, and pattern of development, and efforts to draw wisdom from the tradition tend to bring out the tension between them.[6]

Just war tradition represents a middle ground between two more extreme sorts of positions. On the one hand are the various forms of pacifist opposition to war, notably including sectarian pacifist rejection of participation in warfare and utopian pacifist efforts to transform society so as to bring an end to resort to war.[7] At its most restrictive, just war tradition may produce the same practical judgments as such pacifist approaches; yet it differs fundamentally from them in accepting, in principle, that war is sometimes justified for the protection and preservation of important values. At the other end of the spectrum of attitudes regarding war, the highest values of the culture are defined in terms of religion or other transcendent ideology, and unlimited means of war may be justified as appropriate responses to threats to those values. This is the idea of holy war or ideological war.[8] Within Western culture, this idea is historically and thematically a special, extreme conception within just war tradition, arising when religion or ideology transforms the definition of the categories of the *jus ad bellum*.[9] From the beginnings of the modern period, the main line of just war tradition has rejected religion (and implicitly ideology) as a justifying cause for war, and much of the development of this tradition over the last four centuries has focused on restraints that are to be observed in fighting against any enemy for whatever cause. Thus, in general, the just war idea accepts, against pacifism, the possibility that armed conflict may be justified to protect and preserve values and denies, against the idea of holy/ideological war, the justifiability of unlimited means of war in the service of such values.

The deep roots of just war tradition are in the customs, attitudes, and practices of the cultures that have principally fed it: those of the Hebraic world and the world of classical antiquity and, later, those of the Germanic societies of northern Europe. Even after the coalescence of just war ideas and practices into a coherent tradition (a phenomenon of the Middle Ages), much of its development took place insularly within Western culture. Yet more global claims have been made for the ideas of justification and restraint contained within this tradition. Particularly in the modern period major theorists and apologists for these ideas have identified them as grounded in natural law and thus, in principle, knowable by all people everywhere and binding upon them. The Spanish Scholastic Franciscus de Victoria used a form of natural-law argument to extend just war theory into his consideration of relations between the Spanish explorers and settlers and the Indians of the New World. Two generations later Hugo Grotius made the natural-law grounding of just war concepts the basis of the universal law of nations he described in *Of the Laws of War and Peace*. During the nineteenth and twentieth centuries the political and cultural hegemony exercised by Western nations led to the extension of positive international law, expressing just war concepts conceived as grounded in natural law, over much of the globe. Through the vehicle of the international law of war a version of just war tradition today exists far beyond the cultures in which this tradition originally took root and later developed.

THE ORIGINS OF JUST WAR ATTITUDES, CONCEPTS, AND BEHAVIOR

The Hebraic Contribution

The roots of just war tradition in Hebraic culture are to be found principally in the Old Testament stories of the wars of Israel during the Exodus and the wanderings prior to the entry into Palestine (the books of Exodus and Numbers), the era of the conquest and settlement of Palestine (the books of Joshua and Judges), and the period of existence of Israel as a nation with a king, particularly that segment of this latter history having to do with the reigns of Saul and David. Much of what the Old Testament records about war in the earlier periods has to do with war commanded by God, a form of holy war.[10] In such war not only was God conceived as commanding the conflict, but he was understood to be directly involved in the fighting, warring with the divinities of the enemy on the cosmic level even as the soldiers of Israel dealt with their human counterparts on the earthly level. All Israelite males capable of bearing arms were expected to do so. No quarter was to be given; all the enemy, persons and property, were to be "devoted to the Lord for destruction" (Joshua 6:17). Yet such war was not entirely without examples of mitigation. In Joshua 11, which describes the war between Israel and an alliance of cities and peoples, only those cities are destroyed that actively participated in aggressive action toward the Israelites; this is a form of the idea of noncombatant immunity. In Deuteronomy 20:19–20 the fruit trees and vines are explicitly named not to be destroyed, an idea that later appears as an argument against a scorched-earth policy in warfare, a policy that violates the principle of discrimination.[11]

In a moral tradition whose development extends over centuries, what is most important is the memory and use made of such historical elements by later generations. In normative Jewish thought, as illustrated by the medieval commentator Maimonides, the contribution of the Hebrew Bible to moral tradition on war is summarized in terms of three types of conflict: "religious war" (directly commanded by God), in which participation is mandatory for all males able to bear arms and in which spoils are to be "devoted to the Lord for destruction"; defensive war, in which all males must participate who do not have outstanding religious duties and the prosecution of which involves some mitigation of destruction; and the "optional wars" of kings, offensive wars undertaken at the discretion of kings of Israel, participation in which is excused by a greater range of other obligations and prosecution of which is mitigated by considerations of noncombatancy and proportionality.[12] In Christian thought Ambrose and Augustine both employed the example of the Israelite wars commanded by God as warrant for their own justification of using Roman military force against heterodox forms of Christianity,[13] and the same sources were taken up by later authors in the context of the medieval Crusades and the Protestant-Catholic conflicts of the Reformation era.[14] Largely, though, Christian just war thought focused on other issues, and within the broader just war tradition this holy war concept never moved to the center focus of attitudinal, intellectual, and behavioral development. Rather, just war tradition took from Hebraic culture those insights and practices aimed at mitigating the destructiveness of war.

The Roman Contribution

Much of the specific form of the *jus ad bellum* of just war tradition can be traced to late Roman practice. Augustine of Hippo, widely (if somewhat excessively) regarded as the progenitor of the specifically Christian stream of just war thought, drew heavily from what Rome accepted as normative regarding war. This included the very idea of a "just war," a *bellum justum*, the definition of just cause in terms of three conditions (defense, retaking something wrongly taken, punishment of evildoing), the idea that only the highest authorities in the state could authorize violence on behalf of the state, and such other ideas as the requirements of last resort, proportionality of good to evil done, and the goal of peace. More broadly, the Roman concept of justification of war was part of an overall notion of statecraft in which war is an instrumentality of political sovereignty. The concept of divine involvement in justifying war was, in Roman practice, subordinated to the requirement that the fetial priests, officials of the state religion, review every ostensible cause for war by sacrifice and augury and pronounce it justified or unjustified. They could not, in contrast to Hebraic practice, authorize war by themselves on behalf of the gods. Also connected to an overall concept of statecraft is the grounding of the propriety of defensive war in the need to protect the goods provided in Roman society against the inferior goods represented by other societies who made war against Rome. Defensive war was justified, that is, not because of some abstract raison d'état but because of the values guaranteed by this particular society and its government. This same concept, inverted, justified war for the purpose of punishment toward societies whose political leadership practiced evil activities against their own members or other persons.[15]

The Early Christian Contribution

Despite some early Christian opposition to participation in war (on grounds that military service involved idolatry, created ritual impurity through involvement in human bloodshed, and represented a context in which moral temptations were pervasive),[16] by the second century there were both Christian participation in war and apologetic acceptance of military service for Christians. In the 170s a significant portion of the soldiers in the so-called Thundering Legion (*Legio Fulminata*) were Christians.[17] Only slightly later the writings of Tertullian of Carthage reveal Christian presence in the military units stationed there.[18] Toward the end of the century the theologian Clement of Alexandria wrote that military service was acceptable for Christian "learners," though not for Christian "gnostics," who were to observe a stricter standard of morality and more detachment from things of the world. For Clement one factor that seems to have argued for Christian participation in military service was the need to protect the values provided by the Roman Empire to its inhabitants. By contrast with the radical eschatological beliefs widespread among first-century Christians, which justified a form of sectarian relationship to the Roman state, Clement lived after hope had waned for the imminent Second Coming of Christ, and for him the Roman state represented an earthly peace and stability necessary to the continued prosperity of Christianity until God's purposes for the world had been achieved.[19]

The majority of commentators on Christian just war tradition do not reach as far back as Clement but trace it to Augustine, bishop of Hippo, in the fourth and fifth centuries.[20] However creative a theologian Augustine was, though, his ideas on just war did not spring fresh from his mind without historical antecedents. Clement and the numbers of Christian soldiers who served in the legions beginning in the second century symbolize and exemplify a shift that was already taking place in their own lifetimes, a change in attitude on the part of Christians toward a positive acceptance of participation in the life of the world, including military service to protect the goods represented by the Roman state. This shift provided the background for Augustine's own treatment of the Roman state in *The City of God* and his justification of military service in protection of the political community represented by that state. The same can be said for Augustine's mentor Ambrose, bishop of Milan, who should at least share Augustine's mantle for making important contributions to the establishment of the theological justification for Christian participation in just wars.

Ambrose, rather than Augustine, was the theorist who first realized that a Christian's obligation to the neighbor in love extends to the obligation to protect him or her from harm being inflicted unjustly. When confronting the case of an evildoer attacking an innocent victim, Ambrose argued, the Christian third party should intervene to protect the victim and is justified in using force against the assailant if necessary to keep harm from the victim. The force that may be used against the assailant is limited, however, by the fact that Christ died for him as well.[21]

This paradigm is basic for the theory of just war in Christian doctrine, because it provides a theological justification for the use of force (the obligation of love for neighbor) that sharply counters arguments for pacifism based on Jesus' own nonviolence, his command to turn the other cheek, and his example of "disarming" Peter at the Garden of Gethsemane. These examples, for Ambrose (and Augustine), were identified as having to do with self-defense, not justified war. Extended to the context of society as a whole, Ambrose's paradigmatic case shows how there are Christian, as well as secular, reasons for fighting, if necessary, to protect that society. At the same time, it implies limits on even the justified use of force and respect for the rights and person of the enemy.

Ambrose's paradigm for justified protection of the neighbor as an obligation of Christian love was implicit in Augustine's major creative contribution to just war tradition, the idea that to be justified, resort to force should be rightly motivated or, as the tradition generally has it, undertaken out of "right intention." The locus classicus for this idea is a passage from Augustine that begins by dismissing the idea that "the deaths of some, who would soon die anyway" represent an evil in war. Rather, Augustine went on, what is truly evil is "the love of violence, revengeful cruelty, fierce and implacable enmity, wild resistance and the lust of power, and such like."[22]

This idea that right intention or motivation must be present to justify resort to war on the part of the state—and Christian participation in such war as soldiers—was added, in Augustine's thought and in later systematic accounts of the *jus ad bellum*, to several ideas drawn directly from Roman theory, law, and practice: the general idea of *bellum justum* and, within it, the specific requirements of just cause, right authority, proportionality, last resort, and the goal of peace. Neither Augustine nor Roman doctrine addressed *jus in bello* issues directly, though later theorists (for example, Paul Ramsey) have argued that the principle of discrimination or noncombatant immunity is implicit in Augustine's thought.[23] The later *jus in bello* principles of discrimination and proportionality may also be read, quite straightforwardly, out of Ambrose's paradigmatic case.

The Contribution of Classical Culture

The attitudes and practices of classical culture had their impact on just war tradition both through the idea of the goods represented by a stable political order, to which Christian theologians were gradually converted, and more particularly through the laws and customs of late classical Rome.[24] By Augustine's time an idea of *bellum justum* had coalesced around the requirements that imperial authority alone could rightly authorize force, that there be a just cause (defined as defense, the need to retake something wrongly taken, or the need to punish wrong), and the rest of the *jus ad bellum* ideas previously mentioned. Much later, in the seventeenth century, Hugo Grotius would attribute a form of *jus in bello* restraint to the Romans on the ground that they enslaved their captive enemies instead of killing them, which they were entitled to do by the law of nature.[25] Just cause, in the Roman system, was reinforced by the practice of seeking guidance from the fetial priests, who used sacrifices and auguries to determine their own judgment on the presence or absence of a just cause.

All this has directly to do with formal just war theory as it later developed. Much more in Western attitudes toward justice and restraint in war can, on close scrutiny, be read out of the influence of classical culture. For example, both ancient Greece and republican Rome held it to be an obligation of every male to bear arms in case of emergency, if he was able. Roman culture gradually diminished this requirement, until at the end of the imperial period it was essentially reversed, and citizens were exempted from war, while mercenaries and specialized troops from the fringes of the empire made up the bulk of the armed forces.[26] More broadly, classical culture bequeathed the fundamental concepts of politics and statecraft and of the place of the use of force within the practice of statecraft, which were transmitted to the Middle Ages in legal, philosophical, and theological texts and recovered and elaborated by later theorists. In addition, the concepts of *jus gentium* and *jus naturale* employed by late medieval and early modern thinkers derived directly from Roman culture, as did much of the content placed into these categories.[27]

The Germanic Contribution

Most writers on the idea of just war overlook the influence of Germanic culture on the development of attitudes and practices on war in the Middle Ages. This influence was, however, considerable and was transmitted chiefly through the customs, attitudes, and behavior associated with the knightly class, the direct historical inheritor of the Germanic warrior tradition.[28] It was the knights, more than any other element in medieval culture, who through the code of chivalry shaped the growing tradition on *jus in bello*. The whole idea of a distinction between combatants and noncombatants correlated directly, in the Middle Ages, with the social and functional distinction between knights and nonknights. Observation of the rule of proportionality in combat followed immediately from the recognition that a knight fighting for an enemy was also a member of that larger brotherhood defined by chivalry—as well as from the fact that knights taken prisoner instead of being killed could be redeemed for ransom. Efforts to limit weapons, though formally promulgated by church councils, were aimed at the weapons with which nonknights were typically armed, weapons that killed rather than only injuring and that, in the case of siege weapons, were indiscriminate in their effects.[29]

The traditions of Germanic culture transmitted through medieval chivalry thus contributed to the *jus in bello* of just war tradition, but the major contributions to the *jus ad bellum* are to be found elsewhere, specifically in the inheritance from Roman law and custom and from Christian theology, incorporating elements from Hebraic culture. While Germanic culture certainly had its own conception of when resort to force was justified, who could authorize it, and so on, the direct line of influence in the *jus ad bellum* of just war tradition is from Roman law and custom, transmitted both directly and through Christian theology.[30] Thus the two major aspects of just war tradition, that having to do with just resort to force and that having to do with the proper use and the limits of justified force, derive from essentially distinct cultural heritages that, in the context of medieval Christendom, merged into a single culture. While we have to this point been identifying and examining the sources of just war tradition, the tradition itself, understood as a coherent body of thought and practice including both a *jus ad bellum* and a *jus in bello* and accepted across the breadth of the culture, is a product of the Middle Ages.

THE MEDIEVAL COALESCENCE OF JUST WAR TRADITION

Early Steps

From the breakup of the Roman Empire to the tenth century the just war ideas of the classical world and of late classical Christian theory were ignored in the development of Western culture. At the same time, the Germanic traditions on war had not yet solidified into the attitudes and customs of chivalry. Lack of political unity reinforced the tendency toward general lawlessness on the part of those who bore arms, the descendants of the Germanic warrior class. In the tenth century, as an attempt to put an end to the bullying of landless *milites* (soldiers in the employ of local nobles) and the plundering of peasants and townspeople by armed bands living on the fringes of settled society, several French bishops proclaimed a "peace of God," essentially a declaration that peaceful noncombatants were not to be molested on pain of excommunication for persons who transgressed the peace. The church was immediately supported by the royal officers who bore both political and military authority over the various governmental regions of France, because putting down the bullying *milites* and suppressing bandit bands was clearly in the interest of centralized authority.[31] The idea of the peace of God spread to other regions of Europe but did not become universal. Nonetheless, it represented an important step in the growing cultural consciousness of western Europe, and its provisions for noncombatant protection were picked up in later church doctrine relating to just war tradition.

In the eleventh and twelfth centuries there emerged an idea of a "truce of God," a declaration of certain days as off limits for fighting by Christians.[32] Whereas the peace of God was aimed at ending lawless behavior on the part of miscreants in society—disturbers of the peace, in an apt but later terminology—the truce of God was aimed at restraining people fighting in causes and for authorities that might well be considered just by all affected. The truce of God movement originated in northern Italy, and its effects were strongest there, where it had great popular support. It had no lasting effect, however, on the development of just war tradition.

Nor did the effort to limit specific weapons,[33] already alluded to as one of the approaches made by medieval Western culture to limit the destructiveness of war, work its way into the developing just war tradition as a specific element within the doctrines expressing that tradition. Rather, its long-term effect was to reinforce the broader ideas of discrimination and noncombatant immunity and proportionality, the central concepts of the *jus in bello*. The weapons banned were in fact gradually accepted into the armament of legitimate armies, and eventually the effort to ban them became moot as they were replaced by other weapons. The idea of weapons bans remains seductive, however, and the last century has seen efforts in international law to ban certain types of bullets, air bombardment, certain kinds of naval weapons, gas warfare, and nuclear warfare.[34] Rather than to concentrate on the particular weapons banned, which vary from one historical context to another, it is more instructive to analyze the reasons why they have been banned. These can be traced immediately to the principles of discrimination (such weapons as gas are indiscriminate in their effects) and proportion (dumdum bullets, for example, cause gratuitous harm to their victims). Thus the weapons bans represent a reflection of the consensus on *jus in bello* but are not an independent aspect of it.

The Coalescence of the Tradition

For a tradition to exist, there must be both continuity and convergence of related ideas and associated practices. By such a standard, there is, properly speaking, no just war tradition prior to the Middle Ages, when the various ideas and practices described earlier coalesced into a single, recognizable cultural consensus on the justification and limitation of violence. The benchmark document for the beginnings of this coalescence is the compilation of canon law known as the *Decretum*, written by the monk Gratian in the mid–twelfth century.[35] Gratian's focus was on reducing to essentials and systematizing the Christian tradition as it had been handed down to him, and he knew the influence of the classical and Hebraic cultures only as filtered through the writings of Christian sources. On the subject of war he drew significantly from Augustine, and it was in fact through the *Decretum* that Augustine's importance as a Christian just war theorist was secured. Canonists and theologians writing on war in the next centuries after Gratian depended on his compilation as their window on what was important from earlier writers; Thomas Aquinas, for example, referred only to ideas of Augustine's that had been included by Gratian in the *Decretum*.[36]

The dependence on Gratian was thus at once liberating and constricting. By drawing together and systematizing significant statements on war and Christian morality from acknowledged authorities, he prepared the way for others after him to examine moral issues related to war within the perspective of Christian tradition. The *Decretum* provided a nucleus around which later medieval just war thought formed, as a snowflake crystallizes around a bit of dust. At the same time, though, it was a book of moral definitions and rules, and its perspective on Christian tradition was accordingly restricted to those statements from earlier authorities that matched the purpose of the compilation. Though it provided a base on which later theory could build, this was a narrow base. Gratian's specific concern was to answer the question whether participation in war is ever permitted for Christians. His answer, drawn from Augustine and Isidore of Seville, was that Christians may participate in just wars, defined as those fought to regain something stolen or to repel injury (Isidore) or to revenge injury, punish evil, or restore something wrongly taken (Augustine).[37] Thus the late classical Roman concept of just cause came into the core of the medieval consensus on just war. Other *jus ad bellum* concepts can also be found in the *Decretum*, as well as the germ of a *jus in bello* concept of noncombatant protection. Yet these concepts were sharply truncated and presented without argument or discussion. It remained for later writers to elaborate and build on these ideas that Gratian drew systematically together.

Two successive waves of canonical commentators, known as the Decretists and the Decretalists, followed Gratian in the twelfth and thirteenth centuries.[38] Their major preoccupation was with the juridical definition of right authority, and their collective achievement on this issue was to define and restrict religious authority to wage war and ultimately to reserve authority to make war to secular powers. Their terms of requirements rooted in natural reason, rightly employed. In both respects he was a critical figure, and his work was a crucial step in the development of just war tradition and its transformation into the modern age.

In the *jus ad bellum* Victoria's most creative and far-reaching new idea was what I call "simultaneous ostensible justice"—the recognition that so far as any human observer, however objective, could tell, both sides in a conflict had a just cause for fighting against the other. This idea appears in both *De Indis* and *De Jure Belli* and in contexts applying it to both European and Spanish-Indian conflicts.[47] God, having knowledge superior to humans, can be assumed to know the genuinely just cause in such cases; yet humans alone cannot. Victoria used this reasoning to argue that the belligerents should fight especially scrupulously, not availing themselves of their full rights to injure the enemy—for, after all, one might be mistaken in thinking his own cause just. Grotius, writing in the next century, reiterated essentially the same conception and carried it further: for him, war must be assumed just when duly considered so by the sovereign authority and formally declared by that authority.[48] In Grotius's thought and in the international law tradition after him the *jus ad bellum* thus became closely identified with the existence of sovereign states and their right to exist; the moral concept of just war became a legal concept of duly considered, authorized, and declared war. At the same time, as for Victoria, the implication drawn from this was to strengthen the limitation on violence placed by the *jus in bello*. The great bulk of international law on war accordingly represents elaboration and regularization of the *jus in bello* within the overall framework of just war tradition.

Whereas Gratian, and after him Thomas Aquinas, had focused on the question whether Christians could without sin participate in war, Victoria took this matter as having been settled in the affirmative. Another question that occupied medieval theorists also focused his own attention, however: the question of the relation of religious belief to just war. For the medieval canonists, as we have seen, this was assimilated to the definition of right authority, which was eventually limited to secular sovereigns. For Victoria, writing of the relationship between the Spanish and the Indians, the question was posed differently: might the Indians be converted to Christianity by force of arms? Victoria's answer, consistent with his fundamental position on the natural-law basis of the idea of just war, was a flat no: "Difference of religion is not a cause of just war."[49] Neither is extension of empire nor glory nor advantage to the prince. Just wars may be waged only for causes provided in natural law, for only these bind all men equally.

As in the case of Victoria's position on simultaneous ostensible justice, his denial of religion as affording just cause became consensual among

work on authority to make war was paralleled and reinforced by the work of historians and theorists of Roman law, who sought to make this law the model for a new "international law" of Christendom, and by the social, economic, and political pressures that led to the establishment of centralized monarchies as the normative form of government.

These canonical writers also helped to define the growing consensus on noncombatant immunity, though the church's first concerns seem to have been to protect churchly persons (bishops, priests, monks and nuns, pilgrims) and lands from harm during warfare.[39] The broader development of the idea of noncombatant immunity to include all persons not capable of bearing arms (that is, women, children, the aged, the infirm, and the mentally impaired) or not actually involved in bearing arms (peasants on the land, townspeople, merchants, and other "peaceful folk") came out of the code of chivalry and the self-interest of the knightly class. The concept of proportionality as a *jus in bello* restraint also derives from the values and practices of chivalry; aside from the weapons limits, the church did nothing here. It is fittingly symbolic that the earliest expression of a full idea of *jus in bello*, synthesizing the churchly and chivalric contributions, with both an elaborated conception of noncombatant immunity and a requirement of proportional restraint in combat, appears in the work of a fourteenth-century monk, Honoré Bonet, who was a member of the knightly class and wrote for others of this class who remained in the profession of arms.[40]

The theological contribution to the growing definition of the just war idea in the twelfth through fourteenth centuries appears to have been less influential in its own time than that of the other sectors previously mentioned.[41] In any case, its first effect was on the developing theory of just war, not on the practice. Thomas Aquinas's brief discussion[42] provides a useful benchmark, particularly because of the development of his ideas by Neoscholastic just war theorists like Victoria and Suarez in the early modern period. Thomas, who was a contemporary of the Decretalists, defined the *concept* of just war in terms of three conditions (all part of the *jus ad bellum*): that the war be fought on right authority, have a just cause (which he identified by reference to the role of the prince to punish evil on behalf of God), and be waged with right intention. This rather limited conception implies, but does not say, that just war must always be of a defensive or retributive nature. The concept of right intention (defined by Thomas through the statement of Augustine cited earlier) may be drawn out, though Thomas did not do so, to produce the *jus in bello* ideas of discrimination and proportionality. The *jus ad bellum* mandate that just war aim at the end of peace was also assimilated by Thomas to the requirement of right intention.

As we examine these developments, we should remember that as we look backwards through history from them, there is quite simply no just war tradition to be discerned earlier than this. Even in these developments, considered singly, the full range of the just war idea did not yet exist. If we think of just war theory in the way that has become normative, including a *jus ad bellum* composed of criteria of just cause, right authority, right intention, proportionality of ends, reasonable hope of success, last resort, and the aim of peace, and a *jus in bello* comprising a broad concept of noncombatant immunity and the requirement of proportionality of means, this cannot be found in any of the medieval sources identified earlier. It cannot even be found explicitly, in full form, in the late medieval writers whose work reveals the existence of a general cultural consensus on just war much like the one just stated, writers like Honoré Bonet and his disciple, Christine de Pisan.[43] Yet such a theory can be read through the ideas of these writers. The weight of evidence, then, shows that by the era of the Hundred Years' War, the late fourteenth and early fifteenth centuries, the core doctrine of just war tradition had coalesced and was functioning as a broad cultural consensus within western European culture on the justification and limitation of war. Major writers on these themes from the sixteenth and seventeenth centuries presupposed this consensus. Yet it was they—or more specifically some of them, including Victoria, Suarez, and Grotius—and not any medieval theorist, who stitched them together into a systematic whole. Just war tradition coalesced into a cultural consensus during the Middle Ages; this consensus was then expressed in systematic theoretical fashion by writers of the early modern period, who also transformed this developing doctrine into the base for modern international law. In its medieval coalescence and in the continuity of ideas and practice from the medieval to the modern periods, just war tradition emerged.

JUST WAR TRADITION IN THE MODERN PERIOD

The Early Modern Development of Just War Tradition

For just war tradition, the beginning of the modern era may be said to have been in Spain in the 1530s, when Franciscus de Victoria, then prime professor of theology at the University of Salamanca, "reread" or summarized his two courses of lectures on the Indians of the New World and the rights of the Spanish toward them. The two *relectiones* ("rereadings") were transcribed by Victoria's students and published under the overall title *Of the Indians Newly Discovered* (*De Indis Noviter Inventis*) in two parts, now normally cited as, respectively, *De Indis* and *De Jure Belli*.[44] Victoria's nominal role as a professor of theology in a Dominican university was to comment on the *Sentences* of Peter Lombard, but he

in fact did a great deal more. Earlier he had incorporated the theology of Thomas Aquinas into his lectures, helping to initiate the intensive study of Thomas that established his thought as a principal theological basis for the Catholic church in the modern period. In the two courses of lectures on the Indians, Victoria took the further step of applying Thomas's conception of the perfection and autonomy of the natural in its own sphere to the Indians and their relationship to the Spanish.

The Indians were not Christians, Victoria granted, but they were humans—rational creatures able to know and understand the law of nature and bound to observe it in their dealings with one another and with the Spanish explorers, missionaries, and settlers. As non-Christians the Indians had invincible ignorance regarding the truths of the Christian faith, including the authoritativeness of the pope both directly and mediated downward through bishops and clergy, and so they could not be held to account for not accepting this authority. Yet they could be held to observance of the truths knowable through natural law and to behavior appropriate to this knowledge. Among the contents of the law of nature, Victoria argued, were the values that generated the requirements of just war. The Indians ought to know, understand, and observe these requirements not because of their promulgation in canon law or other authoritative religious teaching, but simply because the Indians were rational beings capable of knowing the law of nature.[45]

This line of argument represents a major step in the development of just war tradition. While the historical sources of just war ideas and practices include much that is nonreligious, medieval just war tradition was in practical terms a doctrine for Christendom alone. When Christian knights fought against infidels, the rules for intra-Christian warfare did not apply, or applied only in part or so far as possible.[46] Apart from the practical problem, alluded to in the first part of this chapter, of extending one culture's concepts on justification and limitation of force across the boundary with another culture, medieval Christendom was not able to produce a mature theoretical basis for attempting to do so. Victoria, employing Thomas Aquinas's concept of an autonomous and perfect natural sphere with its own law knowable by reason, provided such a theory. With this fundamental contribution of a normative basis for just war tradition in natural law, Victoria brought that tradition into the modern age, and in particular he made possible the extension of just war tradition into modern international law.

The just war theory Victoria set on this natural-law basis had the full range of concepts inherited from the medieval consensus. Viewed in relation to the Middle Ages, Victoria's major contribution was to systematize the inherited concepts theoretically and to apply them to his own historical context. Viewed in relation to the modern age, his major contribution was to cast these concepts and the theory they

theorists of the following centuries and, in particular, became central to the developing international legal tradition. Before the consensus could form, though, a century of bloody and exhausting wars of religion between Protestants and Catholics in Europe and in the colonial empires of the European states was necessary to give a last practical test to the justification of war by religious reasons.

Victoria's contributions to the development of the tradition's *jus in bello* were essentially those of a systematizer rather than an innovator. He defined a strong position on noncombatant immunity, listing as noncombatants all those classes of people who by reasons of inability to bear arms or peaceful social function do not participate in war. This was where medieval doctrine had left the matter; Victoria drew out the implications to include "those who are able to bear arms, if . . . they have not shared in the crime nor in the unjust war."[50] Later doctrine on noncombatancy did not improve on this. He employed the rule of double effect, however, to justify the accidental killing of noncombatants in a just war when the normal prosecution of the war could not take place without such killing. Yet he reminded his readers that the right to use any means of war is limited by the principle of proportionality, and that killing even the guilty is allowable only when there is no other way to prosecute a war otherwise just.[51] In all of this Victoria sounds extraordinarily contemporary, for both legal and moral doctrines in the twentieth century have taken essentially the same line.

Though paths of direct influence are difficult to trace, these ideas that surfaced first in Victoria's work became the core of normative moral and legal thought on war in the following centuries. Grotius, as already noted, secured their centrality for the development of international law. In religious thought the Jesuit Suarez and the Puritan William Ames were but two who built essentially similar theories of just war on the newly consensual basis of natural law.[52] Locke and other political theorists of the seventeenth and eighteenth centuries incorporated analogous reasoning into their work.[53] Military codes of conduct, which began to develop in Victoria's own time and became more commonplace in the following two centuries, imposed requirements of military discipline incorporating provisions for noncombatant immunity and restraint by considerations of proportionality that directly paralleled Victoria's.[54]

In the modern period from the seventeenth century to the twentieth the main streams of development of just war tradition have been international law, conceptions of legitimate military practice including military codes of conduct, and political theories that defined and regularized the nature of states and the parameters of their interrelationships. Neither religion nor philosophy had much hand in this. For religion, the conflicts ensuing from the Reformation led to reexamination and efforts to reformulate or reject the inherited tradition, but by the end of the

Reformation era the accepted just war doctrine was essentially as Victoria had cast it. Philosophy had no autonomous voice on just war issues but operated within the parameters of international legal theory or political theory. The reawakening of both theology and philosophy as creative streams of just war tradition is a phenomenon of the twentieth century and particularly of the period since World War II.

Streams of Development of Just War Tradition from Victoria and Grotius to the Present

The Law of War in International Law

International legal tradition on the justification and limitation of war moved from theory, exemplified by Grotius in the seventeenth century, to theory coupled with practical experience in statecraft, exemplified by Vattel in the eighteenth, and to the development of positive international law in the form of conventions and general treaties in the nineteenth and twentieth centuries. Georg Schwarzenberger has called this the progress of the requirements of "civilization"; Geoffrey Best has termed it the growth of "humanitarianism" as a brake on national self-interest.[55] However it is described, this stream of development of legal standards for the behavior of states has been a principal historical carrier of just war tradition from the seventeenth century to the present.

The positive law of war of the nineteenth and twentieth centuries represents a crystallization of this stream of development. As it exists today, the international law of war has three aspects: restraints on the behavior of combatants in their treatment of noncombatants of various sorts, including prisoners of war, the wounded on the battlefield, "protected persons" like medical personnel and chaplains (who though in uniform are not combatants), and civilians; restraints on the means of war, including weapons bans (e.g., dumdum bullets) and nonuse treaties directed toward particular weapons (e.g., poison gas) and restrictions on certain kinds of usage of otherwise permissible weapons (e.g., air bombardment of unprotected, noncombatant areas); and restrictions on resort to military force in the settlement of disputes. The first line of approach began with the Geneva Conference of 1864, which produced the first of the Geneva conventions. The second approach traces to the Hague Conferences of 1899 and 1907 but includes later twentieth-century developments relating to means of warfare that produce gratuitous harm, unnecessary destruction, or indiscriminate effect.[56] Together the first and second approaches constitute the *jus in bello* of positive international law. They correlate closely with the *jus in bello* defined by theory and practice in earlier centuries, and they add the advantages of specificity, widespread formal acceptance by states, and the possibility of imposition of sanctions in cases of violations (e.g., the punishments imposed by the war crimes trials following World War II). They have also had a direct influence on national military codes of regulations, though these are the more direct result of another stream of development of just war tradition.

The third approach taken by international law represents an effort, truncated but real, to define a *jus ad bellum* within international law. The major benchmarks in this approach are the Covenant of the League of Nations after World War I, the Pact of Paris of 1928, and the Charter of the United Nations. Two ideas are common to all three of these specific efforts to establish an international-law *jus ad bellum*: the national integrity of sovereign states and the right of self-defense to protect that integrity. Other ideas flow from these: the emphasis on arbitration to settle disputes found in the League of Nations Covenant and perpetuated in the Charter of the International Court of Justice; the renunciation of first resort to force in the settlement of disputes that formed the centerpiece of the Pact of Paris; and the principle of collective self-defense that is joined to the other two in the United Nations Charter.[57]

It will be remembered that medieval and early modern just war theory, following Roman law and practice, recognized three kinds of justifying cause for war: defense, retaking something wrongly taken, and punishment of evil. Positive international law formally recognizes only defense; yet in practice the concept of defense has been stretched to include the other two, as in the Falklands war of 1982 (retaking something wrongly taken) and the justification of "defensive" nuclear retaliation (punishment of evil). The logic of these international law developments is straightforward, however: if there is no higher judge of justice than the nation-state, then its integrity must be paramount, and defense of that integrity against attack must be the only generally acceptable justifying cause for use of military force. Both as an elaboration and regularization of the just war tradition (in the case of the *jus in bello*) and as a truncated statement of it (in the case of the *jus ad bellum*), international law on war remains a major stream of development of just war tradition.

Codes of Military Conduct and the Phenomenon of Limited War

Specifically military traditions represent another stream of development of just war tradition in the modern age. In the sixteenth and seventeenth centuries formal codes of military conduct began to appear, promulgated by monarchs or their generals as a tool of discipline for armies increasingly composed of common men.[58] The significance of this for just war tradition is that these codes put in the form of regulations for the conduct of soldiers elements of restraint that had in an earlier age been part of the socialization of members of the knightly class. The new common soldiers had received no such socialization, and the codes of conduct took their place. These codes were thoroughly practical in orientation; they laid down a floor below which a soldier's behavior could not slip without punishment rather than holding up ideals to which men under arms could aspire. Might soldiers plunder a church in enemy territory? What were the limits to quartering soldiers on civilians or requisitioning supplies from civilian households? What punishment should be exacted for rape? For pillage? What was the appropriate treatment for prisoners? Under what circumstances could prisoners be put to death? In answering these questions the early modern codes of military conduct drew on the *jus in bello* that had coalesced in the centuries before and expressed that *jus in bello* in terms of regulations and sanctions. Though the codes made use of restraints rooted in deeply held moral values, they were first and foremost tools of discipline for unruly men. Maintaining or enhancing the fighting value of armies composed of such men was a major purpose of the codes: soldiers allowed to plunder freely or live like lords in the civilian households where they were quartered could not be brought together into a unified whole on the march or on the field of battle. For this new type of army, discipline had to be unambiguously imposed and in effect at all times. The codes of military conduct, then, represented an externalization into specific rules and sanctions of what had been for the age of chivalry an internal moral sense of how a warrior should behave. Just war tradition was carried forward into the modern age by these new codes, but it was narrowly focused there by the requirements of military discipline. These codes had no *jus ad bellum* at all; that was no matter for a common soldier. Their establishment of the *jus in bello* as a base for military discipline, however, took the earlier consensus squarely into the realm of practical warfare.

The codes of military conduct were severely strained by the century of totalistic wars for religion ensuing upon the Reformation, and indeed they proved unequal to the task of restraining the conduct of these wars. By the end of the Thirty Years' War the concept of religion as providing a justifying cause for war was generally rejected. In the new political arrangements characteristic of Europe for the next century and a half, there developed a type of warfare characterized by minimal *jus ad bellum* limitations and growing *jus in bello* restraints.[59] The former amounted to a consensual acceptance of the position laid down by Grotius: a sovereign of a particular state represented the only "right authority" to make war; the principal justifying reason for war should be the defense of vital interests of this sovereign; difference of religion should be excluded from among the justifying causes; due care should be given to the balance of harm and good a war would do; diplomacy should precede war in the settlement of disputes; and the purpose of war should be the righting of wrongs and the creating of a more just and stable peace. In fact, resting on the sovereign the broad power to judge his own case led to frequent, if limited, armed conflicts; one commentator calls this the era of "sovereigns' wars."[60] But since the sovereigns had to bear the cost of every war in which they engaged, the numbers of men and amounts of resources committed tended to be relatively small. Such war was limited also as to the area of warfare, the targets deemed legitimate, and the impact upon the populations of belligerent states. The structure of such warfare generally provided noncombatant immunity in belligerent countries outside the immediate area of military operations, though noncombatants inside such areas were protected only by the military discipline of the armies.[61]

This phenomenon of limited war was limited chiefly by the segregation of the military sphere from the rest of society. The armies were chiefly composed of professional soldiers, meaning that the bulk of the civilian population of states at war might be left to its own normal business. Tactics and strategy focused on control of strongpoints (including "magazines," fortified storehouses for powder, shot, weapons, food, and transport), not the civilian subjects of the enemy sovereign.[62] Indeed, the civilians might well be one's own subjects at the end of the war, so there was an incentive not to treat them cruelly and to attempt to keep intact the economic base of the society. This was the kind of war reflected in the writings of eighteenth-century jurists like Vattel, who introduced the language of humanitarianism into the rationale for the *jus in bello*.[63]

These restraints on war from within the sphere of military life and the practice of war carried forward and developed only a portion of the inherited just war tradition. Yet what was adapted and reformulated here was connected directly to the practice of war, and this practice shows the results. Equally importantly, the development of restraints on war within the military sphere provides a historical context for the reciprocal flow of ideas with other streams of development of just war tradition. The interpenetration of international law on war and the national codes and practices of war in the late nineteenth and twentieth centuries is one example of this; more recently, the entry by theologians and philosophers into debate over nuclear strategy exemplifies another sort of interaction bringing two streams of development together.

Within American history, the development of the tradition of codes of military conduct reached a high point in the General Orders no. 100 of 1863, promulgated by the general-in-chief of the United States Army for the guidance of forces in the field during the Civil War.[64] This document was prepared largely by an international lawyer, Francis Lieber, who worked with a committee of high army officers. While less developed codes of military regulations had preceded it, this was a much more thorough exploration of what should be allowed in war and what should not. Lieber in effect encapsulated the international law tradition (or at least his interpretation of it) in a code of conduct for a national army. In turn, it had an influence on international legal theory. Within the American military it was the first example of a new type of document whose present representatives are the manuals on the law of war that exist in all the services today.

Limited warfare has been the norm for international armed conflicts since World War II, despite totalistic ideologies that seemed able to justify global holocaust. This period has also brought a development of limited war theory, exemplified in Robert Osgood's work.[65] William V. O'Brien has analyzed several major armed conflicts of the period since World War II as examples of limited war. He argues that the phenomenon of limited war in the contemporary period represents the closest the practice of war can come to the requirements laid down in just war tradition.[66]

Military theory and practice cannot be overlooked either as a source or as a carrier of just war tradition. Through military practice the ideas of justification and limitation of war are put into practical form; both internally within the military sphere of society and in interaction with other streams of just war tradition, military codes of conduct and the phenomenon of limited war have had a lasting effect on the shape of just war tradition.

The Theological Recovery of Just War Tradition

Though isolated examples of reflection on just war tradition and its implications can be found earlier, the principal period of recovery of this tradition and its meaning is the last forty years, and its principal foci are the debates over nuclear strategy and over American involvement in the Vietnam War. Paul Ramsey, whose *War and the Christian Conscience*, published in 1961, did more than any other one book to begin this renewed reflection on just war as a source for Christian moral guidance relative to war, continued to dominate theological just war theory in the Vietnam War period.[67] By the end of this latter era, though, a good many others had actively entered this arena, and debate swirled over the meaning of just war categories for contemporary war—if indeed, as some critics disputed, these categories were meaningful at all in the present age.

What has characterized the theological recovery of just war tradition is a kind of Renaissance mentality, with the motto *ad fontes* ("to the sources") unheralded but vigorously pursued in practice. Ramsey himself went back to Augustine and Thomas Aquinas. Other Protestant ethicists, including Stanley Hauerwas and John Howard Yoder, sought to ground or test just war theory by reference to the Bible, especially the New Testament.[68] America's Roman Catholic bishops, in their 1983 pastoral letter *The Challenge of Peace*, reached back both into Scripture and into church tradition.[69] In general, the mode of recovery followed established theological fashion in Protestant and Catholic circles, with the Protestants tending to ignore the development that had taken place between the early church and the present and the Catholics looking for normative tradition in established church doctrine. Neither sort of theologian has paid much attention to the broader tradition, in which religious development has been through canon law as well as theology, and in which various streams of thought and practice have produced and carried the consensual body of justifications and restraints that make up just war tradition was a whole. To draw these connections has been the thrust of my own work, in distinction from the more properly theological writers.

The recovery of a specifically religious perspective on just war theory is important because of the balance it restores to the tradition as a whole, which had become dominated by the perspective of international law. With religious concerns now being examined directly, it is possible to explore the relation of individual moral behavior to the practice of war in a way not possible when the religious perspective was dormant. It is also possible now to engage in comparative, cross-cultural discussion about justification and limitation of armed violence in terms of religious beliefs and practices. Moreover, this recovery of the theological perspective allows examination and testing of the religious and cultural values that undergird just war tradition. These are as yet mainly items on the agenda for future work by theorists of just war as an element of Western cultural life.

CONCLUSION

The deep historical roots of just war tradition are the roots of Western culture, and the medieval coalescence of this tradition took place as an activity within Western culture. The discovery of the New World opened two routes along which the just war idea might advance: the route of cultural imperialism, according to which western European conceptions of justification and limitation of war would be imposed as requirements of a dominant, and presumably superior, civilization, and the route of universalizing the just war concept, according to which justifications and limitations of war would be read, in principle, out of a common law of nature equally accessible to all of humankind and equally binding on all. The route actually taken was a combination of these two options. The establishment of a natural-law base for the just war consensus inherited from the Middle Ages provided a theory for a culture-blind just war tradition. In fact, though, the Europeans who explored, colonized, and settled other parts of the globe had a strongly culture-conditioned conception of natural law, and the result was that what was universal in theory became a justification for cultural imperialism on the part of the supposedly culturally superior Europeans.

A vignette from Victoria illustrates how this could happen.[70] Confronted with the question whether the Spanish might use military force to coerce the Indians into accepting Christianity, Victoria responded with a strong negative. Yet he pursued the matter by arguing that of course Spanish missionaries had a right to preach Christianity to all who would hear, and that natural law guaranteed not only this right but also the right of free passage for them through Indian lands. If the Indians refused to let the missionaries enter, or if they made captives of the missionaries, then the Spanish were justified in using military force to enforce the missionaries' rights—in effect making war on the Indians. The rights of which Victoria spoke were conceived by him as universal, as "natural"; yet the Indians knew nothing of them. They were in fact historically derived from the customary practices of European societies. In the name of natural law Victoria was justifying cultural imperialism.

Later theoreticians made no apologies for this: the imposition of international law on the world was justified in the name of requiring civilized behavior from the uncivilized and thus civilizing them. The law of war was presented as imposing requirements of "civilization" as recently as two decades ago.[71] By one means or another, international law on war carried ideas from just war tradition to all parts of the world and imposed practices consistent with that law on cultures greatly removed from the one in which just war tradition had its roots and in which its early systematic development took place. A case can be made, then, that in the form of agreement to the requirements of the international law of war, just war tradition has become global.[72]

The present theoretical task is to reach beyond such de facto acceptance of the international law of war to discover whether it is possible to identify underlying this phenomenon a global consensus as to justice in war. Dominance of other cultures by the West has not entirely run its course, but yet to be explored adequately is the possibility of genuine community of values on matters related to the justification and limitation of force. Identifying exactly where such agreement exists and where it does not is an enterprise that earlier natural law theorists should have engaged in but did not. Doing so in the present context is one way of testing, and perhaps furthering, the development of just war tradition as a global consensus on justification and restraint of war.

NOTES

1. See, for example, James A. Aho, *Religious Mythology and the Art of War* (Westport, Conn.: Greenwood Press, 1981); Michael Barkun, *Law without Sanctions: Order in Primitive Societies and the World Community* (New Haven: Yale

University Press, 1968); John Ferguson, *War and Peace in the World's Religions* (New York: Oxford University Press, 1978); R. Brian Ferguson and Leslie E. Farragher, *The Anthropology of War: A Bibliography* (New York: Harry Frank Guggenheim Foundation, 1988), chap. 14, "Belief Systems, Cognitive Orientations, and Rules of War"; and Quincy Wright, *A Study of War* (Chicago: University of Chicago Press, 1942).

2. See Aho, *Religious Mythology and the Art of War*, chaps. 5 and 6; M. H. Keen, *The Laws of War in the Late Middle Ages* (London: Routledge and Kegan Paul; Toronto: University of Toronto Press, 1965).

3. Cf. Aho, *Religious Mythology and the Art of War*, 187–91 and chap. 11; Philippe Contamine, *War in the Middle Ages* (Oxford: Basil Blackwell, 1984), 434, 436–37.

4. Cf. James Turner Johnson, *Just War Tradition and the Restraint of War* (Princeton: Princeton University Press, 1981), chap. 3.

5. On holy war see Aho, *Religious Mythology and the Art of War*, pt. 2; Roland H. Bainton, *Christian Attitudes toward War and Peace* (Nashville, Tenn.: Abingdon Press, 1960), 148ff.; James Turner Johnson, *Ideology, Reason, and the Limitation of War* (Princeton: Princeton University Press, 1975), chaps. 1 and 2; LeRoy B. Walters, "The Just War and the Crusade: Antitheses or Analogies," *Monist* 57, no. 4 (October 1973): 584–94; Michael Walzer, *The Revolution of the Saints* (Cambridge, Mass.: Harvard University Press, 1965).

6. For a sampling of contemporary renderings of the just war categories and their meanings, see James F. Childress, *Moral Responsibility in Conflicts* (Baton Rouge: Louisiana State University Press, 1982), chap. 3; James Turner Johnson, *Can Modern War Be Just?* (New Haven: Yale University Press, 1984), chap. 1; National Conference of Catholic Bishops, *The Challenge of Peace* (Washington, D.C.: United States Catholic Conference, 1983), sections 80–110; and William V. O'Brien, *The Conduct of Just and Limited War* (New York: Praeger, 1981), chaps. 2 and 3.

7. For definition and analysis of these three positions as major moral traditions of Western culture and consideration of the relationships among them, see James Turner Johnson, *The Quest for Peace* (Princeton: Princeton University Press, 1987).

8. See note 5.

9. See further Walters, "Just War and The Crusade"; cf. Johnson, *Ideology*, chaps. 1 and 2.

10. The principal biblical sources are the books of Numbers, Deuteronomy, Joshua, and Judges. The leading scholarly study of the phenomenon of holy war in the Old Testament is Gerhard von Rad, *Der Heilige Krieg im Alten Israel* (Zurich: n.n., 1951); cf. Aho, *Religious Mythology and the Art of War*, chap. 9.

11. Cf. John Locke, *Two Treatises of Civil Government* (London: J. M. Dent and Sons; New York: E. P. Dutton and Co., 1924), book 2, *An Essay Concerning the True Original, Extent and End of Civil Government*, section 182.

12. Maimonides (Moses ben Maimon), *The Code of Maimonides* (*Mishneh Torah*), book 14, *The Book of Judges* (New Haven: Yale University Press, 1949), treatise 5, "The Laws of Kings and Their Wars."

13. See Ambrose, *Exposition of Psalm 35* and *On the Duties of the Clergy*; Augustine, *To Boniface* (*Letter 189*). For discussion, see John Helgeland, Robert J.

Daly, and J. Patout Burns, *Christians and the Military: The Early Experience* (Philadelphia: Fortress Press, 1985), chap. 11.

14. See note 9.

15. See A. Berger, "Encyclopedic Dictionary of Roman Law," *Transactions of the American Philosophical Society* 43 (1953), 333–809, under the terms *bellum, repetitio rerum, Lex de bello indicendo, indicere bellum, denuntiare bellum, indictio belli, fetiales, Ius fetiale,* and *Senatus.*

16. See further C. John Cadoux, *The Early Christian Attitude to War* (New York: Seabury Press, 1982), pt. II; Adolf von Harnack, *Militia Christi* (Philadelphia: Fortress Press, 1981); and Helgeland, Daly, and Burns, *Christians and the Military,* chaps. 1–9.

17. Cadoux, *Early Christian Attitude to War,* 228f.; Harnack, *Militia Christi,* 73f.; Helgeland, Daly, and Burns, *Christians and the Military,* chap. 4; Johnson, *Quest for Peace,* 44f.

18. Tertullian, *On the Soldier's Crown*; see Cadoux, *Early Christian Attitude to War,* 234f.; Harnack, *Militia Christi,* 75–85; Helgeland, Daly, and Burns, *Christians and the Military,* chap. 3; Johnson, *Quest for Peace,* 22–25.

19. Clement of Alexandria, *Paedagogus* 1.12.98; *Stromata* 4.8.61. Cf. Cadoux, *Early Christian Attitude to War,* 51f.; Johnson, *Quest for Peace,* 20–22.

20. See, for example, National Conference of Catholic Bishops, *Challenge of Peace*; O'Brien, *Conduct of Just and Limited War*; J. David Hollenbach, "Ethics in Distress," chap. 2 in *The Nuclear Dilemma and the Just War Tradition,* ed. William V. O'Brien and John Langan (Lexington, Mass., and Toronto: Lexington Books, 1986); and Paul Ramsey, *War and the Christian Conscience* (Durham, N.C.: Duke University Press, 1961).

21. Ambrose, *On the Duties of the Clergy* 1.41.211.

22. Augustine, *Contra Faustum* 22.74, 78.

23. Ramsey, *War and the Christian Conscience,* chap. 2.

24. For a general treatment of this conception of peace in classical antiquity, see Gerardo Zampaglione, *The Idea of Peace in Antiquity* (Notre Dame, Ind.: University of Notre Dame Press, 1973).

25. Hugo Grotius, *On the Laws of War and Peace,* translated by Francis W. Kelsay (Oxford: Clarendon Press, 1925) bk. 3, chap. 5.

26. Hans Delbrück, *History of the Art of War within the Framework of Political History,* vol. 1, *Antiquity* (Westport, Conn.: Greenwood Press, 1975).

27. See, for example, Alan Gewirth, *Marsilius of Padua: The Defender of Peace,* vol. 1, *Marsilius of Padua and Medieval Political Philosophy,* and vol. 2, *The Defensor Pacis* (New York: Columbia University Press, 1951–56); Lester K. Born, *The Education of a Christian Prince by Desiderius Erasmus* (New York: Octagon Books, 1965).

28. Delbrück, *History of the Art of War,* vol. 2, *The Germans* (Westport, Conn.:, Greenwood Press, 1980).

29. See further Johnson, *Just War Tradition,* 124–31.

30. See further Johnson, *Ideology,* chap. 1, and *Just War Tradition,* chaps. 5–8.

31. See further Contamine, *War in the Middle Ages,* 271f., 434; Frederick H. Russel, *The Just War in the Middle Ages* (Cambridge: Cambridge University Press, 1975), 34, 36, 70, 186, 194, 273, 298.

32. See Contamine, *War in the Middle Ages*, 272; Russell, *Just War in the Middle Ages*, 34–36, 70, 156, 183–86, 194, 244, 272, 298.

33. This appeared first in canon 29 of the Second Lateran Council (1139) but was not included by Gratian in his *Decretum* (see note 35). Cf. Russell, *Just War in the Middle Ages*, 70–71.

34. See Dietrich Schindler and Jiri Toman, eds., *The Laws of Armed Conflicts* (Leiden: A. W. Sijthoff; Geneva: Henry Dunant Institute, 1973), pt. II.

35. *Corpus Juris Canonici Gregorii XIII*, 2 vols, (Graz: Akademische druck-u. Verlaganstalt, 1955), Pars Prior, *Decretum Magistri Gratiani;* the treatment of war appears in Pars Secunda, Causa 23. Cited hereafter as Gratian, *Decretum*.

36. Thomas Aquinas, *Summa Theologica* II/II, Question XL, Article 1.

37. Gratian, *Decretum*, Causa 23, Question 2, Canons 1 and 2.

38. For discussion, see Russell, *Just War in the Middle Ages*, chaps. 4 and 5.

39. See Gratian, *Decretum*, Causa 23, Question 1 and Question 8, Canons 4 and 19. For discussion, see Johnson, *Just War Tradition*, 131–50.

40. See Honoré Bonet, *The Tree of Battles of Honoré Bonet* (Cambridge, Mass.: Harvard University Press, 1949).

41. See Russell, *Just War in the Middle Ages*, chaps. 6 and 7; Johnson, *Ideology*, chap. 1, and *Just War Tradition*, chap. 5.

42. Thomas Aquinas, *Summa Theologica*, II/II, Question XL.

43. See Christine de Pisan, *The Book of Fayttes of Armes and of Chyvalrye* (London: Oxford University Press, 1932).

44. The standard text is Franciscus de Victoria, *De Indis et De Jure Belli Relectiones*, ed. Ernest Nys, trans. John Pawley Bate (Washington, D.C.: Carnegie Institution, 1917). See further James Brown Scott, *The Spanish Origin of International Law* (Oxford: Clarendon Press; London: Humphrey Milford, 1934).

45. See, for example, Victoria, *De Indis*, sections 2 and 3. On Victoria's use of natural law, see further Johnson, *Just War Tradition*, chap. 4.

46. See Richard Barber, *The Knight and Chivalry* (New York: Charles Scribner's Sons, 1970), 213–14.

47. See Victoria, *De Jure Belli*, sections 27–30; *De Indis*, section III, 7.

48. Grotius, *On the Laws of War and Peace*, Bk. 1, chaps. 1, 22, 23, 26.

49. Victoria, *De Jure Belli*, section 10.

50. Ibid., section 36.

51. Ibid., section 37.

52. See Francisco Suarez, *Selections from Three Works of Francisco Suarez, S.J.* (Oxford: Clarendon Press; London: Humphrey Milford, 1944), and William Ames, *Conscience, with the Power and Cases Thereof* (N.p.: n.n., 1639).

53. Locke, *Essay*, sections 179–83, 189, 192, 193.

54. Examples include Balthasar Ayala, *De Jure et Officiis Bellicis et Disciplina Militari* (Duaci: Ioannes Bogardi, 1582).

55. Georg Schwarzenberger, *A Manual of International Law*, 5th ed. (London: Stevens and Sons, 1967), 197–99; Geoffrey Best, *Humanity in Warfare* (New York: Columbia University Press, 1980), 134–57, 175.

56. Schindler and Toman, *Laws of Armed Conflicts*, pts. 2, 4–6.

57. For discussion see Johnson, *Quest for Peace*, 253–66.

58. See note 54.

59. See Best, *Humanity in Warfare*, chap. 1; J.F.C. Fuller, *The Conduct of War*,

1789–1961 (New Brunswick, N.J.: Rutgers University Press, 1961); Johnson, *Just War Tradition*, chap. 7.

60. Fuller, *Conduct of War*, chap. 1.

61. See Delbrück, *History of the Art of War*, vol. 4, *The Modern Era* (Westport, Conn.: Greenwood Press, 1985); Johnson, *Just War Tradition*, pp. 204–18.

62. Delbrück, *History of the Art of War*, vol 4; Johnson, *Just War Tradition*.

63. Emmerich de Vattel, *The Law of Nations; or Principles of Natural Law* (Washington, D.C.: Carnegie Institution, 1916); for discussion see Best, *Humanity in Warfare*, 36–72.

64. *Instructions for the Government of Armies of the United States in the Field*, in Schindler and Toman, *Laws of Armed Conflicts*, 3–23.

65. Robert E. Osgood, *Limited War* (Chicago: University of Chicago Press, 1957).

66. O'Brien, *Conduct of Just and Limited War*, 207–360.

67. Ramsey's major works on war include *War and the Christian Conscience* (see note 20) and *The Just War* (New York: Charles Scribner's Sons, 1968).

68. Stanley Hauerwas, *Against the Nations* (Minneapolis: Winston Press, 1985), especially chaps. 8–10; John Howard Yoder, *When War Is Unjust* (Minneapolis: Augsburg Publishing House, 1984).

69. See especially pt. 1.

70. Victoria, *De Jure Belli*, section 37.

71. See note 55.

72. Such a conception appears to underly Michael Walzer's use of cases from various non-Western cultures in his *Just and Unjust Wars* (New York: Basic Books, 1977).

2

The Sources of Islamic Conceptions of War

Fred M. Donner

PRELIMINARY CONSIDERATIONS

Students of the Islamic tradition have usually sought to define Islam's attitude toward various social and moral issues by scrutinizing what a select number of central Islamic texts have to say about them. Such an examination almost always begins with—and in some cases ends with—Islam's holy book, the Qur'an, which is combed for all verses relating to the issue or institution under study. The examination may then be extended to other texts that the investigator deems representatively "Islamic." In many instances these consist of various juridical and theological writings from the classical Islamic tradition, sometimes with a few later and "modernist" texts thrown in for good measure.[1] Depending on the investigator, this selection of texts may be quite narrow—for example, the Qur'an and the law treatises of one Sunni school of jurisprudence only, or even the Qur'an alone—or it may include a broader range of texts, such as the Qur'an, sayings [*hadiths*] attributed to the Prophet, and the writings of the most eminent jurists from the major Sunni and Shi'i schools of law.[2] In short, these investigators have recourse to a more or less delimited corpus of texts that they consider representative of Islam and use this corpus to determine the "official" Islamic attitude on their given subject.[3]

There is, of course, ample practical justification for proceeding in this way. Clearly one cannot hope to screen all products of a civilization as rich as Islamic civilization. Having recourse to a select canon of theological and juridical texts—that is, to just those texts that are most self-consciously concerned with defining a person's identity as a Muslim—is, therefore, an appropriate way to get some idea of what the "Islamic" attitude on a given issue might be. In the case of Islamic attitudes toward war and peace, the Islamic tradition does in fact discuss many of the issues involved in extensive legal and theological texts.[4] It is still much too early, however, to be able to identify a clear canon of fundamental Islamic texts on warfare. Too many texts remain unstudied, and the influence of one thinker or text on subsequent ones is still largely unexamined. Hence, with a few exceptions, we cannot yet be sure what ideas and thinkers are innovative or imitative, central or marginal to the tradition as a whole.

However, it seems doubtful that one can fully understand the attitude of a particular civilization—in this case, Islamic civilization—toward a phenomenon as complex and as fundamental to human society as war merely by examining the juridical and theological definition of war and its status.[5] To do so would be to strip it of most of its human significance, since what really matters in human terms is how the Muslims of a particular time and place dealt with the vital questions of war and peace. The juridical definition, of course, has been a major force shaping the reactions of Muslims toward war over the centuries, but it would be rash to assume that it has been the only one.[6] Rather, the historian must assume that any particular group of Muslims who wrestled with the question—or threat—of war may have had its thinking on the subject shaped by other factors also. These factors included attitudes that were part of cultural traditions transmitted within a particular ethnic group from its pre-Islamic past, as well as "foreign" (that is, extra-Islamic) ideas that had for some reason become familiar in a particular historical setting. For example, the attitudes of the first Muslims toward war, as toward everything else, were shaped by a host of different cultural backgrounds, depending on whether the individual Muslims originally hailed from Arabia, Syria, Iran, or North Africa. Consequently, as the juridical perspective on war began to crystallize within the Islamic community, it inevitably reflected within itself some diversity of opinion. After the first century A.H. or so, moreover, once the outlines of the juridical Islamic perspectives on warfare had been drawn by the newly emerging specialists in Islamic law and theology, subsequent converts to Islam would have their attitudes shaped not only by their own pre-Islamic cultural background (whether Moroccan, Mongol, or Malay) but by the juridical theories as well, often as refracted through the diverse interpretive prisms of different local *ulama*. For these reasons, one may expect Muslims of various periods to have espoused multiple conceptions of war and diverse opinions on its relationship to statecraft.

This observation suggests that we must distinguish in our analysis between (1) the background and sources of the juridical attitudes toward war and peace and (2) additional factors that may have shaped the attitudes among Muslims in later times, subsequent to the elaboration of a set of juridical attitudes. The latter subject, however, though no less important historically than the former, would require us to range over the full geographical and temporal span of Islamic civilization, so that even a superficial survey of it is beyond the limits of this chapter. Moreover, it has been much less carefully studied than the former. The comments that follow, then, will display a marked imbalance. The next section of this chapter will be the longest; its examination of some possible sources of the juridical tradition's perspective on war and peace will emphasize the diversity of cultural factors that may have contributed to it, hopefully thereby offering a corrective to the view that sees all points of the juridical tradition as direct and organic outgrowths of the Qur'an and the example of the Prophet Muhammad alone. The third section offers a few comments on the substance of the juridical tradition as regards war; because this is the subject of other chapters in this volume, my comments are cursory. The fourth section offers a few suggestions on possible later influences on attitudes toward war in the Islamic world. Since little work has hitherto been done on this subject, and since much of the source material for it lies in historical periods and source languages outside my range of specialization, my comments here are again brief, offered in the hope that they may generate interest in the subject among Islamicists with specialized training in the appropriate periods. The concluding section will attempt to summarize the preceding discussion and to draw some comparisons between the development of attitudes toward war in the Islamic world and in the Western tradition.

BACKGROUND OF THE JURIDICAL TRADITION

The attitudes of the first generations of Muslims toward questions of war and peace were shaped by several factors. Paramount among them were (a) the cultural norms of the pre-Islamic societies to which they had belonged, (b) the attitudes toward war contained, implicitly or explicitly, in the Qur'an, and (c) the dramatic events of their own lifetimes. All of these factors contributed to the formation of the "classical" Islamic conception of war, that is, the juridical notion, as well as to popular attitudes.

Pre-Islamic Cultural Norms

Islam arose in the midst of a great variety of cultural traditions. The Prophet's career in Arabia occurred in a kind of political no-man's-land between several great states (Byzantium, Sasanian Iran, Axum), each of which had quite distinctive cultural traits (including different official languages, official creeds, literary traditions, artistic traditions, legal traditions, and so on). None of these "imperial cultures," if we may so style them, was closely akin to the culture of pre-Islamic Arabia itself, and in any case each empire embraced many groups of people who differed from its dominant "imperial" culture, whether religiously (as, for example, Christians and Jews in the Sasanian Empire), linguistically (as, for example, speakers of Coptic, Aramaic, or Armenian in the Byzantine domains), or in other ways. The earliest Muslims in Arabia were thus in a position to be in contact with a wide range of different cultures; moreover, after the Muslim community started on its rapid expansion as a polity following the death of the Prophet Muhammad in 11 A.H./632 C.E., it quickly absorbed—politically, at least—this most diverse array of cultural groups and had to come to terms with the ideas that they embraced, including their ideas about war and warfare. Out of this great mélange of cultural components, the following seem to me to have been particularly significant in shaping the early Muslims' attitudes toward war and hence the juridical notions of war developed in "classical" Islam.[7]

Pre-Islamic North Arabian Traditions

The fact that northern Arabia, where Islam first arose, had been for centuries a stateless area meant that other mechanisms had been developed to provide a minimum of social order and security for the individual. Essentially, this social order was based on a concept of "tribal" group solidarity against the outsider and on the common assumption that an aggrieved group would try to apply the *lex talionis*—really a threat or promise to get even rather than a law. Power tended to be concentrated particularly among certain large pastoral nomadic groups, who had the mobility, numbers, and mounts to impose their will, within limits, upon other groups that were weaker. The virtues esteemed in this culture were those of loyalty, generosity (as a manner of enhancing one's status), and martial prowess.[8]

In this society war (*harb*, used in the senses both of an activity and of a condition) was in one sense a normal way of life; that is, a "state of war" was assumed to exist between one's own tribe and all others, unless a particular treaty or agreement had been reached with another tribe establishing amicable relations. It is not clear, however, whether actual armed conflict that we might call war (that is, war as an activity) was a frequent phenomenon or not. For one thing, we must assume that many tribal groups living in proximity to one another actually did have agreements establishing amicable relations on some basis. We must also remember that much of the raiding (*ghazw*) that does appear to have been a frequent, almost routine part of life in North Arabia should probably be viewed more as a kind of sport than as true warfare.[9] There appear to have been definite "rules of the game" in raiding that both sides were expected to observe in the interests of fairness; attacking noncombatants with lethal intent, for example, was considered bad form and was generally avoided. Such periodic raids among different groups, which essentially had the effect of redistributing the limited available wealth (particularly livestock) and which seldom involved fatalities, had little in common, conceptually or actually, with more serious clashes between tribes who found themselves in competition for access to (or "ownership" of) a particular grazing ground or wells, or for control of a particular settled community. Conflicts of the latter variety were rarer, were much more bloody, and often involved larger groupings than the usual raid; they were often associated with severe environmental dislocations such as abnormal drought or major political changes that forced one pastoral group to migrate into territories normally claimed by another, and they were sometimes tantamount to battles for the very survival of the groups in conflict, since the resources under dispute could support only one of the groups. In recent times, at least, Arab tribesmen themselves have referred to the two phenomena with different Arabic words—*ghazw* (the origin of European "razzia") for raiding, *manakh* for the more serious clashes.[10]

Pre-Islamic Arabic poetry—one of our few sources for reconstructing the culture of North Arabia on the eve of Islam—frequently describes scenes of battle, often with graphic details regarding a slain enemy's wounds. Nonetheless, war itself is seldom the subject of such poems; rather, their main intent is to celebrate personal or tribal nobility, which in pre-Islamic Arabian society was thought to be manifested through martial valor, generosity, loyalty, and romantic daring. Each of these categories is referred to in order to demonstrate the nobility of the poet (or of his tribe); war is simply accepted as a normal part of life, along with the weather, animals, and (usually) beautiful women, all of which are portrayed in telling detail.[11]

Still, we can gain some idea of the ethic and practice of warfare from these poems. Little quarter was shown to the enemy warrior (at least in the poetry); death or capture against possible ransom is portrayed as their certain fate. The women, too, are likely to be captured, particularly beautiful young ones, but more commonly they are left to mourn their slain men.[12] Harming the women or children, of course, was probably considered a violation of the unwritten code of honorable behavior and hence counterproductive in an enterprise whose purpose was to establish or reaffirm one's honor; but raiding the enemy camp by night—in this case, probably not so much to slay their warriors as to make off with their herds and perhaps some women before the warriors could awake—was permitted.[13]

Occasionally a verse or two suggests some of the reasons for such encounters. One, of course, is to defend the tribe against affronts, real or imagined. "We should shield from harm all our weak ones, and defend the stranger, / and provide for the needs of the widows and

orphan children."[14] Similarly, "It was not for my kinsmen's sake that
'Amir made himself their chief: God forbid that I should exhalt myself
on mother's or father's favor! / But it was because I guard their peculiar
land, and shield them from annoy, and hurl myself against him that
strikes at their peace."[15] But the sense that such clashes are a regular
part of daily life, not caused or legitimized only by aggression from the
outside, comes through in other verses. 'Abid says, "Yea, a son of war
am I—continually do I heighten her blaze, and stir her up to burn when-
soever she is not yet kindled."[16] Even more striking is 'Amir's boast
about a destructive raid launched against the tribe of Hamdan, even
though 'Amir's tribe had no quarrel with it: "No, we had not them in
mind; no excuse had we for falling on them; but what came to pass came
to pass. / We started, intending the Sons of Nahd and their brothers,
Jarm: but God intended Hamdan."[17] Such attitudes toward war must
have been held by many of the North Arabian warriors who fought for
the new faith during the Islamic conquest movement of the seventh
century.

Official Attitudes toward War in Byzantium and Sasanian Persia

The Byzantine emperors inherited from Rome an official ideology of
"charismatic victoriousness,"[18] celebrated in lavish official triumphs in
the imperial capitals following important conquests or the vanquishing
of rebels. There is slight evidence to suggest that some people considered
inappropriate the celebration of a triumph for victories over rivals in
civil war, rather than for victories over external enemies of the empire,
which might imply the existence of a conception of "just" war as being
defined only by war against external enemies; but in fact the celebrations
that resonate most deeply in surviving sources are frequently those
commemorating the fall of usurpers, who were often, from the emperors'
point of view, the more immediate threat to their own rule.[19]

Such triumphs or official imperial victory celebrations, with their underlying theme of the emperor as victor, served several propaganda
purposes that are related to the conception of war in Byzantine official
circles. First and foremost, of course, they suggested to potential rebels
and external enemies the danger of opposing imperial might. But the
official celebrations also provided a way of affirming the conceptual unity
of the empire and of imperial rule, even in periods when the empire
was parcelled out among "mutually recognized imperial colleagues," as
it frequently was in the early Byzantine period.[20] The triumphs also
served to define the subordination to the emperor of lesser centers of
power.[21]

The tradition of celebrating a triumph presumably first sprang from
Roman soil, possibly during the consolidation of the monarchy and early
republic in the Italic wars.[22] Although originally a pagan religious ritual,

the triumph was "Christianized" by the Byzantine emperors, who linked it to the notion that God would aid the empire and emperor against enemies of religion and state. In making this shift, the Byzantine triumph tapped into a very old Judaic notion of war as a kind of judgment in which God renders his verdict by granting victory to the side he favors.[23]

This whole complex of ideas formed part of the background against which emerged the Islamic conceptions of caliphate and *imamate*. Such ideas were current in the former Byzantine provinces conquered by the Muslims (including such distant areas as North Africa and Spain, where the Vandals and Visigoths, respectively, had adopted for their own use the celebration of triumphs and an ideology of victory derived from the Roman-Byzantine model).[24] Moreover, the new Muslim rulers, confronted by such ideas on the part of their Byzantine rivals, doubtless would have felt the need to affirm their own claim to be victorious with God's aid. A detailed examination of Islamic theories regarding the caliphate is beyond the subject of this chapter, but it is impossible to discuss the Islamic conception of legitimate war without making mention of the broader theory of the caliphate/*imamate*. The Islamic conception of legitimate war (*jihad*), once it is systematically developed, is specifically tied to the idea of the unity of the Islamic state against all other non-Islamic states and the legitimacy of the caliph or *imam* as the single ruler of this Islamic state. It is only the state, headed by the legitimate caliph or *imam*, that can launch a *jihad*, so the Islamic conception of legitimate war in particular is inextricably tied to the notions of the unity of the Muslim community and of its rulership. It is also connected to the idea of God-guidedness, which, like the idea of imperial unity, was forcefully projected in Byzantine propaganda, including the triumphs.

It was not merely in official Byzantine ceremonies that this ideology of imperial victory was broadcast, moreover; it also found its way into other forms of expression that affected everyone in the empire. Under Justinian "the texts of the laws echoed the dominant theme to distant audiences: victory was assured for a great Roman emperor with God on his side, a ruler who triumphed over barbarians and through the equity of his laws."[25] Similarly, the Orthodox church liturgy and other Eastern liturgies preserve prayers reflecting the importance of the Byzantine emperors and their victory, aided by God: "Remember . . . our most pious and faithful emperors . . . shelter their heads on the day of battle, strengthen their arm, raise their right hand, confirm their empire, subjugate unto them all the barbarian peoples who want war, grant them deep and lasting peace."[26] Fifth-century and later Orthodox church historians voiced the attitude that the Byzantine emperors were aided by God, especially in their confrontations with would-be enemies.[27] The official conception of the emperor as victor—especially against the barbarians and with the aid of God—is also visible in Byzantine art, which often made it much more accessible to the population at large than the actual victory celebrations, which could only be witnessed by the population of the capital and only occasionally.[28] The most pervasive medium for the dissemination of the imperial ideology of victory, however, was probably through coinage, which of course circulated among all strata of the population. Legends on Byzantine coins commonly referred explicitly to imperial victory; phrases such as "Victoria Augustorum" (or variants thereof) were employed continuously on Byzantine coin issues in the centuries before the rise of Islam.[29] Christian symbolism (particularly the cross, sometimes the name or portrait of Christ) was also prominent on Byzantine coinage and suggested the notion that divine aid supported the imperial power. It is interesting to note, however, that the name of God, which from the start is characteristic of Islamic coinage (even the earliest Islamic coin issues, which are merely modified Byzantine or Sasanian issues), does not appear at all on Byzantine coinage until immediately before the rise of Islam, in the reign of Heraclius, and only seems to last through the seventh century.[30] This suggests, perhaps, that certain religious sentiments were "in the air" at this time, sentiments of which these Byzantine coin issues and Islam itself represent related, albeit different, expressions.

In discussing the issue of divine support, it is also worth noting that in some circumstances Byzantine thinkers could even imagine divine aid, which normally was claimed for the emperors, going to their opponents. A case in point is provided by the historian Theophylact Simocatta's description of the assassination of the emperor Maurice by the usurper Phocas in 602 C.E. According to Theophylact this event led God to withhold his support for the tyrant's armies and even to aid the Persians, who invaded Syria and Egypt in retribution. It was only with the rise of Heraclius, who avenged Maurice and overthrew Phocas, that divine support for the emperor was again forthcoming. Heraclius was therefore able to roll back the Persian occupation of former Byzantine provinces and even to invade the Mesopotamian heartlands of the Persian realm.[31] The implication of this, of course, is that the unjust ruler has no divine aid.

Two extant Byzantine military treatises from the sixth and early seventh centuries C.E. concentrate overwhelmingly on practical details of strategy and tactics and devote little attention to the broader philosophical question of warfare and its justification. The *Strategikon* attributed to Maurice, however, notes at the outset that the general must be concerned above all with the love of God and with justice; "building on these, he should strive to win the favor of God, without which it is impossible to carry out any plan, however well devised it may seem, or to overcome any enemy, however weak he may be thought."[32] This implies that only a war undertaken with God's blessing and guided by the desire to establish justice could be seen as a just war. An anonymous treatise on strategy from the mid–sixth century offers a slightly different emphasis: "I know well that war is a great evil and the worst of all evils. But since our enemies clearly look upon the shedding of our blood as one of their basic duties and the height of virtue, and since each one must stand up for his own country and his own people with word, pen, and deed, we have decided to write about strategy. By putting it into practice we shall be able not only to resist our enemies but even to conquer them."[33] The implication here is that war—which the author frankly deems the "worst of all evils"—is justified primarily in self-defense against one's enemies. The last sentence is ambiguous; it may be taken to imply either that offensive war is also justified, or simply that conquest of one's enemies could even ensue when one embarked upon an essentially defensive war. It is not made clear whether or not an attack launched against an adversary with whom one has a standing "state of war" would similarly qualify as a "defensive war" merely by virtue of the fact of the existence of a state of war, even in the absence of a specific offensive launched by that adversary. In any case, however, such conceptualizations of warfare as especially justified in case of defense may have contributed to the Islamic notion of warfare as requisite and justified in defense of the Islamic community.

A Byzantine manual of statecraft from the sixth century, the *Ekthesis* of Agapetos, stresses the importance to the ruler of securing good counsel and of leading a virtuous and just way of life; like the contemporary manuals of war, it says little that relates to the philosophical understanding of or justification for war. One brief passage, however, is significant in this context. It notes that imperial rule must show armed force to the enemy, but love and mercy to its own subjects; "for this imperial rule makes as great a distinction between friends and enemies, as exists between wild beasts and meek sheep."[34] This brief paragraph implies strongly that the launching of war against external enemies is justified, regardless of the situation; on the other hand, it might be taken to suggest also that the use of armed force against one's own subjects is not permissible in any case, since domestic opposition or unrest could be seen as the result of a failure of the emperor to be adequately just.

About official attitudes in the Sasanian Empire—as about everything else regarding the Sasanians—our documentation is much less secure than it is for corresponding attitudes in the Byzantine Empire. So few direct sources for the reconstruction of Sasanian statecraft and history have survived that we must often be satisfied with comments from books written later, during the Islamic period, and from sources that are only tangentially related to our concerns. There do survive a number of rock reliefs, however, that suggest that the Sasanian great kings exploited an ideology of victory with some parallels to that employed by the Byzantine emperors. The reliefs at Bishapur, dating from the second half of the third century C.E., for example, include a depiction of the triumph of Shapur I over his Roman enemies. In the center panel of the scene we see the Great King Shapur, mounted on horseback, with three Roman emperors in varying postures of submission to him; Gordian III lies prostrate on the ground beneath his horse, Philip the Arab kneels before him pleading, and Valerian stands beside him, his wrist firmly held in Shapur's hand in an ancient gesture of imprisonment.[35] These and other reliefs celebrate the particular victories of Sasanian kings and presumably reflect an ideology of victoriousness. Divine support for the great kings is not only represented by the presence of *putti* and the wearing of the diadem in reliefs such as that at Bishapur but is also explicitly noted in inscriptions. The inscription of Shapur I at Naqsh-i Rustam, for example, after giving a long list of lands subject to the great king, concludes with the observation that this domination is rooted in the Sasanians' serving and adoring the (Zoroastrian) God, who aids them.[36]

Some less direct sources for the Sasanian period confirm the existence of such an ideology of imperial victory regarding the Sasanian great kings. The *Letter of Tosar*, which apparently originated in the third century but has undergone a complex transmission before reaching us,[37] describes how Iran is one of four regions of the earth—the central one and the best. It is legitimate for the great kings of Iran to fight peoples of other regions, and the Iranians are always victorious. But the implication is that the Iranian kings only fight defensively: "A thousand of our soldiers have never met a foe of twenty thousand strong without being victorious and triumphant, because they have never been instigators in tyranny and war and slaughter."[38] The king of kings thus brings the aggressive Turks and Greeks to acknowledge his "pre-eminence" and to send tribute, and he protects the borders of Iran.[39] Religious justification for the legitimacy of defensive war is found in Zoroastrian tradition. The Pahlavi text known as the Book of Arda Viraf describes the invasion of Iran by Alexander the Great in the fourth century B.C.E., with its associated warfare and the burning of Zoroastrian books by the conqueror, as one of the works of Ahriman, the god of evil in Zoroastrian cosmology.[40] The implication, of course, is that since the foreign invader represents the forces of evil, defensive war waged by the Iranian emperor to defend Zoroastrianism and the land of Iran (*Iran zamin*) qualifies as a good work. Hence the Sasanians apparently asserted their claim to Mesopotamia, Syria, and Anatolia as far as the Aegean on the grounds that these regions had formerly belonged to Persia but had been seized by Rome.[41]

As in the Byzantine domain, in Sasanian tradition this ideology of victory is sometimes tied to notions of imperial justice. In the Book of Arda Viraf, for example, which relates the sights witnessed by a Zoroastrian priest of that name during an imaginary journey through heaven and hell—a prefiguration of the theme of the *Divine Comedy*— the narrator tells of seeing in hell "the soul of that wicked man who, in the world, was a bad ruler, and was unmerciful and destructive among men, and caused torment and punishment of various kinds."[42] Similarly, the *Letter of Tosar* notes that violence (obviously considered something evil) came to prevail in society when "men fell upon evil days, under a reign that did not hold fast the welfare of the world, [so that] they fixed their desires upon what was not justly theirs; and destroying decency and neglecting the law, they cast away discretion."[43] Such passages underline the importance of the ruler adhering to proper principles of just rule.

On the other hand, the Sasanian tradition also allowed the king of kings—to be understood here as a God-chosen ruler imbued with justice—quite a free hand in dealing with domestic unrest. According to the *Letter of Tosar*, "When corruption became rife and men ceased to submit to Religion, Reason and the State, and all sense of values disappeared, it was only through bloodshed that honour could be restored to such a realm."[44] This freedom granted to the ruler to shed the blood of obstreperous subjects was closely linked to the Zoroastrian conception of the "right order" of society. A well-ordered society was envisioned in Sasanian Zoroastrian theory as consisting of several sharply differentiated castes or estates, including priests, warriors, peasants, artisans, and shepherds.[45] The smooth functioning of society depended upon everyone remaining in his "right place" in society, and the "unruly," who attempted to break down this divinely established order, were granted no mercy by the ruler: "Punishment and bloodshed among people of this kind [the unruly], even if of a prodigality that seems to have no bound, is recognized by us as life and health."[46] Indeed, the Book of Arda Viraf implies that domestic opposition of almost any kind is reprehensible enough to warrant damnation in the next world (and presumably, therefore, justified chastisement by the ruler in this one), for in hell the priest sees the souls of those wicked people "who have been disobedient unto their rulers in the world, and have been enemies of the armies and troops of their rulers."[47] No requirement that the ruler be just is imposed here; it is simply the duty of the subject to obey and help safeguard the established order. The established order was justice. Similarly, in dealing with alien enemies, the great king was hardly expected to exercise forbearance. In the royal inscription of Shapur at Naqsh-i Rustam, for example, the great king, after describing his conquests, boasts of having burned and pillaged cities of Syria, Cilicia, and Cappadocia and of having deported part of their population.[48]

These concepts of imperial victoriousness, both Byzantine and Sasanian, appear to have been embraced relatively early by Islamic rulers;

we find visual testimony of them, at least, in some of the surviving official monuments of the Umayyad period. Perhaps best known are the frescoes from the little complex of buildings known as Qusayr 'Amra, in the Syrian steppe. The frescoes of this complex, generally considered to have been constructed by the Umayyad caliph al-Walid ibn 'Abd al-Malik (705–715), include figures identified as the kings of the Byzantines, Sasanians, Visigoths, and Axumites (Ethiopians) tendering submission to the caliph, over whose figure the Greek word NIKH (victory) appears to be written.[49] Apparently the Umayyad palace at 'Anjar, situated in Lebanon's Biqa' valley (the ancient Coele-Syria), included column capitals (yet unpublished) depicting the caliph as victor over the Sasanian and Byzantine emperors.[50] The Sasanian tradition of kingship, moreover, would continue to contribute to Islamic conceptions of statecraft for many centuries, notably through the "mirror for princes" genre, about which more will be said later.

War as a Reality of Life

It would be wrong, of course, to assume that these "official" perspectives on war were the only ones that shaped the attitude of the people of the Near East on the eve of the Islamic era. The reality of war must have shaped popular attitudes in these regions as well. In fact, the decades immediately preceding the beginnings of the Islamic conquest were years filled with wars and conflicts of various sorts. These would have included, among others, Justinian's colossal efforts to reconquer the Roman West; Byzantium's continuing struggle with Sasanian Persia, especially the massive Persian invasion of the first decade of the seventh century c.e., by which the Persians seized most of Byzantium's Near Eastern provinces; the civil war between Heraclius and the emperor Phocas (602–610), whom he overthrew; and the emperor Heraclius's bold campaign into the Mesopotamian heartland of the Sasanian empire and his victory over it in the 620s. Countless lesser disturbances, mutinies, and rebellions also took place; the Sasanian invasion of Yemen in 570 c.e. to oust Axumite forces there; the Samaritan revolt in Palestine in the mid–sixth century; and so on.

Such events would have generated a familiarity with war and probably also a horror for it, although we can only guess at their exact impact on particular individuals or groups or at their general contribution to popular attitudes. Most important, perhaps, was the fact that the actual course that wars took in reality was not always—indeed, not even usually—what the "official" attitudes might predict. The Byzantine emperor, for example, despite his ideology of victoriousness, was not always victorious on the battlefield, and his subjects must of course have been aware of this discrepancy between ideology and reality. Such discrepancies may have contributed to the anxiety and volatility of popular opinion that has been said to characterize Byzantine society in the early seventh century C.E.[51] It was a situation that called for extraordinary means to deal with this uncertainty, and this brings us to the final factor we shall consider as part of the pre-Islamic background contributing to Islamic attitudes toward war.

The Apocalyptic Tradition and Popular Attitudes toward War

Another factor in the immediate intellectual background against which early Islam first appeared—in this case, one that had a profound influence especially on popular conceptions of war and peace—was apocalyptic thought. According to this outlook, the world was near its end, about to be surprised by the awesome events of the Last Judgment, which would mark the transition from the eon of the mundane world into the beginning of the new eon, the kingdom of God, when all evil would be banished and only the righteous would exist. By the seventh century C.E. the apocalyptic tradition had a long history, beginning several centuries B.C.E. in Judaism and continuing in Christianity, a faith that itself has deep roots in apocalyptic tradition.[52] On the basis of prophecies ascribed either to the Sibylline oracles or to various biblical prophets (the latter often associated with prophecies in the books of Daniel or Revelation), the authors of these apocalypses offered evidence—including many "signs" of the coming Last Day readily recognizable to their immediate audiences as recent events—that plausibly seemed to show that the end of the world was just around the corner. These "predictions" seemed to confirm the clairvoyance of the prophets who supposedly had uttered them and filled their hearers with an acute sense that the prophecies about the imminent Last Day would also soon be fulfilled.[53]

Apocalyptic thought was not merely a passing fancy of the early Byzantine period nor a movement limited to a narrow sect; it was widely popular and survived for centuries. The intellectual appeal of apocalyptic concepts is borne out by the fact that they have continued to find an ardent following right up to the present day.[54] During the early Byzantine centuries numerous apocalyptic works were composed—in Greek, Syriac, and perhaps other languages—and avidly translated.[55] Latin and Slavic translations of Eastern works circulated widely in medieval Europe and had a great impact on the formation of medieval European religious history and thought.[56] Apocalyptic thought may also have been current in the Christian kingdom of Axum (Ethiopia) on the eve of the Islamic period; recent work on the Ethiopian royal epic, the *Kebra Nagast*, suggests that the text may have been an apocalypse in its earliest form in the sixth or seventh century.[57] The popularity of apocalyptic thought in Axum is further suggested by the fact that the apocalyptic Book of Enoch, considered apocryphal by the Greek and Latin churches, is included in the canon of the Ethiopic Bible.[58]

War played an important part in these apocalyptic speculations. It was generally felt that the Last Days would be ushered in by various calamities, which would serve as "signs" or "portents" of the world's approaching end. Among these calamities, wars of various kinds figured prominently. From the seventh century c.e., if not earlier, for example, apocalypses written by Byzantine Orthodox Christians often presented the end-time as being ushered in by the reign of an expected "last Roman [that is, Byzantine] emperor," who would vanquish the enemies of Rome, restore the universal dominion of Christianity and an era of peace and prosperity, and from Jerusalem hand over imperial power to God, marking the beginning of the end of the kingdom of earth and the beginning of the kingdom to come. But not even the transition to the heavenly kingdom was to be an easy or peaceable one; it was to be marked by the appearance of the Antichrist, who would reign during a period of chaos and war, eventually to be vanquished in his turn by Christ, whose Second Coming would mark the true end of the world, the onset of the Last Judgment, and the beginning of the kingdom of God. Into this kind of general framework Byzantine apocalyptists from the fourth century onward attempted to fit the events of their day and of the recent past. Victorious Byzantine emperors were sometimes portrayed as the expected last Roman emperor; periods of foreign invasion and turbulence were interpreted either as the chaos that was expected to precede the appearance of the victorious last Roman emperor or as signs that the Antichrist was already abroad in the world.[59] The *Kebra Nagast*, for its part, presents the Persian king as an "instrument of divine punishment against Byzantium for her deviation from the true [that is, Monophysite] path"[60] and may well have proposed that the Ethiopian negus, not the Roman emperor, was the one who would vanquish the enemies of the true faith and hand kingship over to God.[61] Generally, people imbued with the apocalyptic outlook watched for portents of the coming Antichrist, including "bad rulers, civil discord, war, drought, famine, plague, comets, sudden deaths of prominent persons and an increase of general sinfulness."[62]

One of the beauties of apocalyptic thought is its flexibility, that is, the ease with which the general apocalyptic vision can be adjusted to fit diverse historical realities. It could, of course, be used to help put the "fear of God" into people, even those of high station who might be held accountable for particular policies and their consequences. But it could also provide a means for believers in a given creed to explain away historical developments that in themselves might seem to undermine the notion that their creed was favored by God. Byzantine (Chalcedonian) Christians, for example, persuaded of the God-aided "victoriousness" of their emperor and state, would have had some difficulty coming to terms with a calamity such as the Persian conquest of much of the Byzantine Near East in the early seventh century c.e. or the Islamic conquest a few years later. But viewed through the lens of apocalyptic thought, such a defeat could be seen as a preliminary (and, indeed, necessary) stage, a sign heralding the imminent advent of the victorious last emperor. That is, apocalyptic thought provided a way of hoping against hope, of retaining one's faith in the face of apparently overwhelming events, and of avoiding the perhaps obvious conclusion that one might have drawn from such events, namely, that God was not on one's own side after all. Apocalyptic thought did not permit one to deny the events of history, but it did provide a means to deny the apparent significance and implications of those events. It would be natural to assume, then, that apocalyptic speculation might be very popular in a period of anxiety and uncertainty, such as that which apparently preceded the appearance of Islam.

Despite the protean variations of apocalyptic thought, however, war always plays a prominent role in the apocalypse, and it always does so in a context that implies that war is among the worst visitations humanity can endure. This much is clear from the bad company it keeps—famine, plague, and so on.[63] On the other hand, despite the fact that the horrors of war are underlined in the apocalyptic worldview, it also presents the picture of a "good" war following on the "bad" wars, that is, a war in which the last emperor or other savior figure vanquishes the enemies of the faith, or in which Christ vanquishes the hordes of the Antichrist. It suggests that people had an ambivalent attitude toward war, decrying it when it resulted in the advancement of their enemies, but accepting it as a valid, indeed even a necessary and inevitable, stage in hoped-for ultimate victory of the forces of goodness and true belief.

Apocalyptic conceptions were taken up by the early Muslims and used for their own purposes. The apocalyptic character of Muhammad's message, as preserved for us in the Qur'an, will be considered in more detail later. But aside from the Qur'an there exists much evidence pointing to the survival of apocalyptic attitudes and their reformulation to fit into an early Islamic context by Muslims of the first century a.h. Indeed, the first century a.h./seventh century c.e. appears to have been a period of intense apocalyptic speculation in the Islamic community (as it was among Christians, who at this time produced such texts as the influential Pseudo-Methodius apocalypse).[64] One of the earliest dated Arabic inscriptions (64 a.h./683–684 c.e.) reveals an apocalyptic outlook by mentioning Israfil, the angel who in Muslim eschatology sounds the trumpet of doom on the Day of Judgment.[65] Numerous apocalyptic traditions—now sometimes presented as sayings of the prophet Muhammad, rather than as sayings of an Old or New Testament figure—were put into circulation during the first century A.H., predicting the imminent end of the world.[66] The South Arabian tribesmen who felt restive under the rule of the North Arabian Umayyad caliphs and their tribal backers generated apocalypses extolling the glories of ancient South Arabian kingship and predicting the eventual appearance of a Qahtani (South Arabian) deliverer, who would drive out the North Arabian oppressors and establish (or reestablish) the true kingship of the South Arabians.[67] The rebel Ibn al-Ash'ath of the South Arabian tribe of Kinda actually presented himself as the Qahtani deliverer during his rebellion in 81–84 A.H./700–703 C.E.[68] Books of oracles modeled on the Book of Daniel were apparently in circulation in Egypt in 61/680.[69] At the end of the Umayyad period an apocalypse attributed to Enoch was apparently composed at the behest of the caliph Marwan ibn Muhammad (127–132/744–750), which included the prediction that Marwan would rule the caliphate and his son after him; and in the Abbasid period another apocalypse stated that the Last Judgment would come with the seventh *imam*, in the reign of the twenty-fourth Arab sovereign.[70]

Much of this apocalyptic speculation in early Islam, as elsewhere, focused on war as a sign or portent of the impending millennium. Key genres of literary composition of the day were traditions about anticipated *fitan* and *malahim*—the "temptations," usually understood as civil strife tearing the eschatological community, and "slaughters" of the final convulsions of the world.[71] Indeed, in some Muslim communities it seems that people may have studied little else in the early Islamic period. In Egypt, for example, people are said to have studied only *malahim* and *fitan* until the efforts of Yazid ibn abi Habib (d. 128 A.H.), who was said to be the first Muslim scholar to occupy himself with "true science," that is, with law and jurisprudence (*fiqh*).[72]

Qur'anic Attitudes

The Qur'an, which for Muslims is literally the word of God, clearly became from an early date in the Islamic era an important guide for the elaboration of Islamic thought on all manner of subjects, not merely regarding war.[73] Since other chapters in this and a companion volume are to discuss the formulation in Islamic law of conceptions of warfare, particularly the notion of *jihad*, and the basis of these legal doctrines in the Qur'an, I will note only a few general points here.[74]

The Qur'an makes occasional reference to "war" (*harb*), frequent reference to "fighting" (*qital* and other words derived from the root q-t-l), and even more frequent reference to "struggle" or striving" (*jihad* and other derivations), by which physical confrontation or fighting appears often—but not always—to be intended. In some passages, of course, the words may well have been used in a symbolic rather than a literal sense. The Qur'anic text as a whole conveys an ambivalent attitude toward violence. On the one hand, oppression of the weak is roundly condemned, and some passages state clearly that the believers are to fight only in self-defense. But a number of passages seem to provide explicit justification for the use of war or fighting to subdue unbelievers, and deciding whether the Qur'an actually condones offensive war for the faith, or only defensive war, is really left to the judgment of the exegete.[75] For example: "Those who disbelieve and divert [others] from the way of God, He will lead their works astray. . . . So when you meet those who disbelieve [during a military campaign], smite the necks; so that, when you have overcome them, you may set [them] in bondage. Afterwards [free them] either as a favor or for ransom; until the war [al-harb] puts down its weapons" (Q. 47:1, 4). Some passages imply that this war is to be defensive in nature, that is, in order to prevent oppression: "And fight [qatilu] in God's way against those who fight you, but do not act aggressively. Indeed God does not love those who act aggressively" (Q. 2:190). But the very next verse states: "And kill them wherever you overtake them, and drive them out from where they drove you out. For fitna [tempting people away from Islam?] is worse than killing. But do not fight them at the Sacred Mosque, unless they fight you in it; but if they do fight you [in it], slay them. Such is the recompense of the unbelievers" (Q. 2:191). The many Qur'anic passages dealing, in one way or another, with warfare thus suggest that war was definitely seen as a valid, indeed even necessary, means of dealing with non-Muslims, at least in cases when non-Muslims attacked Muslims, and perhaps in more general terms.

Apocalyptic conceptions, which, as we have seen, were very widespread in the Near East during the sixth and seventh centuries, may provide an ideological context for these Qur'anic passages. The possibility that Islam may originally have been an apocalyptic movement has been advanced by numerous scholars.[76] According to this view, the Prophet believed that the final Day of Judgment was near and that the present world would soon end, probably during his own lifetime. The Qur'an includes many passages that emphasize the perils of sinful behavior and stress the immediacy of the Last Day.[77] This perception of the approaching Day of Judgment was, of course, what gave Muhammad his sense of moral urgency. He wished to establish a community of true believers (mu'minun) who could live in righteousness and hence be the elect who would be saved and spared the terrible chastisement of the Last Day. Muhammad did not preach merely a passive piety or righteousness in which one looked out for one's own fate, however; rather, he preached a militant piety, one that felt an urgent need not only to adopt righteous behavior in one's own life, but also to stamp out kufr (ingratitude toward God, hence unbelief in the form of impious behavoir)[78] wherever it appeared. "Those believers who remain passive [*al-qaʿidun*, "those who sit"]—unless they be disabled—are not the equal of those who strive [*al-mujahidun*] in the way of God with their property and their selves; God has favored those who strive in the way of God with their property and their selves over those who are passive to a degree" (Q. 4:95).[79] That is, the early Muslims may have felt a responsibility to stamp out unbelief in order to "clean the world up" in preparation for the impending Last Day. The *mujahidun* may thus correspond to the early Christians who viewed themselves as "soldiers of Christ" in contradistinction to the *pagani* or "civilians," nonparticipants in the struggle against evil.[80]

Given the apocalyptic character of Muhammad's message, however, we may wish to go even further and to suggest that the Prophet and the early Muslims may actually have seen themselves as the avenging forces that would punish the unbelievers, that is, as part of the eschatological event itself.[81] They would be playing a role somewhat similar to that reserved for the last Roman emperor in Byzantine Christian apocalyptic, vanquishing the enemies of the true faith and establishing the rule of God. One verse of the Qur'an, for example, states, "It is not fit for a prophet to take captives until he has completely subdued the land [or, made great slaughter in the land? (*athkhana fi l-ʾard*)]. You desire the goods of this world, but God desires [for you] the Hereafter" (Q. 8:67).[82] If the Prophet and the early Muslim "true believers" did see themselves as the avengers who should "completely subdue [make great slaughter in?] the land," their attitude toward war could be quite positive, as they would consider themselves, and the war they waged in God's name, to be the instruments of God's will in the final act of history. Such a self-conception may explain the amazing dynamism displayed in the early Islamic conquests, waged by the early Muslims under the battle cry "*Allahu akbar*," "God is most great."[83]

Historical Circumstances

Regardless of what we conclude the essence of the early Islamic message to have been, and indeed even if we were rashly to make the assumption—to my mind, the incorrect assumption—that Qur'anic statements on war and fighting do not reflect the particular attitude and outlook of the earliest Muslims, we would nevertheless have to take into account in considering the formulation of the "classical" Islamic attitude toward war the historical events that surrounded the rise of Islam. These events, of course, included wars as a significant component. First and foremost, they included the Islamic conquest movement itself (commonly called the "Arab conquest"), a historical phenomenon about the existence of which, in the face of contemporary documentation, there can be no doubt, however much individuals may wish to dispute its ultimate causes or particular details of the received historical picture about it.[84]

If the conquests were in some organic way connected with a new religious movement that came to be called Islam, the very fact of the conquests meant that Muslims of later generations would be forced to come to terms with the concept of war intellectually. Indeed, if later Muslims were not to repudiate the evident consequences of those con-quests—namely, the spread of the faith to distant horizons and the establishment of Muslim hegemony over non-Muslims in large areas of the Near East and North Africa—they were virtually required to develop a view of war that in some way embraced at least the Islamic conquests as a legitimate phenomenon.

If we make the assumption, to me a more natural one, that the earliest Muslims already were motivated by a religiously legitimized zeal to conquer, then the tortured logic of the previous paragraph is unneces-sary. In fact, it seems likely that the crystallization of a "positive" view of legitimate war, if it did not already antedate the beginnings of the conquest movement, took place simultaneously with it, for the conquests continued more or less unabated for well over a century, as a review of the dates of some of the more important conquest landmarks will make immediately obvious.[85] This ongoing process of conquest waged by the new Islamic state, then, would in and of itself have meant the eventual formulation of a conception of war that saw at least some varieties of war as legitimate—in particular, war conducted with the aim of spread-ing the true faith or the rule of the state that ensured the dominance of that faith.

Not all the wars of the early Islamic period were conducive to a positive view among Muslims regarding war, however. Just over thirty years after the death of the Prophet, political and religious disagreements within the Muslim community boiled over in a conflict that, for the first time, saw Muslims taking up arms against other Muslims. This first civil war (35–40 A.H./656–661 C.E.) and the second civil war that divided the Muslims again a few decades later (60–72 A.H./680–692 C.E.) were trau-matic events for the community, and it is noteworthy that later Islamic tradition—already by the end of the first century A.H., if not even ear-lier—referred to these events with the term *fitna*, "test, trial, tempta-tion," a Qur'anic word with decidedly negative moral overtones.[86] From these intracommunal conflicts, particularly from the first civil war, emerged the main religiopolitical subdivisions ("sects" or "parties," de-pending on whether one emphasizes mainly the religious or the political aspect) within the Islamic community: the Shi'is, the Kharijites, and the Murji'a or proto-Sunnites (the last-named essentially comprising those Muslims who were identified neither as Shi'is nor as Kharijites). The fundamental difference between these groups had nothing to do with their attitude toward war, however, but rather with their conception of how the limits defining the community of believers were to be drawn—that is, with who is "us" and who is "them." When radical Kharijites in Iraq and Iran attacked communities of people who considered themselves Muslims during the early Islamic period, while leaving communities of Christians, Jews, and others unmolested, it was because they believed that those Muslims had committed apostasy through their failure to challenge openly the impiety of the established rulers. Hence in Kharijite eyes, such people, even though they called themselves Muslims, were unbelievers, not even deserving the grudging acceptance accorded "peoples of the book" such as Christians. Their vicious attacks, however, would hardly have given their victims (or those who feared that they might become their victims) reason to think of war in positive terms.

The very events of the early Islamic period, then, since they included both wars of conquest and civil wars, meant that Muslims would almost inevitably adopt an ambivalent attitude toward war in general and had to make an effort to distinguish "good" from "bad" wars, depending upon the motivations and objectives for which war was being conducted. Whereas the "good" wars, for the purposes of conquest, came to be called *futuh*, "openings" (that is, occasions when God helped the believers "open" or conquer a given territory for the imposition of divine law and Islamic rule), the "bad" wars were dismissed as *fitan*, "temptations," as a result of which believers had turned their back on God's ordinances and the duty to keep solidarity with other believers. The word *harb* appears to have remained morally neutral and to have referred above all to the actual process of fighting, whether in a "good" or "bad" war.[87] But it could refer to a state of war also, and standard juristic usage came to distinguish the *dar al-islam* ("abode of Islam")—the territory of the united Islamic state—from the *dar al-harb* ("abode of war"), which was all of the world not yet subjected by the Islamic state. That is, the *dar al-harb* was all territory with which the Islamic state could be said to have been in a "state of war," regardless of whether hostilities were actually taking place. This distinction between abodes of Islam and of war, however, must be subsequent to, and an outgrowth of, a clear-cut notion of "legitimate" war (*jihad*) as distinct from *fitna* or internal dissension. Indeed, the terms *dar al-harb* and *dar al-islam* do not appear in the juristic literature until the late second century A.H./late eight century C.E.[88]

THE ISLAMIC JURIDICAL TRADITION ON WAR

All of the factors described in the preceding section—and, doubtless, many others—contributed to the way the first generations of Muslims thought about war and hence to the Islamic juristic tradition regarding war, peace, and statecraft. Given the vast scope of the juristic literature and the fact that the majority of general works of Islamic jurisprudence include a section on *jihad*, we can make here only a few brief observations on the content of the juristic tradition. First, we must recall that the literature of Islamic jurisprudence—whether Sunni or Shi'i—is based on the assumption that the Islamic community is, or should be, not only a religious unity but also a political unity, governed by a single Islamic government headed by the caliph (*khalifa*) or *imam*. According to this conception, the unified Islamic state stood apart from all other states, the governments of which were not dedicated to fostering the perfor- mance of Muslims' religious duties. As we have seen, by the end of the second century A.H./eighth century C.E. the juristic tradition had devel- oped the notion of the "abode of Islam" (*dar al-islam*) and "abode of war" (*dar al-harb*) as a succinct expression of this political dichotomy.

From a relatively early date, however, the Islamic world no longer was unified politically. Already by the middle of the second century A.H./eighth century C.E., when Spain remained in the hands of the Umayyad dynasty while the rest of the empire fell to the Abbasids, there existed two essentially independent and mutually antagonistic Muslim states, and from the fourth/tenth century onward, independent Muslim states proliferated.

This inconsistency between juristic theory and political reality affected how Muslims viewed the legitimacy of waging war—what in European tradition would be called the *jus ad bellum*. Against states of the *dar al- harb*, the legitimate ruler of the Islamic empire, in juristic theory, was justified in making war at any time; indeed, to wage *jihad* in an effort to subdue the *dar al-harb* and to incorporate it into the *dar al-islam* was seen as a religious duty of the *imam*/caliph. Moreover, only the *imam* was authorized to declare an offensive *jihad* against unbelievers with a view to subduing them; the individual Muslim was discouraged from "striking out on his own." Given the existence in most historical periods of many Islamic states, however, this latter provision of the holy law posed a problem, since presumably only one of those states—whichever could best claim to be the legitimate one—could be justified in declaring *jihad*. What resulted in practice was a curious inversion of the juristic ideal: Muslim rulers did not consult the jurists to discover whether they were legitimate and therefore entitled to wage *jihad*, but rather by waging *jihad* they offered evidence of the legitimacy of their claim to rule.

Given the proliferation of independent Muslim states, the juristic norms also meant that a Muslim ruler could only make war against another Muslim by declaring him to be a rebel or apostate, since the law reserved *jihad* for efforts against unbelievers. Each Muslim regime had to see itself as the sole legitimate Muslim state and considered other

Muslim regimes to be rebels or usurpers of the legitimate state's sovereign rights. Consequently, discussions of relations between Islamic states fall under the headings *fitna* (internal dissension) or *bughat* (rebels) in the juristic literature.[89] Generally speaking, there is a strong tendency in the juristic literature to uphold the authority of the established ruler and to discourage rebellion. For example, there are numerous sayings attributed to the Prophet in which he relates the punishment that will befall anyone who breaks the unity of the community, or enjoins the Muslims to disobey the *imam*—even, according to some sayings, if the *imam* is unjust.[90] Moreover, the assumption of political unity among Muslims that undergirds the juridical tradition may have made it difficult for the jurists to develop a pragmatic system of interstate law to regulate hostilities such as those that arose in early modern Europe, where different rulers or governments viewed one another as sovereign peers, each equally legitimate within his own territory.

This attitude toward the legitimacy of waging war against other Muslims not only affected the juristic literature but seems to have spread also to the more practical literature of statecraft. For example, in Ibn al-Muqaffa''s *Risalat al-khamis* (epistle to the army), written for the Abbasid caliph al-Ma'mun during his struggle for control of the caliphate against his brother al-Amin, al-Ma'mun's war is called an effort to subdue apostasy (*ridda*) inspired by Satan.[91] Another passage defines the role of the ruler: the community, it says, needs a commander who will assure a good state of religion and justice, guard the rights of each Muslim, and organize campaigns against non-Muslim enemies.[92]

The juristic tradition also contains significant guidance on how Muslims are to conduct themselves in war—discussions corresponding to the Western *jus in bello*. The early juristic literature already contains plentiful examples of injunctions against killing women, children, and other noncombatants; similarly, it bars attacks on the enemy without first inviting them to embrace Islam, discusses the problem of "double effect" (for example, unintended death of noncombatants during a night assault), and so on.[93] These early juristic principles of *jus in bello* were elaborated by later authors. Sometimes they were treated in the sections on *jihad*, *ghaza'* (raiding), or *siyar* (campaigns) in full-scale juristic compilations and commentaries, with an effort to bring the discussion "up to date"; for example, the Ottoman author Muhammad Mawqufati (d. 1065/1654), in his commentary on the *Multaqa' al-'abhur* of Ibrahim ibn Muhammad al-Halabi (d. 956/1549), debates whether guidelines and limitations on using ballistae and mangonels refer also to cannons.[94]

OTHER FACTORS AFFECTING THE CONCEPTUALIZATION OF WAR IN ISLAM

As diverse groups of people embraced Islam, they brought with them their traditional attitudes toward war, and one can expect that at the very least they would have interpreted the Islamic legal doctrines on war in the light of their own traditional attitudes and personal experience. In long-established Muslim communities, moreover, the events of a particular historical epoch may have contributed to a modification in their popular attitudes toward war, even if they did not greatly affect the juridical doctrines toward war. We can thus propose that there may be as many varieties of "Islamic" attitudes toward war—that is, attitudes held by significant communities of Muslims—as there have been communities. Since, as noted earlier, there can be no question of attempting a comprehensive survey of all the possible attitudes (even if one could recover historical evidence about them), we will merely note here a few specific historical instances that suggest interesting problems regarding attitudes toward war held by Muslims.

The Crusaders in the East and Muslim Attitudes toward War

Orientalists have paid considerable attention to the question of the Crusaders' notions of "holy war" and to the question of whether the Muslims in response (or beforehand) developed a corresponding concept to deal with the threat posed by the Crusaders.[95] In a recent essay on this theme Albrecht Noth has demonstrated that the Crusades had no major impact on either the theory or the practice of *jihad* among Muslims. The Crusades never produced a "counter-Crusade" because the Frankish invasion was never seen as a particularly serious threat to Islam as a whole, however much it threatened specific localities in the Levantine fringe of the central Islamic lands.[96]

True though this may be, it does not permit us to conclude that the Crusades had no impact on the attitudes toward war among some Muslims. We cannot know, of course, what most Muslims who were affected by the arrival of the Crusaders thought personally of the events of their day. We cannot know whether their attitudes as individuals were influenced in any special way because the adversary consisted of Frankish Christians rather than the usual Arab bedouins, Turkoman or Kurdish tribesmen serving a Seljuk prince, or the Berber, African, or Armenian infantrymen of the Fatimid army, all of whom periodically intervened militarily in the Levant in the decades preceding and following the first appearance of the Crusaders. But we can see a reflection of what may have been a heightened sense of the importance of warfare fought "for the faith" against non-Muslims (for example, against Frankish invaders) in the appearance of a new genre of literature that has been called "pseudo-*futuh*" literature. It is at this time and in this place—geographical Syria—that we see the appearance of a number of Arabic works ostensibly dealing, in a romanticized way, with the first great Islamic conquests.[97] These late "pseudo-*futuh*" works often have little, if any, documentary value for the history of the early Islamic conquests and contain telltale anachronisms that reveal them to be products of the age of the Crusades. But they are filled with an idealized and nostalgic vision of the successful *jihad* launched against non-Muslim powers—especially Christian Byzantium—by the earliest Muslims of the golden age. The mere existence of these works thus provides some testimony to a heightened popular interest among Syrians in the theme of Islamic conquest of non-Muslims, particularly of Christians, who would (in Byzantine form) have been the main adversary in the initial Syrian conquests. That such a theme should suddenly have become of special interest at the time of the Crusades can hardly be coincidence.[98]

The Sasanian Tradition of Statecraft and the "Mirror for Princes" Literature

The Sasanian tradition of kingship and statecraft, some aspects of which we have discussed in the context of the pre-Islamic background of the juristic tradition on war, continued to exert a powerful influence on the Islamic world, particularly in the Islamic east. From an early date in the Islamic era, ministers and advisers began to compose "mirrors for princes," in which they offered to the ruler or prince sage advice on how to manage the affairs of state. The content of these works, which were written in Arabic, Persian, Turkish, or Urdu, varied considerably. Some were essentially practical manuals of administration or handbooks of manners, others were treatises on the theory of government; some presented Sasanian political concepts virtually unchanged, others attempted in varying degrees to subordinate the old Sasanian tradition to the political conceptions of Islamic law; some hardly treated the question of war at all, others took it up at considerable length.[99]

A few examples can help convey this diversity. The famous *Siyar al-muluk* or *Siyaset-nama*, written by the vizier Nizam al-Mulk (d. 485/1092) for the Seljuk sultan Malik-Shah, presents the Sasanian conception of kingship with little change. The king is chosen by God for the good of mankind, in order to preserve the equilibrium within society. God gives the king those qualities of wisdom and justice necessary to rule and holds him accountable for his acts. Religion and kingship are called "two brothers"—that is, related, but neither subordinate to the other.[100] While the text devotes considerable attention to the proper organization of the army, it has little to say about the legitimacy of war, whether against the infidel or against other Muslims. It is interesting to note, however, that one passage, at least, refers in a matter-of-fact way to the conquest of other Muslim rulers: "The rulers of the Arabs, Kurds, Dailamites, Rumis, and others who have only recently come to terms of submission" to the Seljuks should provide close relatives as hostages to be held at the Seljuk court.[101] There is no elaborate justification for this conquest of other Muslims; evidently, in the minds of author and recipient, none was required.

A second "mirror," written only slightly later and within a similar political context, offers a dramatic contrast to the *Siyar al-muluk*: the anonymous Bahr al-fawa'id, written around 555/1160 in northern Syria for a Seljuk *atabeg* (military ruler). This text is noteworthy for the degree to which its political theory, implicit and explicit, is subordinated to the regulations of Islamic law. Moreover, in further contrast to the *Siyar al-muluk*, the work contains a great deal on *jihad*.[102]

A third example, an early eighteenth-century C.E. Ottoman manual of statecraft written by Sari Mehmet Pasha, deals in passing with such issues as preventing troops on campaign from committing excesses against their coreligionists and discusses the need for proper preparation and precautions on the part of commanders.[103] But the reasons given are entirely practical, not ethical, in character. Generally, the work appeals more to earlier "mirrors" (including the *Siyaset-nama*) than it does to the Islamic religious literature.

Many of these "mirrors for princes" served as vehicles for the expression of conceptions of statecraft and attitudes toward war that were at least in some measure divergent from those of the juristic tradition. Their impact was increased, moreover, by the arrival in the central Islamic lands of yet another political tradition, that of the central Asian steppe. Because the people who brought it—mainly Turks and Mongols—entered the Islamic world primarily through Iran, this steppe tradition was combined with the old Iranian tradition of statecraft to form a new, hybrid "Perso-Turkish" tradition.

The Eurasian Steppe Tradition and Its Impact on Islamic Attitudes toward War

The steppe traditions of warfare and of statecraft were introduced into the Islamic world by a variety of channels. Many generations of Turkish slaves, captured in central Asia and shipped into the Islamic heartlands from the ninth century C.E. onwards, were converted to Islam, were given military training, and, when freed upon completion of their training, served as bodyguards and army cadres for the caliphs or their rivals. Eventually, troops of this kind—notable both for their military effectiveness and their high cost—set themselves up as independent regimes in Egypt, India, and elsewhere by the thirteenth century C.E. Moreover, beginning in the eleventh century, Islamized (or partly Islamized) Turkish tribes, and later Mongol tribes who had not embraced Islam, migrated into the Islamic world—particularly into the Iranian and Anatolian plateaus—and established independent states. A long series of regimes, beginning with the Seljuks (11th–14th centuries) and continuing through many others including the Il-Khans (13th–14th centuries), Timurids (14th–16th centuries), Dehli Sultans (13th–16th centuries), and Ottomans (13th–20th centuries), were Turkish or Turko-Mongol in origin, and the steppe traditions of statecraft flourished in them. As already noted, however, these steppe traditions were powerfully modified not only by the juristic tradition of Islam, but also by the Iranian tradition of statecraft, as many of the early Turkish and Mongol rulers employed highly educated Iranians to staff their bureaucracies once they had established their rule in the central Islamic lands.[104]

The steppe tradition differed markedly from the Islamic juristic tradition in its approach to political authority. The Sunni juristic tradition came to see legitimate political authority growing out of adherence to the holy law and recognition by the majority of the community; the Shi'i tradition stressed both the holy law and the primacy of the Prophet's family, among whom the *imamate* was considered to reside. The steppe tradition, on the other hand, granted the ruler absolute authority to make laws for the state, independent of any existing religious law.[105] Such concepts became particularly firmly established after the conquest of the Middle Eastern Islamic lands by the Mongols, who brought with them their concept of the ruler's *yasa* or personal legislation. Consequently, there occurred in many later Islamic states, such as the Ottoman Empire, a continuing tension between the *shari'a*, or religious law, and the *qanun*, or "secular" state law.[106] The latter was especially important in matters of statecraft and administration, including establishing the governance and tax policies in newly conquered territories. This tension came to be summed up among the Ottomans in the phrase *din ve devlet* (religion and state) as the two (presumably somewhat independent) spheres of responsibility of the sultan.

Whatever the reason, Islamic states of the early modern period do not seem to have evolved the kind of pragmatic agreements and practical literature on war and its limitation among themselves that evolved among states in early modern Europe. It must be remembered, however, that no concerted search for such a pragmatic literature on statecraft, war, and the limitation of war, to the best of my knowledge, has ever been made, so that works of this kind may be buried from view somewhere among the millions of unpublished manuscript sources for the Ottoman, Safavi, Qajar, or Moghul empires. We must hope that scholars concerned with the history of these states will keep a weather eye out for such works as they comb through various archives.

CONCLUSIONS

We are not yet in a position to catalog unequivocally the main elements contributing to the way Muslims thought about war and its limitation, as James Turner Johnson has so succinctly done for the Western tradition.[107] The reason for this is mainly a practical one: too little preliminary work on a vast subject.

Islamic jurisprudence offers relatively rich discussions on many issues relating to war, its limitation, and its justification. As we have seen, this juristic tradition on war grew out of a combination of original Islamic values and of traditions stretching back into the distant pre-Islamic past, and it was likely subjected to continuous reshaping as new historical situations created the conditions for successive reinterpretations of previously established juristic norms. But, as noted at the beginning of this chapter, the details—indeed, even the main contours—of the historical development of this rich juristic tradition (on war as on everything else) are still relatively poorly known. Too many works of Islamic jurisprudence from all periods remain unpublished, and the lines of affiliation among even those works published to date are not yet always understood.

Moreover, despite the vibrancy within the Islamic world of certain traditions of statecraft that were in origin independent of the religious law, it is not clear whether purely secular or pragmatic treatises discussing war and the limitation of war from an ethical perspective emerged within the Islamic world.[108] There did arise a genre of specialized manuals of war in Arabic, which seems to have flourished especially in Mamluk Egypt and Syria, but we cannot yet say whether these manuals are merely a distillation of the juristic tradition on war, or whether they represent a pragmatic tradition essentially independent of the jurists' thinking—and if so, whether they go beyond mere questions of tactics and organization to discuss the ethics and legitimacy of war. One example that has been published, dating from the Mamluk period (1250–1517), is overwhelmingly practical and shows little concern for ethical questions;[109] but most of these Arabic works remain unpublished, and this one example may not be characteristic.[110] The existence of similar works in Persian, Turkish, Urdu, and other Islamic languages remains to be explored. In the Ottoman Empire there apparently was a genre of literature aimed at the common people that offered guidance on proper conduct, including proper conduct for warriors on campaign (*ghaza'*). This so-called *'ilm-i hal* literature also remains to be closely studied, but in all probability it was an effort to communicate to a popular audience the norms of the juristic tradition.[111]

Thus it is not clear whether and to what extent Muslims developed a literature on war that was truly independent of the juristic norms, beyond what is known from the "mirrors for princes" genre. It may be that the juristic conception of war as *jihad* was too strong to be ignored by Muslim rulers, even at their most autocratic, particularly as many of these states—notably the Ottomans—justified their legitimacy precisely by claiming for themselves the role of *ghazis*, that is, warriors for the faith against the infidel.

It must be remembered, however, that there was a vibrant tradition of statecraft in Islamic culture, whatever its particular contribution to the question of war and its limitation may have been. This tradition was effectively cut off by European colonialism during the nineteenth and twentieth centuries, as the great Islamic states that carried the living tradition of Islamic statecraft (Ottomans, Qajars, Sharifs of Morocco, etc.) were dismantled by European powers.[112] In many cases the European colonial authorities introduced European legal systems to the Islamic territories they ruled, above all in the area of foreign relations. In some instances, European law was voluntarily self-imposed; after World War I, for example, the young republican government of Turkey, which had—barely—managed to escape colonial occupation, embarked decisively upon the course of secularization (i.e., of de-Islamization) that had already begun in the last century of Ottoman rule. Virtually the only Islamic state to escape Western colonial rule between 1850 and 1950, the Kingdom of Saudi Arabia was culturally backward and in any case was a regime staunchly committed, in principle at least, to the *shariʿa* and to traditional Islamic jurisprudence. As a result, Muslims in the late twentieth century who wish to find Islamic principles to guide their behavior on all sorts of issues, including those relating to war, have turned almost exclusively to the religious (i.e., juristic) tradition, because it alone survived the colonial onslaught unscathed.

The recovery and reconstruction of the full Islamic tradition of statecraft and war should be a desideratum for all historians of the Islamic lands. But while the task may initially be a labor for historians, it might in the long run also have significant practical implications for modern Muslims by providing states of the Islamic world with a basis for the adjudication of their disputes that is rooted in the Islamic cultural tradition and independent of current "international law." "International law," which now serves as the basis for most interstate adjudication, in fact originated as the European law of nations—that is, as agreements concluded by various European states in their efforts to regulate hostile relations among themselves. Given the European origin of modern "international law," however, it seems obvious that this law will reflect in many ways the ethical values of the Western just war tradition. Although its advocates usually assume that "international law" is a system of universal validity and acceptability, it seems highly probable that it contains embedded within it some cultural values that, being Western in origin, are at variance with Islamic traditions of statecraft.[113] A reconstructed Islamic tradition of statecraft would permit governments in the Islamic world to deal with one another in terms of a system that they might find more culturally palatable to them than "international law."

It would also set the stage for fruitful discussion between advocates of the two systems of adjudication, with a view to discovering the common ground shared by both. Only on this basis could one begin to move toward a truly universal system of international adjudications.[114]

NOTES

I am indebted to several colleagues who offered constructive comments on an earlier draft of this chapter, particularly Lawrence I. Conrad (Wellcome Institute, London), Walter E. Kaegi, Jr. (University of Chicago), and the participants in the symposia where this chapter was first presented, especially the organizers, James Turner Johnson and John Kelsay. I would also like to thank Richard L. Chambers, Robert Dankoff, Halil Inalcik, Robert S. Nelson (all of the University of Chicago), and Carl Petry (Northwestern University) for helpful advice and references.

1. The "classical" period of Islamic civilization is usually considered to embrace its first six centuries (ca. 600–1200 C.E.); "modernist" writings begin to appear in the later nineteenth century and are the products of Muslims' efforts to come to grips, intellectually, with the increasing pressure of European civilization and power. A typical "later" text—postclassical, but premodern—that might be consulted is the famous *Muqaddima* of Ibn Khaldun (d. 780 A.H./1378–79 C.E.).

2. Seldom do such investigators include writings by adherents of the third major religiopolitical sect in Islam, the Kharijites, even though they were of undisputed importance in the earlier Islamic centuries and still exist as a significant minority today.

3. Since the Islamic community traditionally had no organized hierarchy of priests, there can of course be no question of an "official" Islamic position in the same sense that we might speak of the official policy of the papacy in Catholic Christianity. By "official" here we mean only that the attitude represents a certain consensus of leading religious scholars.

4. Classic studies of Islamic attitudes to war, conducted along these lines, are Majid Khadduri, *The Law of War and Peace in Islam* (London: Luzac, 1940), and the relevant chapters of Muhammad Hamidullah, *The Muslim Conduct of State*, rev. 5th ed. (Lahore: Sh. Muhammad Ashraf, 1968) (first partial German edition, Bonn-Leipzig-Berlin, 1935; first complete English version, 1941–42). A more recent example—noteworthy for its concise effort to discuss issues from the perspective of the categories of *jus ad bellum* and *jus in bello*, and for its use of Shi'i sources (especially recent ones) generally neglected by Khadduri and Hamidullah—is the editors' introduction in Mehdi Abedi and Gary Legenhausen, eds., *Jihad and Shahadat: Struggle and Martyrdom in Islam* (Houston: Institute for Research and Islamic Studies, 1986), 1–46.

5. For some general thoughts on the definition of war," see Quincy Wright, "War. I. The Study of War," *International Encyclopedia of the Social Sciences* (New York: Macmillan, 1968), 16: 453–68. A fuller discussion of the problem can be found in his classic study, *A Study of War*, 2d ed. (Chicago: University of Chicago

Press, 1965), 8ff. War can be conceptualized either as an activity or as a condition. In the former case we may define war as "conflict among organized political groups, including but not limited to sovereign states, carried out by armed force" (a slight modification of the definition of war "in the ordinary sense" offered by Wright, "War," 453); as such, it embraces most situations in which serious armed conflict occurs, whether between sovereign states or between organized political factions within a given state. But viewing war as an activity leaves out situations in which a "state of war" is said to exist between two entities even though no actual fighting may currently be taking place. Such situations are covered by viewing war as a condition; this provides a neat, essentially legal distinction between war and peace, but it has the drawback of failing to embrace many cases of armed conflict, even between sovereign states, where no formal declaration or theory of war has been promulgated. In the present chapter war as understood by both definitions will be considered. A well-informed general discussion of the Islamic vocabulary for war, peace, and related concepts and its evolution can be found in Bernard Lewis, *The Political Language of Islam* (Chicago: University of Chicago Press, 1988), especially chap. 4, "War and Peace." Unfortunately the study by Ibrahim Mustafa al-Mahmud, *Fi l'harb'inda l-'Arab* (On war among the Arabs) (Damascus: Ministry of Culture and National Guidance, 1975), despite its promising title, offers nothing on conceptions of war and peace and dwells on organization and the history of particular military campaigns.

6. The argument here rests on a distinction between Islamic religion in the strict sense (including its juridical and theological disciplines) and the broader culture or civilization of which Islam was the dominant element. This distinction was first rigorously made by Marshall G.S. Hodgson, *The Venture of Islam*, 3 vols. (Chicago: University of Chicago Press, 1974), 1:56–60. Hodgson favored reserving the adjective "Islamic" for the former and coined the term "Islamicate" for the latter. In the present chapter I will generally use Islamic" in the more usual manner to refer to both strictly religious and broader cultural phenomena, making clear which is intended by further definition when required.

7. Other sources of opinion might also, on closer examination, be confirmed as important for the background of Islamic conceptions of war, but will not be treated here. Among them we may note South Arabian civilization, which appears to have contributed to Arabic (that is, to North Arabic, a Semitic language group distinct from the old South Arabian languages) numerous loanwords for military institutions (e.g., *misr*, South Arabic "army," North Arabic "cantonment city"; *khamis*, South Arabic "main army force," North Arabic "army"; and so on). On this see A. F. L. Beeston, *Warfare in Ancient South Arabia (2nd–3rd Centuries A.D.)*, Qahtan: Studies in Old South Arabian Epigraphy, no. 3 (London: Luzac, 1976). Another possibility worth closer attention is Samaritanism, given great significance in the background of Islamic concepts of statehood and religious legitimacy by Patricia Crone and Michael Cook, *Hagarism* (Cambridge: Cambridge University Press, 1977), especially 14ff.

8. For a fuller discussion of these themes, see Fred M. Donner, *The Early Islamic Conquests* (Princeton: Princeton University Press, 1981), chap. 1, "State and Society in Pre-Islamic Arabia."

9. The sporting or gamelike nature of pre-Islamic Arabian raiding may be

compared with similar qualities in medieval chivalry in western Europe mentioned by James T. Johnson at the beginning of his chapter on "Historical Roots and Sources of the Just War Tradition in Western Culture" in this volume.

10. Louise E. Sweet, "Camel Raiding of North Arabian Bedouin: A Mechanism of Cultural Adaptation," *American Anthropologist* 67 (1965):1132–50; T. M. Johnstone, "Ghazw," *Encyclopaedia of Islam*, 2d ed., edited by H.A.R. Gibb, et al., (Leiden: E.J. Brill, 1960-continuing), hereafter EI2; A. Musil, *The Manners and Customs of the Rwala Bedouin* (New York: American Geographical Society, 1928), 540, on *ghazw* and *manakh*.

11. A good sense for this poetry can be obtained by reading the selections in Charles Lyall's *Translations of Ancient Arabian Poetry* (London: Williams and Norgate, 1930; New York: Columbia University Press, 1930) and his *The Diwans of ʿAbid ibn al-Abras, of Asad, and ʿAmir ibn al-Tufail, of ʿAmir ibn Saʿsaʿa* (London: Luzac; Leiden: E. J. Brill, 1913).

12. ʿAmir ibn al-Tufail, poem 17; poem 2, verse 15.

13. ʿAmir, 2, v. 16; ʿAbid ibn al-Abras, 4, v. 16.

14. ʿAbid, 4, v. 16.

15. ʿAmir, 1, vv. 2–3.

16. ʿAmir, 29, v. 10. Cf. ʿAbid, 4, v. 17.

17. ʿAmir, 37, vv. 5–6. One wonders whether the word "God" is not an emendation introduced by a Muslim scribe in place of "Fate."

18. The phrase is that of Michael McCormick, *Eternal Victory: Triumphal Rulership in Late Antiquity, Byzantium, and the Early Medieval West* (Cambridge: Cambridge University Press; Paris: Editions de la Maison des sciences de l'homme, 1986), 26, whose valuable study forms the basis for the following remarks.

19. Ibid., 81–82.

20. Ibid., 111ff.

21. Ibid., 120ff.

22. I am indebted to Professor Walter E. Kaegi, Jr., for discussion of this subject.

23. See Robert M. Good, "The Just War in Ancient Israel," *Journal of Biblical Literature* 104 (1985): 385–400.

24. On the Vandal and Visigothic cases, see McCormick, *Eternal Victory*, 261ff. and 297ff.

25. Ibid., 68, citing Justinian's *Institutiones*, preface.

26. P. N. Trempelas, "Hai treis leitourgiai kata tous en Athenais kodikas," *Texte und Forschungen zur byzantinisch-neugriechischen Philologie* 15 (Athens, 1935), 185–86, quoted in McCormick, *Eternal Victory*, 239.

27. On this subject, see the examination of such church historians as Socrates Scholasticus, Sozomen, and Theodoret in Walter Emil Kaegi, Jr., *Byzantium and the Decline of Rome* (Princeton: Princeton University Press, 1968), especially chap. 5,"Divine Providence and the Roman Empire."

28. See André Grabar, *L'Empereur dans l'art byzantin* (Paris: Les Belles Lettres, 1936, fasc. 75 of "Publications de la Faculté des lettres de l'Université de Strasbourg; reprint, London: Variorum, 1971), 32ff. I owe this reference to Robert S. Nelson.

29. Legends for this period can be conveniently surveyed in Cécile Morrison,

Catalogue des monnaies byzantines de la Bibliothèque nationale. I. D'Anastase ler à Justinien II (491–711) (Paris: Bibliothèque nationale, 1970).

30. The name of God appears in the phrase "Deus adiuta Romanis" (God is the helper of the Romans) on a few gold and silver issues from Heraclius (610–641) to Justinian II (first reign, 685–695). See Morrison, *Catalogue des monnaies byzantins*, 310, 323, 381, 406.

31. *The History of Theophylact Simocatta*, trans. Michael Whitby and Mary Whitby (Oxford: Clarendon Press, 1986), 229–30. Theophylact wrote under Heraclius.

32. George T. Dennis, transl., *Maurice's Strategikon* (Philadelphia: University of Pennsylvania Press, 1984), 9. The work is probably to be dated to the reign of Heraclius (Walter E. Kaegi, Jr., and Lawrence I. Conrad, personal communications).

33. George T. Dennis, ed. and transl., *Three Byzantine Military Treatises* (Washington, D.C.: Dumbarton Oaks, 1985), "Anonymous Byzantine Treatise on Strategy," 21.

34. Wilhelm Blum, translator and commentator, *Byzantinische Fürstenspiegel* (Stuttgart: Hiersemann, 1981), 65 (*Ekthesis*, chap. 20).

35. Roman Ghirshman, *Persian Art, Parthian and Sassanian Dynasties, 249 B.C.–A.D. 651* (New York: Golden Press, 1962), 152, pl. 196.

36. André Maricq, "Res Gestae Divi Saporis," *Syria* 35 (1958): 295–360, at 330.

37. The assumed third-century text in Pahlavi (Middle Persian), now lost, was evidently translated in the eighth century into Arabic. The Arabic version (also now lost) was then retranslated in the thirteenth century into New Persian. Various additions were made to the text in the course of transmission. On the transmission, see Mary Boyce, transl., *The Letter of Tansar* (Rome: Istituto Italiano per il Medio ed Estremo Oriente, 1968), 1. On the proper form of the name (Tansar vs. Tōsar), see Boyce, 7–8.

38. Boyce, *Letter of Tansar*, 63–64.

39. Ibid., 65.

40. *The Book of Arda Viraf*, the Pahlavi text prepared by Destur Hoshangji Jamaspji Asa, with an English translation and introduction by Martin Haug and E. W. West (Bombay: Government Central Book Depot; London: Trübner, 1872), 141–43 (chap. 1).

41. Dio Cassius 80.3.1–4, cited in Fergus Millar, "Government and Diplomacy in the Roman Empire during the First Three Centuries," *International History Review* 10 (1988): 345–47.

42. *Book of Arda Viraf*, 173 (chap. 28).

43. Boyce, *Letter of Tansar*, 39.

44. Ibid., 40.

45. Slightly different "caste" groupings are given in Boyce, *Letter of Tansar*, 38, and *Book of Arda Viraf*, 163–64 (chaps. 14 and 15).

46. Boyce, *Letter of Tansar*, 40.

47. *Book of Arda Viraf*, 202 (chap. 99).

48. Maricq, "Res Gestae Divi Saporis," 312–14; cf. Millar, "Government and Diplomacy," 346.

49. For excellent plates of the newly cleaned frescoes and brief discussion

with references to earlier literature on the inscriptions, see Martin Almagro, Luis Caballero, Juan Zozaya, and Antonio Almagro, *Qusayr 'Amra* (Madrid: Instituto Hispano-Arabe de Cultura, 1975), 56–57, 119, and pls. 14, 16, and 17.

50. Heinz Gaube, *Ein arabischer Palast in Südsyrien, Hirbet el-Baida* (Beirut: Orient-Institut der Deutschen Morgenländischen Gesellschaft, in Kommission bei Franz Steiner Verlag, Wiesbaden, 1974), 123.

51. On this, see Walter Emil Kaegi, Jr., *Byzantium and the Early Islamic Conquests* (forthcoming), chap. 1. I am indebted to Professor Kaegi for allowing me to read a prepublication version of this important work. Factors other than war, of course, could well have contributed to this mood of anxiety and uncertainty— for example, the prevalence of plague, which had appeared in the Near East in the mid–sixth century. See Lawrence I. Conrad, "The Plague in the Early Medieval Near East" (Ph.D. diss., Princeton University, 1981).

52. The word "apocalyptic" can be used to refer either to a literary form or to an outlook or cosmology; the latter in particular is intended here. For a concise general survey of apocalyptic, see Walter Schmithals, *The Apocalyptic Movement* (Nashville, Tenn.: Abingdon Press, 1975); on early background, see H. H. Rowley, *The Relevance of Apocalyptic*, rev. ed. (Greenwood, S.C.: Attic Press, 1980); the special volume of *Journal for Theology and the Church* 6 (1969), devoted to apocalypticism; also Norman Cohn, *The Pursuit of the Millennium*, rev. ed. (New York: Oxford University Press, 1970), 19–36. The classic study of early Jewish apocalyptic is Paul Volz, *Die Eschatologie der jüdischen Gemeinde im neutestamentlichen Zeitalter* (Tübingen: J.C.B. Mohr, 1934).

53. On the historical content of these apocalypses, see Paul J. Alexander, "Medieval Apocalypses as Historical Sources," *American Historical Review* 73 (1968): 997–1018.

54. For a glimpse of the importance of apocalyptic in the late twentieth-century United States, see Randall Balmer, *Mine Eyes Have Seen the Glory* (New York and Oxford: Oxford University Press, 1989).

55. On Byzantine apocalyptic in general, see Paul J. Alexander, *The Byzantine Apocalyptic Tradition* (Berkeley: University of California Press, 1985).

56. On the continuing vitality of apocalyptic ideas in the Middle Ages, see Bernard McGinn, *Visions of the End: Apocalyptic Traditions in the Middle Ages* (New York: Columbia University Press, 1979); also Werner Verbeke, Daniel Verhelst, and Andries Welkenhuysen, eds., *The Use and Abuse of Eschatology in the Middle Ages* (Leuven: Leuven University Press, 1988), especially Richard Landes, "Lest the Millennium Be Fulfilled: Apocalyptic Expectations and the Pattern of Western Chronography, 100–800 c.e.," 137–211; and Cohn, *Pursuit of the Millennium*, to be read in light of McGinn's survey of its shortcomings (*Visions of the End*, 28ff.).

57. Irfan Shahid, "The Kebra Nagast in the Light of Recent Research," *Le Muséon* 89 (1976): 133–78, at 173. The current form of the *Kebra Nagast* apparently dates to the late "middle ages." On the early origins of the *Kebra Nagast*, see Shahid, "Kebra Negast," 143ff.; Shahid suggests that the text may originally have been written in Coptic (in Egypt? or by a Copt in Axum or Nubia, which were culturally dependent on Egypt in this period?) and subsequently translated into Ethiopic, since the Copts of Egypt, like other Monophysites, came to look to the Ethiopian monarchy as the bulwark of their faith after Byzantium returned to the Chalcedonian creed under Justin I.

58. Shahid, "Kebra Nagast," 173. On Enoch, see R. H. Charles, transl., *The Book of Enoch* (London: SPCK, 1917); it originated in Galilee in the late second century B.C.E.

59. Alexander, *Byzantine Apocalyptic Tradition*, see the modifications proposed by G.J. Reinink, "Pseudo-Methodius und die Legende vom römischen Endkaiser," in Verbeke, Verhelst, and Welkenhuysen, *Use and Abuse of Eschatology*, 82–111.

60. Shahid, "Kebra Nagast," 165.

61. In accordance with Ps. 68:31, a verse that Byzantine apocalyptists such as Pseudo-Methodius had to explain away by ingenious means. On this, see Paul J. Alexander, "Psevdo-Mefodiy i Efiopiya," *Antichnaya Drevnost'i Srednie Veka, Sbornik* 10 (Sverdlosk, 1973), 21–27, reprinted in Alexander, *Religious and Political History and Thought in the Byzantine Empire* (London: Variorum, 1978), selection 11, with English summary.

62. Cohn, *Pursuit of the Millennium*, 35, referring particularly to early medieval Europe, but equally applicable to the contemporary Near East.

63. Cf, for example, the Oracle of Baalbek, an apocalypse of late fourth-century origin that was recast in Baalbek in the first decade of the sixth century: Paul J. Alexander, *The Oracle of Baalbek: The Tiburtine Sibyl in Greek Dress* (Washington, D.C.: Dumbarton Oaks, 1967), especially 26 (translation), where war occurs among other portents—locust plagues, famines, incest, sorcery, fornication, greed, and so on.

64. On Pseudo-Methodius generally, see Francisco Javier Martinez, "Eastern Christian Apocalyptic in the Early Muslim Period: Pseudo-Methodius and Pseudo-Athanasius" (Ph.D. diss., Catholic University of America, 1985); Reinink, "Pseudo-Methodius"; Alexander, *Byzantine Apocalyptic Tradition*; McGinn, *Visions of the End*, 70–73.

65. ʿIzz al-Din al-Sanduq, "Hajar Hafnat al-ʾUbayyid," *Sumer* 11 (1955): 213–17 (Arabic).

66. Lawrence I. Conrad, "Portents of the Hour: History and Hadith in the First Century A.H.," *Der Islam* (forthcoming). I am indebted to Dr. Conrad for making available to me a draft of this paper. Cf. A. J. Wensinck, *A Handbook of Early Muhammadan Tradition* (Leiden: E. J. Brill, 1927), s.v. "Hour," for scores of references to supposedly prophetic predictions of the End. E.g., Abu Daʾud, *Sunan* (n.p. [Beirut?]: Dar al-Fikr, n.d.), vol. 4, p. 94, no. 4241: the prophet said, "In this community there will be four civil wars, in the last of which will be the annihilation," a tradition probably put into circulation during the fourth civil war in the early third/ninth century.

67. Wilferd Madelung, "Apocalyptic Prophecies in Hims in the Umayyad Age," *Journal of Semitic Studies* 31 (1986): 141–85.

68. W. Madelung, "al-Mahdi," *Encyclopaedia of Islam* (2d ed.).

69. Muhammad ibn Jarir al-Tabari, *Taʾrikh al-rusul waʾl-muluk*, ed. M.J. de Gioeje et al. (Leiden: E.J. Brill, 1879–1901, sec. ii, p. 399); cf. T. Fahd, "Djafr," *EI* (2).

70. Armand Abel, "Changements politiques et littérature eschatologique dans le monde musulman," *Studia Islamica* 2 (1954): 23–43, at 28–30. In the latter case, assuming that al-Hasan ibn ʿAli ibn Abi Talib's brief "reign" was counted, the tradition would have a terminus ad quem of 183/799, the date of death of

the seventh *imam* of the Imami Shiʿa, Musa al-Kazim, during the reign of the twenty-fourth caliph, Harun al-Rashid (r. 170/786–193/809).

71. Cf. D. B. MacDonald, "Malahim," *EI* (1); T. Fahd, "Djafr," *EI* (2). The *Kitab al-fitan* of Nuʿaym ibn Hammad, on which Madelung, "Apocalyptic Prophecies," relied for much of his information, is a typical product of the genre; cf. also the chapters on *fitan* and *malahim* in the *hadith* collections.

72. Ignaz Goldziher, *Muhammedanische Studien*, vol. 2 (Halle: Max Niemeyer: 1890), 73; English translation: *Muslim Studies*, vol. 2 (London: George Allen and Unwin, 1971), 77.

73. Recent revisionist theories proposing that the Qurʾanic scriptural canon only assumed its present form much later than Islamic tradition claims—in the late first or even second or third centuries A.H.—do not strike me as convincing, and in this chapter I assume that the Qurʾan existed in something akin to its present form virtually from the date of the Prophet's death in 632 C.E. For revisionist views, see especially John Wansbrough, *Quranic Studies* (Oxford: Oxford University Press, 1977); Crone and Cook, *Hagarism*, 17ff. For a very different revisionist view, see John Burton, *The Collection of the Qurʾan* (Cambridge: Cambridge University Press, 1977), who argues that the Qurʾan text as we now have it was already fixed during the lifetime of the Prophet himself and hence is older than claimed by Muslim dogma, which states that the text was only codified a few decades after the Prophet's death.

74. See especially Abdulaziz A. Sachedina, "The Development of *Jihad* in Islamic Revelation and History," in *Cross, Crescent, and Sword*, ed. James Turner Johnson and John Kelsay (Westport, Conn.: Greenwood Press, 1990).

75. Most recent Muslim commentators take the view that the Qurʾan condones only defensive war; see, for example, the many passages in the translation and commentary by Maulana Muhammad ʿAli, *The Holy Qurʾan, Arabic Text, English Translation, and Commentary*, rev. ed. (Lahore: Ahmadiyya Ajnuman Ishaʿat Islam, 1951); see index s.v. "Muslim War." Using the same verses, the Christian cleric Jacques Jomier decided the opposite; in his opinion, from the beginning "Islam had an active warlike character" (*The Bible and the Koran*, transl. Edward P. Arbez [New York: Desclee, 1964], 102–3). In the passages that follow herein, translations from the Qurʾan are my own unless noted otherwise.

76. First and foremost by Paul Casanova, *Mohammed et la fin du monde: Étude critique sur l'Islam primitif*, 2 vols. (Paris: Paul Geuthner, 1911–24); most recently, reemphasized in Conrad, "Portents of the Hour." The latter includes brief references to other scholars who have discussed the apocalyptic outlook of Muhammad or the early community of Muslims, including C. Snouck Hurgronje, Tor Andrae, Frants Buhl, and M. J. Kister.

77. For the latter, see the examples adduced by Conrad, "Portents of the Hour," e.g., Q. 21:1; Q. 33:63; Q. 7:187; Q. 47:18; Q. 43:61; or generally in a concordance to the Qurʾan, s.v. "*saʿa*."

78. On *kufr* as ingratitude, see Toshihiko Izutzu, *Ethico-religious Concepts in the Qurʾan* (Montreal: McGill University Press, 1966), 105–77.

79. Paret, in his translation and commentary on this verse, renders it in a strictly military sense: *al-qaʿidun* are those who "remain at home" instead of going to war; *al-mujahidun* are those who go to war (Rudi Paret, *Der Koran* [Stuttgart: Kohlhammer, 1962 and 1971/1977]). This interpretation is possible,

indeed highly plausible, but to me it also seems possible that the verse may have been intended in a more general, moral sense and not merely in the military sense.

80. Cf. Henry Chadwick, *The Early Church* (Harmondsworth: Penguin, 1967), 152 n. 1. In the Christian case, the "soldiery" image was generally metaphorical; in the Islamic case, it seems sometimes to have been metaphorical, but at others it could be literal, as suggested in the text.

81. David Noah Freedman, "The Flowering of Apocalyptic," *Journal for Theology and the Church* 6 (1968): 166–74, makes the following general comments regarding apocalyptic communities (171): "In classic fashion the apocalyptic group withdraws from the corrupt society of this world to form a pure and holy community of the elect. . . . In practice, such a community tends to be passive . . . [but this] is not so much a matter of basic policy as of timing. When the decisive moment arrives the apocalyptic army must be ready to swing into action in God's warfare."

82. See the Arabic lexicons, such as Ibn Manzur's *Lisan al-ʿArab*, 15 vols. (Beirut: Dar Sadir, n.d.), for the meanings of the phrase *athkhana fi l-ʾard*. It is worth noting that modernist Muslim translators often tone down the meaning: e.g., "fought and triumphed in the land" (Muhammad ʿAli); "thoroughly subdued the land" (Yusuf ʿAli). Compare the less pacifistic translations of Marmaduke Pickthall ("made slaughter in the land") and A. J. Arberry ("until he make wide slaughter in the land"). Others hedge, e.g. "solange er nicht (die Gegner überall) im Land (ard) niedergekämpft hat (yuthina)" (Rudi Paret).

83. A confirmation of the use of this slogan by the Muslims in a source contemporary with the conquests is noted by Patricia Crone, *Slaves on Horses* (Cambridge: Cambridge University Press, 1977), 12. Jomier, *The Bible and the Koran*, 103–4, quoting Q. 24:55, states that it "promises the earth to the believers, in God's name, as an inheritance, and justifies in advance any attempt, peaceful or, within certain limits, warlike, for the purpose of attaining world hegemony." Jan-Olaf Blichfeldt, *Early Mahdism* (Leiden: E. J. Brill, 1985), seems to borrow Jomier's insight and speaks of an original "Islamic principle" according to which the Muslims believed that God promised them not only rewards in heaven, but rewards in this life as well, in the form of possession of the lands and goods of the conquered peoples.

84. For two divergent reconstructions of the possible motivations, see Donner, *Early Islamic Conquests*, and Crone and Cook, *Hagarism*. Contemporary documents regarding the conquest are very few, but nonetheless confirm that something that we must identify as the Islamic or Arab conquest did occur: cf. Adolf Grohmann, "Greek Papyri of the Early Islamic Period in the Collection of the Archduke Rainer," *Études de papyrologie* 8 (1957): 5–40; also the early sources surveyed in Walter Emil Kaegi, Jr., "Initial Byzantine Reactions to the Arab Conquest," *Church History* 38 (1969): 139–49, such as the Christmas Sermon of the patriarch of Jerusalem, Sophronius, from the year 634 C.E., and an epistle of Maximus Confessor, probably written in Egypt or North Africa before 653 C.E.

85. E.g., Yarmuk (Syria), ca. 636 C.E.; Qadisiyya (Iraq), ca. 637 C.E.; Egypt entered, 639 C.E.; Nihawand (western Iran), 642 C.E.; Marv (northeastern Iran) conquered, 651 C.E.; Qayrawan (Tunisia) founded, 670 C.E.; Constantinople be-

sieged, 669, 674–80, and 717 c.e.; first expedition to the Indus valley, ca. 710 c.e.; Spain invaded, 711 c.e.; Shash (Tashkent) conquered, 712 c.e.; Narbonne (southern France) occupied, ca. 715 c.e.; Battle of Tours or Poitiers (central France), 732 c.e.; Battle of Talas (central Asia), 751 c.e. In this context we should recall also the tradition of annual, or almost annual, "summer campaigns" (sing. *sa'ifa*) against Byzantine forces in Anatolia, which continued from the early days of the conquests well into Abbasid times.

86. In Qur'anic usage *fitna* refers both to those temptations that might seduce true believers from their faith and also to the painful consequences of sinfulness on the part of unbelievers. For a review of the term's meaning in the Qur'an and in later Islamic usage, see L. Gardet, "Fitna," *Encyclopaedia of Islam* (2d ed.).

87. Thus we have the *hurub al-ridda*, "wars of apostasy" (a legitimate variety) during which the Muslims subjected the rebellious tribesmen of Arabia during the caliphate of Abu Bakr (11–13 a.h./632–34 c.e.); al-Tabari, *Ta'rikh*, vol. 1, p. 3453, 'Ali and Mu'awiya negotiate a truce to bring to an end the *harb* between them (referring to events of the first *fitna*, a "bad" war)—here meaning merely "fighting" (war as activity), or "state of war"?

88. I hope to develop this point in a publication currently in preparation.

89. Cf. Lewis, *Political Language of Islam*, 80–82.

90. For references to these, see Wensinck, *Handbook of Early Muhammadan Tradition*, under the headings "Imam(s)," "Rebellion," "Community," and so on. Of course there are also prophetic sayings that assert that obedience is due to the *imam* only if he acts justly, but the general tendency is to support royal authority.

91. Albert Arazi and 'Amikam El'ad, "«L'Épitre à l'armée.» Al-Ma'mun et la seconde da'wa," part 1, *Studia Islamica* 66 (1987): 59–60.

92. Ibid, 55.

93. For references, see Wensinck, *Handbook of Early Muhammadan Tradition*, under "War (*jihad*)."

94. Mawqufati, *Sharh Multaqa' al-abhur li-Ibrahim Halabi* (Istanbul, 1318 a.h./ 1900 c.e.), 339–41 ("Kitab al-siyar"). I owe this reference to Professor Halil Inalcik. On Mawqufati, see Bursali Mehmed Tahir Bey, *Osmanli Müellifleri*, vol. 2 (Istanbul: Meral, 1972), 228.

95. Marius Canard, "La guerre sainte dans le monde islamique et dans le monde chrétien," *Revue Africaine* 79 (1936): 605–23; Albrecht Noth, *Heiliger Krieg und heiliger Kampf in Islam und Christentum*, Bonner Historische Forschungen, Band 28 (Bonn: Ludwig Röhrscheid, 1966); Emmanuel Sivan, *L'Islam et la croisade: Idéologie et propagande dans les réactions musulmans aux croisades* (Paris: Maisonneuve, 1968).

96. Albrecht Noth, "Heiliger Kampf (Gihad) gegen die 'Franken': Zur Position der Kreuzzüge im Rahmen der Islamgeschichte," *Saeculum* 37 (1986): 240–59.

97. An example is the *Futuh al-Sham* ascribed to al-Waqidi (d. 823), usually called "Pseudo-Waqidi." On this and similar works, see Rudi Paret, "Die legendäre Futuh-Literatur, ein arabisches Volksepos?" in *Atti del convegno internazionale sul tema: La poesia epica e la sua formazione (Roma, 28 marzo–3 aprile 1969)*. Problemi attuali di scienza e di cultura, quaderno no. 139 (Rome: Accademia nazionale dei Lincei, 1970), 735–49.

98. Another genre of Islamic literature—the so-called "merits of Jerusalem" material—began before the Crusades, but got a significant boost as a result of the Crusaders' activity. See Emmanuel Sivan, "The Beginnings of the *Fada'il al-Quds* Literature," *Israel Oriental Studies* 1 (1971): 263–71.

99. A survey of this literature, stressing the political ideals it projects, is Ann K. S. Lambton, "Islamic Mirrors for Princes," in *Atti del convegno internazionale sul tema: La Persia nel Medioevo*, Problemi attuali di scienza e di cultura, quaderno no. 160 (Rome: Accademia Nazionale dei Lincei, 1971), 419–42. We may wish to begin the genre already with the *Rasa'il* of ʿAbd al-Hamid ibn Yahya (d. 132/750), on whom see the entry by H.A.R. Gibb in *Encyclopedia of Islam* (2d ed.).

100. Nizam al-Mulk, *The Book of Government; or, Rules for Kings: The Siyar al-muluk or Siyaset-nama of Nizam al-Mulk*, trans. Hubert Darke, 2d ed. (London, Henley, and Boston: Routledge and Kegan Paul, 1978), xviii–xxi. Cf. Lambton, "Islamic Mirrors for Princes," 420.

101. Al-Mulk, *Book of Government*, 101 (chap. 25).

102. Muhammad Taqi Danishʿpazhuh, ed., *Bahr al-fawa'id* (Tehran: B.T.N.K., 1345 solar A.H./1966 C.E.). The discussions in the opening chapter on *jihad* (12–45) are squarely based on the juristic tradition. A fairly detailed description of the contents of the whole work is provided in Lambton, "Islamic Mirrors for Princes," 426–36.

103. *Ottoman Statecraft: The Book of Counsel for Vezirs and Governors (Nasa'ih ul-vüzera re'l-ümera) of Sari Mehmed Pasha, the defterdar; Turkish text, with introduction, translation, and notes* by Walter Livingston Wright, Jr. (London: H. Milford, Oxford Univ. Press; Princeton: Princeton University Press, 1935), 126–27, 129–31.

104. The previously mentioned Ottoman manual on statecraft by Sari Mehmet Pasha is a perfect example; it appeals both to the Iranian "Mirrors" tradition and to such works as *Kutadu Bilig*, the earliest extant Turkish treatise on government.

105. There were, of course, numerous efforts to establish the principle of independent royal authority within the Islamic tradition prior to the arrival of the steppe peoples, but these were never particularly successful until they were reinforced by the steppe tradition.

106. For an introduction to this, see Halil Inalcik, "Kanun—iii. Financial and Public Administration," *Encyclopaedia of Islam* (2d ed.). See also Inalcik, "Ottoman Methods of Conquest," *Studia Islamica* 2 (1954): 103–29, at 112–13; Inalcik, *The Ottoman Empire* (New York and Washington, D.C.: Praeger, 1973), 66–67.

107. James Turner Johnson, "Historical Roots and Sources of the Just War Tradition in Western Culture," in this volume.

108. To confirm this, further study of the "mirrors for princes" and of some of the later works on politics and statecraft is needed. Some of those known in Arabic—again, mostly unpublished—can be traced in Carl Brockelmann, *Geschichte der arabischen Litteratur*, rev. ed., vol. 2 (Leiden: E. J. Brill, 1949), 165f., 272, 330, 343, 593.

109. ʿUmar ibn Ibrahim al-Ansari al-Awsi, *Tafrij al-kurub fi tadbir al-hurub: A Muslim Manual of War*, ed. and transl. George T. Scanlon (Cairo: American University at Cairo Press, 1961). Brief mention is made in book 7, chapter 2 (pp. 44–46 of text; pp. 74–75 of translation) of the need for the commander to restrain his troops from indiscriminate plunder and abuse of "people of obedience," by

which is meant other subjects of the Muslim state. In book 7, chapter 2 (p. 50 of text, p. 79 of translation), the author urges commanders to strive for submission of the enemy, not for their slaughter when it can be avoided, but the reason given is simply that those who have submitted may prove to be useful later on. The discussion of siege warfare in Book 19 (pp. 89–94 of text, pp. 114–119 of translation) evinces no special concern for noncombatants, who are hardly mentioned in the work.

110. For a number of such works, see Carl Brockelmann, *Geschichte der arabischen Litteratur*, rev. ed., vol. 1 (Leiden: E. J. Brill, 1943), 653; 2:168f., 477, 617–18.

111. On *ghaza* in Ottoman ʿ*ilm-i hal* literature, see Sinasi Tekin, "XIV. Yuzyilda Yazilmmis Gazilik Tarikasi 'Gaziligin Yollari' Adli Bir Eski Anadolu Turkcesi Metni ve Gaza/Cihad Karramlari Hakkinda," *Journal of Turkish Studies* 13 (1989): 139–204. I am indebted to Prof. Halil Inalcik for this reference.

112. Political theorists in the Islamic world today do not take as their points of departure the principles of statecraft of the Ottomans, Safavis, and others. Instead, they draw on systems of legitimization of Western origin (capitalism, Marxism, socialism, European law of nations, and so on) or consult the Islamic juristic tradition. The precolonial Islamic tradition of statecraft has simply been allowed to die.

113. The fact that most states of the Islamic world today adjudicate their disputes, even among themselves, using "international law" is no argument in favor of its universal acceptability, for "international law" was essentially imposed upon the world community by the victorious powers following World War I and World War II through the agency of the United Nations and its predecessor, the League of Nations. Moreover, virtually every country in the Islamic world was at some time between 1850 and 1950 a Western colony or protectorate. It is noteworthy that the only case in which a modern government appealed to Islamic law rather than to Western "international law" in litigation before the International Court of Justice was one brought by the Kingdom of Saudi Arabia. (This point was made in the symposium discussions by Ann E. Mayer.) Is it merely coincidence that Saudi Arabia is virtually the only Islamic state with no colonial past?

114. To complete this process, one would, of course, also have to incorporate all other major traditions of law and statecraft, not just the Islamic and Western.

3

The Western Moral Tradition on War: Christian Theology and Warfare

John Langan, S.J.

PRELIMINARY CONSIDERATIONS

One graphic way of illustrating the ambivalence and complexity of the Western tradition on war would be through a quick overview of some of the defining places of the Western tradition: Jerusalem, the city of David's kingdom and Jesus' crucifixion; Rome, the city of empire and of law, the shrine of martyrs and the seat of papal monarchs; Geneva, the city of Calvin's reform and of the League of Nations; Paris, the city of the Rights of Man and the Arc de Triomphe. But I would focus for a moment on a place that is of secondary importance, the city of Würzburg in the center of Germany. Overlooking the city is the fortress of Marienberg; in the chapel of the fortress the prince-bishops who ruled Würzburg and much of Franconia from the tenth to the nineteenth centuries are buried. Each of the tombs is covered by a stone effigy of a bishop holding in one hand the crozier or staff of his episcopal office and in the other the sword appropriate to his princely position as duke of Franconia. The effigy serves as a vivid illustration of the integration of force and war within the dominant religious and theological tradition of the West. The guns of the fortress, the guide tells us, were used for quelling the intermittently rebellious burgers and artisans of the town, not least during the period of the Reformation. The prince-bishops of medieval and baroque Catholicism are long vanished; but the problem for whose solution they served as one temporally and culturally conditioned element remains. It presses on us in new ways and with new intensity in an age of international interdependence and technological innovation and ideological division. The problem is how to integrate in both practical and theoretical terms the basic affirmations of the Christian theological tradition with the demands for justice and peace in a political order marked by division and violence. This political order has always had military institutions and has been periodically made and remade by wars, but it has also been marked by repeated efforts to realize high moral and religious ideals.

This major problem can be broken into three more specific problems that any justification of war in the Western tradition has to confront, regardless of the particular form of the Western tradition within which the argument is made and the assessment of war is carried on. The first of these problems is whether the concept of a justifiable war is compatible with the basic affirmations of the tradition or traditions that provide the intellectual context for the moral assessment. This is a question that is raised about war in general, and it is logically prior to our assessment of particular wars. Sometimes, however, it happens that people actually proceed from convictions about the justifiability of particular wars, such as the American Civil War or World War II, where the justice of the cause seems especially evident. At the same time, they can be very reluctant to affirm the justifiability of war in general, partly because of intellectual confusion but partly from an understandable anxiety about condoning future conflicts that are not well defined and that have, because of the ongoing development of technology, an increasing potential for higher levels of destruction.

It is in the moral assessment of particular wars that we encounter the other two fundamental problems, namely, the determination of the specific circumstances that legitimate in particular cases the resort to the use of force by states and by political movements that aspire to statehood, and the establishment of norms that will enable impartial judgments to be made on whether the war is being conducted in a morally acceptable way. These are the concerns of what is commonly discussed as the *jus ad bellum* and the *jus in bello*, the right to initiate war and the right that is to be observed in the conduct of war. These subjects are dealt with elsewhere in this volume. A satisfactory resolution of these two problems is necessary if any affirmative answer to the first problem is to retain credibility. But it is the first problem that is of the most fundamental interest to philosophers and theologians and to the religious conscience.

I have put this first problem in terms of compatibility with the basic affirmations of one or several traditions that provide the intellectual context for moral assessments. In doing this, I have wanted to make several points. First, the restriction to "basic affirmations" comes from a recognition that not all affirmations in a complex religious or philosophical tradition are on an equal footing. We need some interpretative standpoint from which we judge that some affirmations are peripheral or incidental to the tradition and that others are central or essential, that some are privileged and can serve as a guide for the interpretation of others. This preliminary observation, while obvious to nearly all reflective exponents of particular traditions, is in reality a superficial glance at a nest of complex and subtle problems in epistemology, hermeneutics, and ecclesiology, that part of theology that reflects specifically on the mission and the authority of the community of belief itself.

Second, the reference to one or more traditions is a way of indicating the dialogical clustering of traditions within the West and the plural allegiances of many thinkers on these issues in the West. The subtitle of this volume suggests a juxtaposition of two traditions, one Islamic and one Western. For certain purposes, such as the structuring of this volume, or from a sufficiently great distance (say, from the interior highlands of New Guinea or the "canals" of Mars), such a way of setting out the elements in this work's dialogue may be completely satisfactory. But as all of the contributors would admit, both the traditions from which we are speaking are marked by internal divisions and by considerable internal complexity. Whether it is possible to say much that is useful about the Western tradition in general is not a question that can be answered in the abstract. More specifically, whether we can deal in any rigorous fashion with issues of coherence and consistency if we remain at the level of the Western tradition in general seems to me to be very doubtful. We can, however, find significant similarities and convergences among the various strands constituting the Western tradition if we direct our attention to the ways in which questions are put and to the cognitive sources and cultural values that are taken seriously rather than to common conclusions.

Furthermore, for our purposes we have to bear in mind the fact that the major Western religious and intellectual traditions have been locked in dialogue and dispute over the centuries and that they have been intimately related to the developing professional consciousness of such concerned groups as international lawyers, military officers, diplomats, political advisors, and technical experts, who are called on in different ways to think about the problems of war and statecraft and to cope with these problems in practice. Thus the contemporary Western tradition in these matters can mold and be molded by Catholic bishops, Episcopalian diplomats, Jewish political theorists, agnostic physicists, atheistic military strategists, Methodist theologians, Lutheran generals, Baptist politicians, and Mennonite pastors. We also have to bear in mind that because of their internal complexity and flexibility, the constituent traditions of the West are likely to contain within themselves tendencies that are in sharp conflict with each other. Here too we have to look to dominant tendencies and fundamental orientations rather than for clear and distinct divisions or unanimous affirmations.

Third, I have referred to an "intellectual context for moral assessment." In doing this, I have wanted to leave open questions about the precise relationship between religious affirmations and moral conclusions, while at the same time allowing for the real possibility of contradiction within a religious ethical system. For my own part, I hold to the logical independence of moral evaluations from religious affirmations, while treating the affirmations of faith as altering in decisive ways the horizons within which moral judgments are made.[1] There have been within the Western tradition, broadly conceived, a number of different ways of understanding the relationship between religion and morality; and, as already mentioned, the Western tradition includes constituent traditions that are theological and atheological, moral and amoral. It includes Machiavelli as well as Kant, Nietzsche as well as St. Augustine. But it is clear that particularly for the Christian theological traditions in the West, the moral affirmations of just war theory present a serious, frequently renewed problem, since they legitimate violence that seems to be at variance with important elements in the teaching of Jesus and with common ways of conceiving God as supremely wise, benevolent, and powerful.

There are two main ways of presenting the norms of just war theory or any more general set of norms on war, peace, and relations among states and political communities. One is to stress their independence of particular belief systems and their function of regulating and limiting conflicts between groups with contradictory systems of belief and with no commonly acknowledged moral or religious authority over them. The classic expression of this approach is found in the remark of the Protestant Hugo Grotius that the norms would hold even if there were no God.[2] But features of this approach can be found in many Catholic and secular presentations of the norms as well. The alternative approach is to present the norms as integrated within a body of theological or metaphysical beliefs, an approach that can be traced from St. Augustine to Paul Ramsey. In this approach there is a better prospect of achieving systematic compatibility with basic theological doctrines, but at the same time there may be no guarantee of acceptability to those who are working from within other belief systems. It should not, however, be thought that these two approaches are always neatly and sharply contrasted with each other. Both theologians and ordinary citizens or church members make use of both approaches. Indeed, the 1983 letter of the U.S. Catholic Bishops, *The Challenge of Peace*, explicitly takes advantage of both approaches in its effort to reach both "the community of the faithful and the civil community."[3]

We have to keep the pluralism of the Western tradition or traditions in mind, as well as the fact that the Western tradition over the last five centuries and especially during the last two centuries has undergone a long process of modernization and internal self-criticism. We can make some headway in laying out the first and most theoretical of our three problems if we take as our benchmark the place of just war theory within Roman Catholic theology, if we note relevant divergences from that theological framework either within Roman Catholicism or in the various Protestant churches, and if we indicate the necessary transformations of the problem when we deal with the perspectives on the problem taken by nontheistic or agnostic philosophical and humanitarian movements.

The usefulness of taking the Roman Catholic form of just war theory as a benchmark rests on the centrality of Roman Catholicism in the religious traditions of the West. This in turn rests on five major factors:

1. Its long period of religious monopoly, from the decline of Arianism in the early Germanic kingdoms to the Protestant Reformation
2. Its even longer period of interaction with the centers of political and military power
3. Its long tradition of transnational centralization of both jurisdiction and religious teaching
4. Its cultivation of a tradition of comprehensive and logically disciplined systematic theology
5. Its place as the paradigmatic example of church even for those who rejected its authority

We can also note in passing that three of the major Catholic cultures of Europe have had sustained and significant contact with the Islamic world: Spain (which was dominated by Islam for several centuries and which developed strong anti-Muslim tendencies), Italy (mainly through the trading activities of the maritime republics), and France (both in the Crusades and in its active role as protector of Christians in the Levant).

It should also be noted that at least with regard to the range of issues about which the contributors are concerned in this volume, the sharpest and deepest divisions within Christian communities have not been between Roman Catholicism and Protestantism but within Protestantism. Acceptance of the legitimacy of some forms of warfare has been common ground among Catholics, Orthodox churches, Lutherans, Anglicans, Presbyterians and other Reformed churches, and many smaller groups, whereas the pacifist challenge to this acceptance has prevailed in the sects and church groups that carry on the traditions of the radical Reformers. Protestantism in Germany and the English-speaking world, as well as in those areas of Europe where Calvinism prevailed (the Netherlands, Switzerland, and Scotland), has been more deeply involved with the process of modernization and with the transformation and renewal of theological traditions. But even here we should note that Roman Catholicism, while laggard and even reactionary in many ways, continued to enunciate positions that provide a benchmark for comparisons with new forms of theology and philosophy. Roman Catholicism, however, has recently developed much higher levels of internal dissent and divergence, much of which can be traced to its recent recognition of the historically conditioned character of its previous teaching and of the tensions found in the sources, biblical and other, from which it draws for that teaching, as well as to its own recent experiences of transformation, modernization, and enculturation. In the future it will be less appropriate to regard Roman Catholicism as simply a fixed core element in the Western tradition, and it will be more accurate to see it as carrying within itself many of the divisions and complexities of that tradition.

THE GOD OF PEACE AND THE GOD OF BATTLES: THE TENSION BETWEEN CHRISTIAN THEOLOGY AND WARFARE

When we take up the task of integrating just war theory or any doctrine affirming the legitimacy of war into the systematic framework of Christian and, more specifically, Roman Catholic theology, we can set out a number of points of difficulty that are immediately apparent, even though they are not always recognized by those who accept unquestioningly the classic resolutions of these difficulties. In characterizing these issues as "difficulties," I do not wish to trivialize them, to separate them from "doubts," or to prejudge whether they require major revisions of either just war theory or the systematic theological framework. The multiplication of these difficulties serves to underline the paradoxical combination within Christianity of a general acceptance of war and military institutions along with a series of affirmations that seem to lead simply and directly to pacifist conclusions. Principal among the difficulties in my view are these:

1. *The moral character of God.* The God proclaimed by Jesus Christ is a God of forgiveness and generosity, a God that requires justice and is abounding in love. How is it possible for such a being to authorize the bloody and destructive acts of war? How is it possible for those who identify themselves as his children to carry out such acts without violating their religious identity?

2. *The power of God.* If the God of Christianity is indeed perfectly benevolent and wise, then it seems that the occurrence of something so evil as war shows that his power to bring about good and to overcome evil must be limited.

3. *The unity of God.* If God is indeed one, how is it possible for those who proclaim their obedience to the one Lord to be so divided and hostile to each other? If political authority is derived from one creator, how can it be so divided and so bent on the destruction of its peers and rivals?

4. *The justice of God.* If God deals justly with creatures, treating them according to their merits or according to some recognized canon of distributive justice,

how can he accept the outcomes of war, which frequently involve grave and irreparable suffering for innocent people and from which the vicious frequently escape either unpunished or victorious? Can war be an instrument of a just God?

5. *The providence of God.* If God truly cares for human creatures as individuals and as ends in themselves, can it be that God would abandon them to the weapons of war and to its attendant calamities such as famine, pillage, and enslavement?

6. *The kingdom of God.* Jesus came to proclaim the coming of the kingdom of God (Mark 1:15), which is a kingdom of justice and peace. If the kingdom has indeed come in his person and ministry, then war can have no place in the community of his disciples and in the world that he came to save. The continuation of war and military institutions among Christians shows either the falseness of the claim that Jesus is the Messiah or the blindness and unfaithfulness of Christians or perhaps both.

7. *The commandment of love.* The New Testament, echoing the Hebrew Bible, reminds us in numerous places that Christians are to love their neighbors and their enemies. Is it really possible to hold that the deliberate infliction of harm and even death on other persons, many of them innocent of any specific offense, is consistent with or even, as some suggest, demanded by the commandment of love?

8. *The example of Christ.* Christ gave his life for the salvation of human beings and accepted death even on the cross without offering resistance to those who used force against him. Are not Christians, who profess themselves to be his disciples, bound to follow his example in this central regard?

9. *The teaching of Christ.* Particularly in the Sermon on the Mount (Matthew 5–7), but also elsewhere throughout the Gospels, Jesus teaches his disciples that they are to forgive injuries and that they are not to return evil for evil. How then is it justifiable for them to take up arms even against aggressive enemies?

10. *The hierarchy of goods.* War at best involves the taking of human life and a profound disorientation of society for the sake of goods such as economic freedom and political self-determination, which are goods that in the Christian view are not of ultimate importance. Efforts to legitimate war must then rely on a distortion of the proper order or hierarchy of human goods.

11. *The universality of natural law.* If natural law provides norms for right human conduct that are cognitively available to all and that direct human beings to the common good, then it cannot include norms that allow the deliberately destructive and contradictory behavior of war.

These eleven difficulties are not offered as an exhaustive list of problems that one might raise about including just war theory within the systematic framework of Christian theology. They are intended to be illustrative of a range of difficulties that people would raise within and about that framework. They are objections that in some form would come to people spontaneously, even though the formulation of some of them requires a certain academic sophistication.

If we look at these eleven difficulties, we can see that the first five raise problems of theodicy, of the justification of "the ways of God to men."[4] The next six raise questions of the compatibility of the deeds of war with ethical norms either taught by Christ or embedded within the Catholic theological tradition. The difficulties in the first set suggest that the mainstream Christian tradition, which has propounded the principles of just war theory or at least accepted analogous attitudes and practices, errs and that its error is one of intellectual inconsistency arising from a failure to think through the implications of its doctrine of God, its theology in the strict sense. They present a situation of intellectual conflict in which political realism about armed conflict points toward atheism or at least a denial of the Christian understanding of God. The difficulties in the second set imply that Christianity in its acceptance of war and military institutions and practices and its teaching of just war theory is offering an inconsistent set of moral norms. Consistency here can be achieved by dropping the norms of just war theory in favor of the more specifically Christian norms mentioned in the difficulties, that is, by accepting the pacifist position. The problem of reconciling the occurrence of wars with the divine attributes remains for the pacifist believer.

My intention here is not to review the various ways in which Christian theologians have dealt with these difficulties. Rather, it is to focus our attention on the kinds of considerations that are necessary if the difficulties are to be contained within the tradition and to acknowledge some of the ways in which the tradition has changed over time so that these difficulties are either lessened or intensified.

All of the difficulties, it should be noted, start from the assumption that performing the acts of war involves doing deeds of violence to other persons, deeds that inflict physical and psychological harm on them and that may do lasting damage to the societies to which they belong. Some of them make the further assumption that performing the acts of war involves attitudes of intending to injure others, even lethally. As stated, they are consonant with the Platonic judgment, often echoed in Christian ethics and exemplified in the long and highly esteemed tradition of Christian martyrs, that it is better to suffer evil than to do evil.[5] These views, with the exception of the last, are not particularly controversial. The arguments for which these claims provide backing are simple and direct. They are familiar as standard responses by people to the real evils inflicted by war and to the disparity between clearly stated and lofty Christian norms and the practice of purportedly Christian societies. If we consider them cumulatively, we may wonder why it took centuries before Pope Paul VI came to stand before the United Nations in 1966 to proclaim, "No more war, war never again." But of course we know that this array of arguments and questions, while widely available in some form or other to most Christians down through the ages, did not lead any more than a small minority of them to a pacifist denial of the legitimacy of all wars. Christianity, as Sir Michael Howard reminds us, has for over fifteen hundred years functioned as "one of the great warrior religions of mankind."[6] Why mainstream Christianity has persisted in maintaining the just war tradition despite the prima facie pacifist implications of its views about God, Christ, and fundamental moral norms is a matter both for historical research and explanation and for systematic questioning and reflection.

BASES FOR INCLUDING THE MILITARY
WITHIN CHRISTIANITY

My purpose here, as mentioned earlier, is to set out some of the main considerations that make it possible for Christianity to combine its basic theological affirmations with acceptance of the institutions and practices of war. But first we have to look at three factors in the life of the Christian community that have counted heavily against a simple exclusion of military institutions and personnel from the Christian world.

The first of them is the pretheoretical experience of the presence of Christian virtues and Christian witness in military personnel. This is acknowledged in the New Testament and has continued to be both a reality and an ideal down through the centuries. The idealized medieval figures of the Christian knight (for example, Chaucer's knight) and of the Christian king (St. Louis) are not unproblematic, both by reason of the many ways in which performance fell short of the ideal (not least during the Crusades) and by reason of the potential for hypocrisy and manipulation of others that ideals of the powerful normally contain. Contemporary critics may find in these ideals an instance of a too-easy harmony between Christ and culture and even of a corruption of Christian witness by a violent society bent on self-justification. But even when these points are acknowledged, there remains the massive socioreligious fact of military piety and ecclesial recognition of and support for that piety down through the centuries. This fact and the practices and judgments constituting it carry a certain systematic weight, particularly within a tradition of ecclesiology that affirms God's continuing guidance of the church in its basic magisterial and pastoral roles. Such an ecclesiology is, of course, central in Roman Catholicism's understanding of itself.

Second, there is a long history of military images and analogies within the traditions of Christian theology and spirituality. This begins with Paul's exhortation in Ephesians 6:10–20 to "put on the whole armor of

God" and his admonition that we are contending "against the world rulers of this present darkness, against the spiritual hosts of wickedness in the heavenly places." The imagery of Christ as victor, of the individual Christian as warrior against the passions, of the Christian community as carrying on its missionary activity in a conquering spirit, and of the angels as quasi-military agents of God (beginning with Genesis 3, continuing through the cult of St. Michael, and finding its most elaborate expression in the heavenly battle in *Paradise Lost*) does not entail acceptance of earthly and political just wars, much less a blanket endorsement of military activity as such. Nor does it ensure that religious and spiritual activities will not be corrupted by militarizing tendencies. But it does invoke some congruence of values and attitudes that makes it appropriate for Christians to think about their spiritual lives in terms of a set of institutions and practices that are not inherently and inescapably at odds with God's kingdom.

A third consideration is drawn from the explicit affirmations in the Hebrew Bible that Yahweh is a man of war (Exodus 15:3), that he intervenes in battle in order that his people may be victorious, and that he calls forth judges and kings to lead his people in battle. Whatever theologians may make of these affirmations at the present time, it has to be recognized that these affirmations enjoy biblical authority and were taken during the most formative periods of Christian theology as clear indications of God's will. For long, they stood firmly in the way of any argument from the divine attributes to the unacceptability of war. Mainstream Christianity through the centuries resisted proposals to set aside the Hebrew Bible and to dismiss Yahweh as a being morally inferior to the Father of Jesus. It also resisted efforts to treat the Torah as definitive for Christian moral understanding. In contemporary discussions it may seem attractive to treat the biblical affirmations as expressions of an imperfect stage of religious development, in which the emphasis should be put either on God's accommodation to human ignorance or on the deep and pervasive influence of the existing culture on the human understanding of the divine message. For it is a clear matter of historical fact that God's revelation was communicated to a world with well-established military institutions and practices, the necessity and legitimacy of which were taken for granted. People were well aware of the contrast between the blessings of peace and the evils of war[7] but did not regard war as a realm shut off from the sacred and the divine.

Reconciling these explicit biblical affirmations with the affirmations made in our previous list of difficulties requires a fuller study of how the institutions and practices of war came to be and how they can function as instruments of God's providence and action in history. The traditional Christian view has not involved denying the reality of the evils of war or separating these from the realm of decisive action for salvation.

Rather, the mainstream of Christian theology has responded to these difficulties in three ways. First, it has incorporated a recognition of the evils of war within a historical theodicy in which God's justice is manifested over time and in which the evils of war are both an expression of and the consequences of the sinfulness of human creatures. Second, it has adopted an interpretation of God's kingdom with its fullness of justice and peace that effectively postpones its realization until some future time of fulfillment. This interpretation enables the Christian community to offer two sets of norms: one for the interim between now and the kingdom and one for the fullness of the kingdom. Third, and this approach has been particularly prominent within Roman Catholicism, it has developed a division between clergy and religious on one side and laity on the other that is accompanied by a series of prohibitions on the first group entering into a number of worldly, dangerous, or inferior activities (such as making money, waging war, having sexual relations, or conducting political activities).

The third manner of response does little to resolve the general problem, but it does offer the example of a group of people who attempt to live a life that is more responsive to the moral norms and aspirations that are cited in difficulties six through ten. It is this move that the bishops of Würzburg and other prelates in the Middle Ages and the Renaissance failed to make, and their failure to act in accordance with the letter of canon law and the spirit of the Gospels scandalized many, most notably Erasmus.[8] In Catholic religious orders as well as in some similar Protestant groups, this response to moral or religious norms that imply a rejection of violence is embedded within a larger church that teaches the justifiability of war in certain circumstances. It is thus different from the affirmation made by the historic Protestant peace churches as well as by some recent Catholic movements that participation in war and in military institutions is incompatible with Christian discipleship, an affirmation that should in principle hold for all Christians.

The second response itself is provisional and incomplete, though in a less obvious way than the third, since it affirms the acceptability of certain types of conduct under one set of norms that are not compatible with ultimately valid norms. Such an approach needs both a rationale for accepting some deviations from the ultimately valid norms and not others (for example, accepting war but not slavery) and an account of those factors in the human situation that require our temporary acceptance of these deviations. (This is the general form of the task that confronted the U.S. Catholic Bishops when they had to take up the task of explaining their conditional acceptance of nuclear deterrence.) So the fundamental way of resolving the difficulties, in my view, has to be the first one, the construction of a historical theodicy.

THE STRUCTURE AND LIMITS OF HISTORICAL THEODICY

The standard form of historical theodicy in Western theology is that laid down in St. Augustine's *De Civitate Dei*. Augustine undertook this enormous work after the Gothic seizure of Rome in 410, and he continued to work on it until near the end of his life in 431. *The City of God* was in its origins a polemical work intended to refute "those who refer the disasters of the Roman republic to our religion."[9] But it grew to include a synoptic account of the history of salvation, or more specifically, an account of the "earthly and heavenly cities, in their origin, progress, and destiny."[10] This grand structure became one of the central works of the Western tradition, and it provided one outline for a comprehensive understanding of history, elements of which have survived even in secularized form down into Enlightenment and Marxist philosophies of history.[11] A particularly prominent and admired late exponent of the Augustinian scheme was Jacques-Benigne Bossuet, who in the *Discourse on Universal History*, which he composed for the son of Louis XIV, set forth "those facts that show us the perpetual duration of religion and finally those that show us the causes of the great changes in empires."[12] This task naturally led Bossuet to focus heavily on military and political history, but the dominant themes in his work were the providential governance of the world and the continuity of true religion, specifically in its Catholic form.

Augustine's opus begins with a reflection on the disasters of a recent unsuccessful war, but his concern is not with the moral rightness or wrongness of warfare but with the possibility that the outcome of the war would undermine the credibility of the Christian religion. This may seem to be a deflection from the proper object of a theodicy, which is to make evident the rightness of what God does. But it is not an irrelevance, for in Augustine's view it is precisely by accepting the Christian faith and the mediation of Christ Jesus who is the way and the truth that human beings attain salvation (11.2) and entry into the everlasting Sabbath of the heavenly city (22.30). Acceptance of the Christian faith helps to bring about the favorable outcome, which in some sense justifies the risks, sufferings, and evils of the present life. As generations of Christian piety and art testify, the expectation is that the narrative ends with a grand tableau in which the good are united with God, are triumphant over various threats and past sufferings, and are clearly shown to be so. In the working out of this grand tableau, the losses and harms suffered by individuals are seen to be of temporary and secondary importance (10.10). In the Augustinian form of historical theodicy, it is not God who is tested, but human beings: "For as the same fire causes gold to glow brightly, and chaff to smoke . . . so the same violence of affliction proves, purges, clarifies the good, but damns, ruins, exterminates the wicked."[13]

Augustine's interest does not lie primarily in showing the internal consistency of the Christian faith, but in defending it against its competitors, principally the syncretistic polytheism of late imperial Rome, astrology, and the doctrines of the philosophers. Augustine states his objective as asserting "the city of God, and true piety, and the worship of God, to which alone the promise of true and everlasting felicity is attached."[14] This project involves Augustine in a good deal of argument about the interpretation and evaluation of Roman history, but his fundamental position is that "God can never be believed to have left the kingdoms of men, their dominations and servitudes, outside of the laws of His providence."[15] But while Augustine affirms that God distributes kingdoms and determines the duration and outcomes of wars (5.21–22) and that his "good pleasure is always just,"[16] he keeps a considerable agnostic element in his interpretation of history. As he concedes, "It . . . far surpasses our strength to discuss the hidden things of men's hearts, and by a clear examination to determine the merits of various kingdoms."[17] He recognizes that God gives power to Julian the Apostate as well as to the Christian Constantine. So some empires and some successes, notably the establishment of the Roman Empire, are the result of virtue, even though virtue in such cases is not the full and authentic virtue that God produces in those who have the true faith.

The key elements in Augustine's historical theodicy that allow for the inclusion of warfare within a moral and religious system that, like the ethos of the peace churches, is both highly demanding and strongly otherworldly can now be identified. First, war, even when conducted by non-Christian states, is a matter of religious significance and falls within the scope of God's providential governance of the world. Second, war always involves serious evils and is excluded from the eternal peace, which is the ultimate satisfaction of our desires. Third, war is an instrument for the distribution of power and the creation of political units that are major historical actors in the world's movement through time to the ultimate destiny of the two cities. Fourth, the outcomes of war correspond, but only in a rough and partial way, to the virtues possessed by the protagonists; so war has a moral element internal to it. Fifth, there is enough interpretative flexibility in linking moral attitudes and dispositions to outcomes in war that virtually all outcomes are compatible with the principles of the true (that is, Christian) religion. This is a consequence of Augustine's liberal reliance on appeals to agnosticism both about God's judgments and about the moral dispositions of human persons in this life. Sixth, the hierarchy of goods that Augustine affirms and the sharp disjunctions that he makes among the various types of goods (union with God in the peace of the heavenly city, true virtue, success and power in the earthly city, and the apparent virtues present in civic life) are set forth in such a way that it is impossible to produce situations in which the morally worthy are deprived of the most important goods or are harmed in a lasting or irreversible way.

The end result is a picture of world history in which religious faith can trace the workings of God's providential governance in the rise and fall of empires and the outcomes of wars without subjecting the basic religious affirmations to any possibility of falsification. Whatever happens will fall within the order of God's providence, and more specific hypotheses will be adjusted to ensure that evils are either overcome or made stepping stones to further and higher goods or are justified as proportionate to previous sins. The radical depreciation of temporal or this-worldly goods that is involved in the sixth point ensures that those pacifist arguments that rely on the harm that war does to earthly interests will in effect miss their mark. The exaltation of God's sovereignty, the insistence on God's wisdom, and the belief that war and the large-scale changes in human society that are often found with it are instruments of God's providence all combine to produce an acceptance of the general course of the world in which war continues to play a significant part. The various moral norms referred to in the list of difficulties serve as principles to be applied within the course of the world, not as norms directing us in the reconstruction and reorientation of the world. Since the cause of the just ultimately prevails in this historical theodicy, God is justified in using war as an instrument for the provisional rewarding and punishing of his creatures and for redirecting their minds and hearts to himself. This may seem to be an evasion of the difficulties listed earlier. I certainly would not want to contend here that these difficulties are solved by Augustine's historical theodicy. Rather, I am underlining the fact that Augustine, along with most mainstream theologians and most ordinary Christians, thinks about wars in a broad context that recognizes them as morally significant and allows for the raising of critical questions about specific wars and acts of warfare, but that is quite inhospitable to raising fundamental questions about the consistency between military institutions and actions, on the one hand, and moral norms and divine attributes, on the other.

Proposing a historical theodicy brings to the center the questions of how to understand human responsibility and freedom and how to reconcile these with divine sovereignty and grace, questions on which Christian theology became profoundly divided at the time of the Reformation. A robust affirmation of human freedom obviously lessens the problem about God's moral attributes, since it leads to a greater separation between the doing and suffering of evils in wars and God's action. On the other hand, it requires a softening or dilution of much of the biblical language, in effect relying on a series of free secondary causes to take responsibility for these evils. Resolution of the debate in favor of a strong theory of divine sovereignty, a resolution that is favored by the greatest classical theologians of the West (Augustine, Aquinas, Luther, and Calvin), sticks closer to the original biblical affirmations.

Emphasis on divine sovereignty also fits well with an understanding of God as a judge who rewards and punishes. Punishment necessarily involves the infliction of evils, and so it is an institution or activity presenting serious theoretical problems of its own.[18] War can be regarded as a punishment, an instrument by which God punishes Israel or the Christian community for its sins; but it is a notoriously inexact instrument. So a serious difficulty remains about how it can be just for an omnipotent, omniscient, benevolent deity to punish creatures, some of whom may well be innocent of grave offenses. The classic theological way of surmounting this difficulty is to insist that we are all sinners and are in no position to complain about receiving unmerited punishment. This follows from the Christian doctrine of original sin, which affirms the inclusion of all human persons in the sin of Adam and which serves as the negative correlate of the inclusion of all in the redemptive action of Christ (Romans 5). More specifically, the coercive institutions of society (criminal law, war, slavery) were justified by Christian theologians as appropriate to or required by the sinful condition of humanity.[19] Original sin does not function merely as a justification for the essentially retrospective activity of punishment. Because it points to continuing aspects of the human condition, it can serve to justify continuing institutions that provide ways of countering evils that may arise in the present and in the future.

A theological approach to the understanding of war that stresses the punitive functions of the evils of war and that treats war as a given within the human condition provides a framework for dealing with the passive side of the problem of war, that is, reconciling the evils suffered by human beings with the divine justice and goodness. But it does little to illuminate the active side of the problem, that is, the decision to inflict such evils. It seems to require that human beings take on themselves the judicial and punitive functions that this approach assigns to God or to imply that they are authorized to do so by God. This second possibility is one that is present in the reliance of many Christians on the functions that Paul assigns to the state in Romans 13, though there his concern is not explicitly with war. The objective of protecting rights and restoring the order of justice is one that has been recognized in just war theorizing, but the assigning of divinely authorized functions in this area to a secular state is a move that is not likely to strike either Christian theologians or secular political theorists as fully satisfactory. The potential for abuse of power by the state seems to be increased, and the prospects for democratic control of military power seem to be lessened when the decisions of the state are identified with the work of God in the world.

There is the further risk that the working out of God's providence and the manifestation of his lordship of the world are interpreted in such a way that God is presented as the God of victors. This is at odds with the biblical insistence on God's special concern for the poor and the oppressed, an insistence that has been given a central place in liberation theology. Progressivist interpretations of the struggles of history in religious terms also run the risk of subordinating the welfare and the moral standing of earlier generations to those that come later and that are closer to the time of fulfillment. This raises problems of justice in God's treatment of his creatures, problems that can be alleviated by allowing the salvation of persons and the manifestation of God's lordship beyond the limits of time and history. Otherwise, history and its wars serve as "the slaughter bench of the peoples"[20] and become an indictment of God's providence and justice.

From a biblical perspective, it is also necessary to recall that God's covenant with Israel allows for both victory and defeat, for the fulfillment of promises of deliverance and for the chastisement of the chosen people through defeat. Christianity has sometimes allowed itself to serve as the ideology of the powerful and the victorious, but it has also struggled to recover its mission of ministering to the afflicted, the despised, and the powerless. The course of recent debates within the church in Latin America, however, makes it clear that this renewal of mission and the demand for social justice that it includes as a constitutive element do not of themselves resolve the problem of choosing between pacifism and the justification of at least some violence.[21] On the one hand, God is presented as a source of consolation and strength for the poor and the oppressed and as the Father of Jesus, who suffers evil without violent resistance. On the other hand, he is the one who demands justice and the transformation of society, which may well require the use of force.

THE CONTEMPORARY SITUATION

The difficulties of the task of integrating the different aspects of God presented in Scripture and of reconciling these with the rational demands of theodicy become less acute once large numbers of Christians come to believe that it is possible and therefore morally imperative to transform the world in such a way that war is eliminated. This presupposes that the violence and destruction of war are no longer taken as given and somehow appropriate elements in our human condition as sinful creatures but are instead seen as evils that are to be eliminated. This has been a significant response to the problem of war since the time of Erasmus, and it has gained strength and influence in this century, especially in reaction to the massive casualties of World War I and the development of nuclear weapons. This response directs the attention of the Christian community to the second set of difficulties enumerated in the second part of this chapter, which, as I mentioned, can be resolved by the renunciation of just war norms in favor of pacifism.

A plausible brief account of the deepening concern about the acceptability of war in this century would see it as proceeding from the recognition that it is necessary to eliminate total war if advanced industrial societies are to survive to the hope that it may be possible to eliminate war, whether through international consent (the Kellogg-Briand Pact) or through an international organization taking collective security as its goal (the United Nations) or through nuclear deterrence. This change may well be dismissed as an extratheological event, a consequence of technological, military, political, and diplomatic activities occurring well after the formation of our religious traditions and in realms of life in which religious influence has for a long time been diminishing. But I would argue on the one hand that the religious traditions are themselves living and developing realities that are continually reinterpreted to provide guidance for communities interacting with a changing world, and on the other hand that this change has brought into question the consistency of the integration of the institutions of war with the basic theological affirmations about God that was provided by just war theory and its accompanying historical theodicy.

For once the elimination of war itself becomes part of the agenda, then we are at a different level of questioning. The conclusion that if war can be eliminated it should be eliminated seems to require our acceptance. The possibility of war, on this view, is taken to be a crippling defect in an international system for whose maintenance and modification human beings are responsible. The affirmation of full human responsibility in this area may be an appropriate response for a "humanity come of age," in Dietrich Bonhoeffer's phrase. It transforms the problem of war from an issue of theodicy to an item in the agenda of social reform. The problem of war from the Christian standpoint ceases to be one of how we are to reconcile military institutions and the rightness of participating in some wars with our beliefs about the nature of God and about the appropriate way of life for those who have accepted his call to conversion. It becomes instead a problem of how we are to change human institutions and human attitudes so that war is eliminated. The problem ceases to be a problem about God and history and becomes a problem about ourselves and our failure to do what our situation requires. This, I submit, is the way in which contemporary Protestantism, especially liberal Protestantism, read the problem of war in the aftermath of 1914 and 1945. It is increasingly the way in which Roman Catholicism tends to read the problem. Catholicism experiences profound tensions between its traditional commitment to just war theory and the aspiration to an international order united in peaceful acknowledgment of the moral imperatives arising from human solidarity, as we can clearly see in the recent encyclical of John Paul II, *Sollicitudo Rei Socialis* (1988).[22]

But reflection also suggests that there is something seriously flawed in this line of argument. It trades on certain confusions about the "we" who are being urged to take responsibility for the elimination of war. "We" can refer to all human beings; or it can refer to the citizens of one or more states; or it can refer to committed Christians. The people who are addressed by a moral argument or a religious exhortation and who are likely to be swayed by it rarely coincide with those who are in a position to make decisions for one or more political units. Political disputes of sufficient gravity and intensity to prompt people to resort to violence are unlikely to allow for convergent readings of the moral imperatives of a particular situation. The major long-standing political disputes (with the possible exception of the civil strife in Ulster) cut across preexisting communities of moral and religious discourse. While it may be possible for us (human beings taken collectively) to eliminate both war and the conditions that produce and partly justify wars, it does not follow that it is possible for us (members of a particular confessional group) to eliminate either. Even if it is argued that surrender or nonviolent resistance by one side would eliminate war, such conduct increases the likelihood of conditions of oppression and injustice. In a complex, modern, pluralistic, industrial society, the connections between conversion of heart and the making of political decisions and the achievement of morally acceptable outcomes in situations of conflict are matters of hope rather than demonstration or even plausible prediction. When this point is taken seriously, then the appeals and denunciations of church leaders urging "us" to make an end of war and establish a just and lasting peace are seen not as commands to do what is clearly feasible but as urgings to explore the bounds of the possible. In this matter the possible is not the logically or the nomologically possible but the possible in political action. These urgings can range from impersonally rational assessments of risks and benefits to expressions of pious utopianism, depending on what the prospects and arguments are in a particular situation and how precisely we can formulate them.

The waging of even conventional war between powers with nuclear weapons is obviously a very dangerous activity, and it is noteworthy that the superpowers have generally (though not always) refrained from provocative behavior of the sort indulged in by great powers with fair frequency before 1939. But to conclude from this that we are in a position to eliminate war and the situations that provoke it is a long and uncertain step.

The churches and the religious critics of modern warfare confront a dilemma here. On the one hand, the way in which the contemporary world has arrived at an uneasy and threatening peace through mutual deterrence between hostile blocs grows out of motives and practices that are suspect and justifiable only with difficulty from a Christian standpoint. Even then, justification will have to make use of either just war categories or some form of utilitarianism or proportionalism. On the other hand, appeals calling for a conversion of hearts to a new set of values in the political order, while easily reconcilable with Christian beliefs about the moral character of God and with norms for Christian behavior, are likely to rely on unrealistic assumptions about the behavior of societies in situations of conflict, assumptions that are more consonant with hope than with experience.

That the attitude of the Christian churches (including Roman Catholicism) toward nuclear deterrence and the real possibility of modern warfare that comes with it should be somewhere between reluctant acceptance and rejection should not be surprising. There are two kinds of reasons for this pained and ambivalent reaction. The first group of reasons is felt by contemporary men and women in general, regardless of their religious convictions, and arises from the general revulsion at the destruction that would be produced by the use of any significant fraction of the world's arsenal of nuclear weapons, a revulsion that is combined with a sense of the irreversibility of technological change and the indispensability of the weapons. The other and deeper set of reasons arises from the fact that the Christian tradition has never been able to give more than a limited and conditional moral justification for the use of violence. Its endorsement of violence is never stronger than "yes, but."[23] The bishop of Würzburg kept his crozier but lost his sword.

NOTES

1. For a clear presentation of arguments for the logical independence of morality from religion, see William Frankena, "Is Morality Logically Dependent on Religion?" in *Religion and Morality*, ed. Gene Outka and John P. Reeder, Jr. (Garden City, N.Y.: Doubleday Anchor, 1973), 295–317.

2. Hugo Grotius, *De Jure Belli ac Pacis*, Prolegomena, 11.

3. National Conference of Catholic Bishops, *The Challenge of Peace* (Washington, D.C.: United States Catholic Conference, 1983), Section 17.

4. John Milton, *Paradise Lost* 1.26.

5. Plato, *Gorgias* 475d.

6. Sir Michael Howard, *War and the Liberal Conscience* (Oxford: Oxford University Press, 1978), 13.

7. See, for instance, the contrast between peace and war depicted on the shield of Achilles as described in Homer, *Iliad* 18.477–608.

8. Desiderius Erasmus, *Julius Exclusus*, trans. Paul Pascal and ed. J. Kelley

Sowards (Bloomington: Indiana University Press, 1968). This is the famous satire depicting Pope Julius II's exclusion from heaven for his military exploits and corruption.

9. St. Augustine, *The City of God* 1.3, trans. M. Dods (New York: Modern Library, 1950).

10. Ibid., 11.11.

11. For an account of the transformations of the Augustinian and biblical scheme of history, see Karl Lowith, *Meaning in History* (Chicago: University of Chicago Press, 1950).

12. Jacques-Bénigne Bossuet, *Discourse on Universal History*, trans. Elborg Forster and ed. Orest Ranum (Chicago: University of Chicago Press, 1976), 6.

13. Augustine, *City of God* 1.8.

14. Ibid., 1.36.

15. Ibid., 5.11.

16. Ibid., 5.21.

17. Ibid.

18. See Mary Mackenzie, *Plato on Punishment* (Berkeley: University of California Press, 1981), for a vigorous statement of difficulties presented by the practice of punishment.

19. See Herbert Deane, *The Political and Social Ideas of St. Augustine* (New York: Columbia University Press, 1963), chap. 2, "The Psychology of Fallen Man," 39–77.

20. G.W.F. Hegel, *Philosophy of History*, trans. J. Sibree (New York: Dover, 1956), 28.

21. See John Langan, "Violence and Injustice in Society in Recent Catholic Teaching," *Theological Studies* 46 (1985): 685–99.

22. John Paul II, *Sollicitudo Rei Socialis*, in *National Catholic Reporter*, May 27, 1988, 14–27. Cf, paragraphs 22–24.

23. For an elaboration of this theme, see John Langan, "Just War Theory and Decisionmaking in a Democracy," *Naval War College Review* 38 (1985): 67–79.

4

The Religious Foundations of War, Peace, and Statecraft in Islam

Richard C. Martin

al-Salamu ʿalaykum, "Peace be unto you" (Qurʾanic phrase and common greeting among Muslims)

Alladhina amanu yuqatiluna fi sabil allah, "Those who believe fight-to-kill in the path of God" (Qurʾan 4:76)

The purpose of this chapter is to introduce students of just war theory to the religious foundations of war, peace, and statecraft in Islam.[1] As the two epigraphic quotations that begin this chapter suggest, both peace and war are fundamental to the Islamic worldview, although war and violence have tended to receive more attention in popular media representations of Islam. The question arises, then: Does conflict with enemies form a significant theme in Islam? If so, the historian of religion must account for and interpret this theme for comparative studies of religions.

In this regard, Earle Waugh has suggested the possibility of discovering in the Qurʾan "an enthronement of peace within the context of conflict."[2] In fact, Islam makes a strong claim that both peace and war are ultimately rooted in divine purposes for human history. Hence the analysis of Muslim reflections on peace and war must take into account the primary sources of the revealed divine will. These are primarily the sacred texts of the Qurʾan (scripture) and the Sunna (exemplary "practice" of the Prophet Muhammad). Yet our attention is naturally drawn to Muslim worldviews and to social behavior as evinced by Muslims themselves in the course of history. Actual expressions of Muslim thought and action on matters of peace and war, now and in the past, must also be evaluated. Ultimately, historical experience for the

Islamic as for the other confessional communities leads to moral tensions between the ideal and the actual; existential crises arise when violence and human tragedy erupt and cannot be made to fit into one's operative worldview and when the darker side of life emerges and must painfully be acknowledged.

Among these different textual and contextual dimensions of our topic, the first matter at hand is to discuss the fundamental symbols and representations of peace, war, and statecraft in Islam. The first section of this chapter aims to meet this requirement. In the second section we turn to a consideration of how the "other," the non-Muslim and/or anti-Muslim antagonist, is construed within the Islamic symbol system. In the third section we take up the problem of how the historian of religion is to analyze the interrelated textual and contextual fields of data that comprise our topic. The final section of this chapter reflects on the different approaches to problems of war and violence represented by students of ethics and ritual studies. Insofar as rules exist for the justification of violence and bloodletting and for the prevention or control thereof, and insofar as conflict often assumes cultural and symbolic forms other than outright bloodshed, the ethical and ritual dimensions of human violence are especially apropos to scholarship on the history of religions.

It follows from these introductory remarks that this chapter is not organized around the prevailing ethical problems of Western just war theory, *jus ad bellum* and *jus in bello*. How Muslims have justified going to war and have restricted violence in war involves a broader range of issues in comparative religious studies than just war theorists are generally accustomed to allow.

WAR AND PEACE, TRUTH AND LIE IN THE PATH OF ALLAH

Majid Khadduri has observed that the ultimate objective in the Islamic worldview is peace, not war.[3] More specifically, no purpose for war exists save that which fulfills the religious purpose of defending the interests of the Muslim community (*umma*), whose members—contrary to the enemies of the divine truth—fear God and obey his prophets. War (*harb*), to the extent that it finds justification in Islamic law, is counted among the religious duties (*'ibadat*) and is defined by the Qur'anic notion of *jihad (fi sabil allah)*, "striving (in the Path of God)." *Jihad* comprises a large variety of individual and collective efforts to implement the life of pious submission (that is, *islam*) to the will of God and requires, significantly, an Islamic polity to ensure worldly success.[4] Peace (*salam*) is also a semantically rich concept in the Qur'an in passages such as "Those whom God wills to guide, He expands their breast to *islam*. . . . Theirs is the dwelling-place of *salam* with their Lord, and He is their friend [literally 'He is one close to them'], in what they practice [i.e., righteousness]."[5] Sura (chapter) 37 of the Qur'an admonishes uttering the divine blessing of peace upon all prophets, and, as Waugh concludes, "The parallelism [between Muslim historical experience and the Qur'an] carries the truth of 'If they are granted the greeting [of peace, *salam*] by God, [believers] will be too.'"[6] Even so intense a critic of traditionalist and modernist Islam as the Muslim Brotherhood's Sayyid Qutb could construct the agenda of fundamentalist Islam around the notion of ultimate peace in the divine will.[7] The moral requirement to strive (*jihad*) in the path of God is a fundamental notion in Islam; closely related to it is the injunction to "command the good and combat evil." Both phrases occur frequently in the Qur'an and appear as scriptural warrants in Islamic law for taking moral action in the world. It is to the cosmological dimensions of moral order in the Qur'an, then, that we now turn in order to grasp better the significance of Qur'anic symbolism for our topic.

The second sura of the Qur'an begins with a long account of generic distinctions between beings who believe in God and his revelation and fear him, those who reject God, and those who attempt to deceive both believers and God by professing faith falsely (Q. 2:1–29).[8] The latter, the deceiving hypocrites in particular, are described in striking metaphors (deafness, lightning that blinds, covenant breakers, followers of Satan). The struggle between Truth (*sidq*) and Lie (*kadhb*) and between acceptance (*iman*, "faith") and rejection (*kufr*, literally "ingratitude") is a powerful thematic characterization in the opening verses that speak of inherent conflict in the human condition.

The opening passage of the second sura is followed by verses on the creation of Adam and the refusal of Iblis among the angels to obey God's command to "bow down" to Adam, and then by the story of the primal man and his wife in the Garden, God's instruction of Adam in the names of things and in obedience to him, and Satan's successful deception of the first parents, which caused them to be expelled from the Garden (2:30–39). Thus the struggle between truth and lie, doing good and sowing disorder, is a cosmological problem and a fundamental one in Islamic symbolism. The story continues in the second sura with an account of Israel's covenant with God (brief mention is also made of the Christians and Sabaeans—other people with scriptures, signs from God), their breaking of the covenant and rejection of God's signs, and their consequent punishment, in which it is said that God made an example of them (2:40–86). The following passage dwells on the role of prophets sent by God to various communities to warn them to fear God and obey his prophets:

We gave Moses the Book and after him followed up with Messengers, and gave Jesus son of Mary clear [signs] and confirmed him with the Holy Spirit. So whenever a Messenger comes to you with that which you desire not, do you yourselves [literally, your spirits, souls] become inflated with arrogance? (2:87)

Then follows the judgment on those confessional communities that reject their messengers:

The Jews say "the Christians have nothing [true to stand] on" and the Christians say "the Jews have nothing [true to stand] on," although they recite the same [or a similar] Book. In a similar vein, those without knowledge say the likes of what [Christians and Jews] say. On the Day of Resurrection God will judge among them regarding that in which they differ. (2:113)

With 2:122 begins a section on Abraham, the founder of the Ka'ba in Mecca, who prays: "O Lord, make Muslims [literally, those who submit to You] and [make] our progeny your *umma muslima* ['community that submits to You']" (2:128).

The focus on the *umma* in Arabia and on the Messenger to the Arabs (Muhammad is meant but not named) begins at 2:142. Here the themes of going in the Straight Path (*sirat al-mustaqim*) versus going astray or being led astray are brought to bear on the Arabs and their Prophet in particular. To stay on the Straight Path requires effort in the path of God (*jihad fi sabil allah*), a root metaphor in the Qur'an, as noted earlier. The Qur'anic cosmology can be represented with the following diagram:

```
                    Divine - Hereafter
          Angels                |              Iblis
                                |
   Truth                        |                    Lie
   _____ |Satans_____
          Obedience            |Satans    Disobedience
                               |
          Muslims              | Hypocrites, non-Muslims
          Jinn                 |               Jinn
                    Human  -  This world
```

This diagram represents a state of affairs in the cosmos ("worlds," al-'*alamun*) within the cosmogonic framework of creation of the worlds and of humankind. Elsewhere in the Qur'an, in a well-known passage, the primordial unity of humankind in the seed of Adam is presented as follows:

And when your Lord drew forth from the descendants of Adam, from their loins, their seed, and caused them to testify concerning themselves [saying]: Am I not your Lord? They said: Truly, we so testify; Lest you say on the Day of Resurrection: Verily, of this we were unmindful. (Q. 7:172)

Among the implications of this passage is that the seed of Adam, the whole of humankind, is born Muslim and thus in a state of primal peace (*salam*). To be non-Muslim or to fall from Islam appears to be a product of history in this world (*al-dunya*), not a primordial attribute of humanity as defined in the Qur'anic cosmology (*al-akhira*).

The dynamics of heavenly/earthly conflict among the creatures of God stand in sharp contrast—both as a preponderant theme and in textual clarity—to the Qur'anic vision of peace.[9] Nonetheless, peace is what underpins the whole of the Qur'anic cosmology; it is the eschatological goal toward which sacred history moves and for which the sending of prophets from Adam to Jesus and culminating in Muhammad's mission to the pagan Arabs receives its implicit rationale. Prophets come as messengers to instruct in the Guidance, the Book, which should be studied, recited, and obeyed. God sent it down to prepare human communities for judgment on the Last Day, when all contentious parties and opponents of those who followed the Guidance will endure a terrible punishment. Believers, on the other side, will have no more fear, but rather will have peace, as the following passage promises characteristically:

And the Trumpet shall be blown; then behold, they are sliding down from their tombs unto their Lord. They say, "Alas for us! Who roused us out of our sleeping-places? This is what the All-merciful promised, and the Envoys spoke truly." It was only one cry; then behold, they are all arraigned before us. So today no souls shall be wronged anything, and you shall not be recompensed, except according to what you have been doing. See, the inhabitants of Paradise today are busy in their rejoicing, they and their spouses, reclining upon couches in the shade; therein they have fruits, and they have all they call for. Peace!—Such is the greeting, from a Lord All-Compassionate.[10]

In sura 48, known as "the Victory," we read: "He [God] is the One who sent down the *sikina* in the hearts of the believers that they might increase, faith upon faith" (Q. 48:4). The widely read Jalalayn commentary defines the mysterious term *sikina* as a synonym of *tuma'nina*, "peace, tranquility, calm, confidence." The implication of this and related passages is that victory in the Path of God is tantamount to peace and tranquility; like the Qur'an itself, "the Tranquility (*sikina*)" is also "sent down" (revealed, given) to those who walk (go through life) in the Straight Path.

The Qur'an stresses in this regard that humans who walk in the Path must be morally aware of their actions. Moral awareness is framed in the concept of *taqwa* (piety, fear of God), which Fazlur Rahman translates as "to protect oneself against the harmful or evil consequences of one's conduct."[11] Again, the consequences are unavoidable on the Day of Judgment (*al-akhira*, "last") and hence are "ultimate." Thus only a life of service to God (*'ibada*), a life governed by the *'ibadat* (the Five Pillars and other religious duties, such as *jihad*) is appropriate to this result, this overcoming of conflict, this *salam*.

The Qur'anic cosmology, therefore, admonishes humanity to live by the Book of Guidance, to follow the prophets/messengers sent to them, and to build a community (*umma*) that will ensure the ability of humans to accomplish these ultimate ends. It is with this communal sense of obligation and effort in the Path that Islamic religious theories of state-craft have been articulated. Sura 2 makes this explicit in addressing the *umma* of the Prophet: "Even so we have constituted you as a median community that you be witnesses to mankind and that the Messenger be a witness over you" (Q. 2:143). Rahman's commentary on this passage ties the various themes we have been discussing together into the ine-luctable Islamic conclusion that a Muslim polity, one capable of sup-porting and enforcing a life of walking in the Straight Path, is necessary and a duty for Muslims to establish, maintain, and extend.

There is no doubt that the Qur'an wanted Muslims to establish a political order on earth *for the sake of creating an egalitarian and just moral-social order*. Such an order should, by definition, eliminate "corruption on the earth . . . " and "reform the earth." To fulfill this task, to which every people whose vision is neither truncated nor introverted pays at least lip-service, the Qur'an created the in-strument of *jihad*.

Rahman then cites Q. 3:64 ("O People of the Book! Come [let us join] in a formula that may be common between us—that we may serve naught except God") and comments:

It should also be noted that this invitation is for cooperation in building a certain kind of ethico-social world order and is not of the nature of contemporary forms of "ecumenism," where every "religious" community is expected to be nice to others and extend its typical brand of "salvation" to others as much as it can! For Islam there is no particular "salvation": there is only "success (*falah*)" or "failure (*khursan*)" in the task of building the type of world order we are describing.[12]

To summarize the implications of the Islamic cosmology for peace, war, and statecraft, the cosmological dilemma that Islam exists to over-come is alienation from the Truth, from life on the Straight Path. Islam is self-consciously a universal missionary religion that seeks to restore humankind to its original condition in the seed of Adam, the condition in which all of humankind testifies to its submission to Allah. To achieve this goal of life on the Straight Path and service to God, a political entity governed by the Guidance must be established and enforced. Until the final condition—of the original in the seed of Adam—has been restored, Muslims must struggle, make effort (*jihad*) in the Path of God against the forces of deception and unbelief. In this framework the "other" presents a condition of conflict in the world, one that is potentially violent. The end or final return to God (*akhira*), however, is peace, peace for all humankind.

Of particular interest and importance in this cosmology, as stressed earlier, is how the Qur'an construes the "other," those who are blameworthy for not striving in the Path of God. In the following section, Islamic categorizations of the "other" derived from Qur'anic symbolism are briefly discussed.

MUSLIM PERCEPTIONS OF THE OTHER

The Islamic view of social life is reflective of events that took place in the sacred history of the time of revelation (the sending down of the *ayas* of the Qur'an and the prophecy of Muhammad in Mecca and Medina. The grounds for Muslim self-identity implied, as in other traditions, criteria for perceiving other religions and opponents of *islam*, which, as noted earlier, means "submission" to the will of Allah but also carries the connotation of peace.[13] Pious recollection of the historical experience of the Muslim community during and after the time of revelation, which ended with the death of the Prophet in 632, gave greater definition to the other, the forces of deception and unbelief.

The obligation of Muslims to make effort in the Path of God is expressed by the Qur'anic phrase *al-amr bil-ma'ruf wal-nahya 'an al-munkar*, which is loosely translated as "command the good and combat evil."[14] Theological and legal discourses expound upon this basic obligation of Muslims in pursuit of what we might call "Islamization." A related concept is that of the *da'wa*, the "invitation" (sometimes rendered "propagandizing") to become Muslim. Both the normative and historical texts of Islamic civilization are rich in expounding on these concepts, as other chapters in this volume demonstrate. In what context was this "effort" made?

The difference between the nascent Muslim and Christian communities is instructive in this regard. Christianity was born outside the councils of Judean and Roman political power. For the first few centuries the "other" was Caesar and his realm. The language differentiating insiders from outsiders was formed by a semantics of religious community versus secular world that culminated, when Christianity came to power in the fourth century, in Augustine's dichotomy: city of God/ city of man. The moral problem posed by military conflict was not a profound theme of the cosmology of the preeminent Christian text, the New Testament. Christianity did not escape the moral dilemma of war thereby, but rather was drawn into moral reasoning without the support of symbolic, cosmological clarity about the need to cope with human resistance in the Path of God.

Islam, on the other hand, was born within the ethos of tribal conflict and the military ascendancy of the Arabs in the Middle East. The "other" was defined in terms of non-Muslim pagans, scripturaries, and cultural traditions (for example, Persians) that resisted the rising Muslim hegemony over this expansion. The language that differentiated insiders from outsiders was at once political and religious. The conflictual and military implications of otherness were, as shown earlier, a profound aspect of the cosmology of the Muslim text, which contained the basis for a highly sophisticated sorting out of the problems posed by the existence of various opponents of Islam.

The most immediate problem addressed by the Qur'an is *Shirk*, associating other beings with Allah. Those who resisted Allah and his Messenger by clinging to other gods were the *Mushrikun*. No more repugnant epithet for opponents exists in the Qur'anic lexicon. Historically, the discourse against *Shirk* and the *Mushrikun* centered first upon polytheism and the clans of Mecca and Arabia that opposed Muhammad. *Shirk*, however, became a powerful symbol in later Islamic discourse against unbelief and sociopolitical movements perceived as opposing Islam.

Another perception of "otherness" was defined by the concept of *ahl al-kitab*, People of the Book, mentioned in the Qur'anic cosmology and identified specifically with Jews, Christians, and Sabaeans (and, later, Zoroastrians). As the Qur'anic cosmology specifies, the People of the Book had previously received a book of divine revelation and had been sent prophets; the Qur'an was the final revelation, and the Prophet Muhammad was the Seal of the Prophets. The older confessional communities had rejected their prophets and distorted their scriptures, whose existing historical textual versions no longer completely reflected the original archetype of the Text, known as the *umm al-kitab*, "Mother of the Book," and *al-lawh al-mahfuz*, "the Preserved Tablet." In the Islamic worldview these communities have a special sacred legal status (*dhimma*), which indicates a protected confessional group authorized to pursue its religion within the framework of its own rituals and authoritative structures, but not to proselytize or otherwise encroach upon the Muslim community. *Dhimmis*, as members of protected confessional communities were called, were under obligation to pay to the central treasury a poll tax known as the *jizya*.

Another important construction of otherness in the early Muslim worldview was the distinction between *dar al-islam*, "the abode of Islam," where Muslim rule and the *shari'a* were in force, and *dar al-harb*, "the abode of conflict," where Islam was not accepted and hostility toward Islam was experienced. A later category of *dar al-sulh*, "abode of treaty," classified those bordering non-Muslim states with which it was deemed permissible temporarily to avoid conflict that would not be in the momentary best interests of Muslim forces to pursue. In other words, dar al-Islam was in theory in a state of conflict with dar al-Harb, with provisions for a temporary stalemate on some fronts.[15]

Conversion to Islam of a *harbi*, "resident of Dar al-Harb," or *Mushrik* or *Dhimmi* was regulated by classifying them as belonging to a special class of Muslims known as *mawlas* "clients" of a Muslim Arab individual or clan. The degree of otherness Arab Muslims perceived in *mawlas* and vice versa was epitomized in the ninth century in a movement known as the *shuʿubiyya*, in which racial and cultural overtones of conflict appeared in popular poetry and prose.[16]

Still another form of otherness pertained to developments within the community, for example, when *ridda*, "apostasy," and *ikhraj*, "dissent, rising in rebellion against the orthodox creed," took place. The wars of apostasy waged by the nascent Muslim community after Muhammad's death and the early Muslim struggle with the Kharijite movement presented the paradigms for later understanding of dissent from within.[17]

In confronting the *harbi*, the non-Muslim beyond the rule of Islam, the Islamic worldview, as encoded in Islamic law, provided for several measures to be taken before violent force was warranted. The *jihad* in this particular case must first be declared by the *imam* of the Muslim community. An invitation to submit to the will of Allah must then be extended. If the *daʿwa* is declined, assault against the recalcitrant enemy is then justified. The kinds of violence permitted and against whom (the question of women, children, and the enfeebled comes in here) are further adumbrated in the legal sources. The treatment of prisoners once the assault has been successfully completed is another important category in the treatment of the "other" (non-Muslim). The terms of coming under Islamic rule as *dhimmis* or as *mawlas* are also discussed in detail in Islamic jurisprudence, as is the treatment of non-Muslim combatants and noncombatants.[18]

METHODOLOGICAL CONSIDERATIONS

The next task of this chapter is to discuss appropriate methods for the interpretation of Islamic religious texts and contexts. For purposes of this discussion, I shall consider the relevance of four interrelated fields of inquiry: (1) cosmology, (2) worldview, (3) ethos, and (4) pathos. These can be characterized as follows. Cosmology is the cosmic structure and dynamics of total reality that is represented in a foundational text and/ or performative ritual system. Worldview reflects historically rooted perceptions of the physical and social environment.[19] Ethos is the local system of cultural values and norms of behavior that the community self-consciously attempts to set in practice and to preserve (socially transmit) from one generation to the next. Pathos is the manifestation of moral and spiritual crises of conflicts between the ideal and the actual when these lead to tragic moral and/or physical consequences as experienced by the actors themselves.[20] Although identification of these fields is meant to address comparative studies in religion more generally, they are applied here to Islam, in particular as it is represented in formative religious texts. These aspects or fields are not meant to be reductive categories; obviously scripture cannot be adequately understood solely in terms of cosmology, and violence cannot be reduced to social pathos, or vice versa. Rather, these fields provide a way to construe the semiotic range of religious discourse and action at work within a given religious tradition in particular historical circumstances.

Cosmology

Islamic cosmology is presented primarily in the Qur'an, the text that Muslims accept as the authoritative divine word to humankind, and in the Sunna, the textual representation of the exemplary practice of the Prophet Muhammad and his closest companions. Both the Qur'an and the Sunna can be analyzed in terms of the relationship between a particular, cultural context and an authoritative, ritualized depiction of the structure of the totality of reality, the cosmos, and the forces that operate within it.[21] There are important distinctions between the two sources, however. The content of the Sunna points to the sacred in terms that are clearly part of the historical space and time of Muhammad and the Arabs in Mecca and Medina. The process of the oral transmission of the Sunna from the time of the Prophet to the time of the authoritative collections (*sahih*) of these prophetic logia (the ninth century) clearly indicates that one is dealing with a humanly transmitted and written text.

The Qur'an, on the other hand, is the eternal Word of God. While it too is related to Muhammad's career in Mecca and Medina, it is not subject to the same processes of historical revision and review as the Sunna. In principle, the Qur'an articulates a message that is beyond history, while the Sunna corresponds to and illustrates the Qur'anic cosmology on the earthy plane. For example, one aspect of Sunna literature provides the earthy occasions (*asbab*) for the sending down or revelation (*tanzil*) of the heavenly text. In Qur'an and Sunna, heaven and earth reach out toward each other and interact textually in ways that define the ultimate significance of human history for Muslims.

The Qur'an plays a distinct and central role in Islam as the a priori text. In other words, we might ask: What distinguishes a "scripture" such as the Qur'an from any other written text? Seen from within Islam, the Qur'an is the Word of God (*kalam allah*). Seen from without, it may be viewed in the manner of Robert Scharlemann, who puts it this way: "A [scripture] is a writing upon which commentaries can be written but which itself is not a commentary upon another text."[22] Islam allows that all other texts, including the *hadith* reports that transmit the Sunna of the Prophet, are humanly produced. That the Qur'anic text (and its cosmology) are rigorously separated in Muslim thought from human production calls for special consideration of its role in Islamic conceptions of textuality.[23]

Worldview

The primal texts or scripture (Qur'an) and prophetic logia (*hadith*) are continually consulted by the community (*umma*), which may be called in this regard a "textual community."[24] Meaning is a product of interpretation, although it is often a part of the theology of the text to claim that a literal or, as in the case of the Qur'an, a "clear" or "plain" meaning (*zahir, muhkam*) is explicit in the text and requires no special explication. Conversely, Islam also holds that some passages are unclear at the surface of the text and/or possessed of inner or recondite meanings (*batin, mutashabih*) known only to God or to a special leader (*imam*) or one "close" to God (*wali*). Thus interpretation can also be privileged; a charismatic individual or school of interpretation (*madhhab*) has the culturally recognized authority to interpret the text. Erich Auerbach has described this aspect, this "need of interpretation" (*Deutungsbeduerftigkeit*), with respect to the text of the Bible in relation to other classical textual "representations" of reality.[25] The most important and authoritative interpretive materials in Islam are the Sunna or practice of the Prophet Muhammad and his companions (*ashab*), which are recorded in *hadith* and interpreted in Islamic law, the biographies of the Prophet (*sira*), and the commentaries (*tafsir*) of the Qur'an. The *hadith* reports in particular are characterized by *Deutungsbeduerftigkeit*; hence the Islamic worldview is presented historically by an ever-expanding textual system with a high degree of oral transmission. The traditional Islamic cultural system places the heuristic situation of teacher (reciter) and pupil (auditor) at the forefront of authoritative modes of learning the Islamic worldview— even when that which is recited is from a written text (taken in dictation from a teacher/reciter) and when that which is heard is in turn written down, but passed on to the next generation as a recited text.[26]

A distinctive religious concept to evolve in the Islamic worldview is that of *shariʿa*. The primary texts of the Islamic cosmology and worldview—Qur'an and Sunna—present both the divine purpose of human life and the textual, ritual, and legal means for carrying it out in the formation and implementation of a Muslim polity, as we have seen earlier. *Shariʿa* frames the distinctively Islamic system of moral reasoning. *Shariʿa* is theoretically a "closed" system, bounded by the authoritative texts of Qurʾan and Sunna, which reveal the divine will.[27] In practice, however, *shariʿa* operates as an open system that is made to be responsive to each new moral question put to it arising out of virtually any historical, social, or potentially legal circumstance in which Muslims might find themselves. If Qurʾan and Sunna comprise the textual "diet" that restricts what ought to be done in the Muslim ethos, *shariʿa* is the hermeneutical "cuisine" that is able to accommodate varieties of taste and purpose, although not without cultural disputation and conflict.[28]

Worldview differs from cosmology insofar as the materials of *hadith*, prophetic biography, Qurʾanic commentary, and legal discourses on the *shariʿa* are, as already stated, humanly produced texts—a part of a continuing textual, semiotic process. Aside from the specific genres of texts that present the Islamic worldview, then, we must also account for how worldviews are socially reproduced through the process of transmission from one generation to the next. Local cultural determinants play a role in how a given group at a particular time and place puts together a worldview and acts in terms of it.

Ethos

Assessing the moral ethos of Islam, insofar as a common "ethos" of Islamic society can be constructed and described, takes the scholar beyond the more normative kinds of evidence for social and cultural descriptions. According to Clifford Geertz, the ethos of a group, community, or civilization is seen in how its members go about the conduct of their lives according to certain cultural patterns. Ethos, then, includes social relations such as kinship patterns and the etiquette practiced among social strata; the structure, content, and sources of education; and the celebration of life crises, such as birth, puberty, marriage, and death, in communal rituals. Since ethos is primarily social and behavioral rather than textual,[29] scholarly focus is less on what authoritative sacred sources say "ought" to be done and more on what the historical record suggests actually took place. Islamic historical texts—for example, annals, travel literature, and poetry—and, more recently, ethnographic descriptions project and describe the Islamic ethos in great detail (and variety).

The religious ethos of a tradition is but another dimension of worldview. Both comprise symbols whose meanings are often difficult for outsiders to interpret, for the referents of such symbols are in fact other symbols within the same system rather than constituents of a universal empirical or semantic world. Geertz says of worldview and ethos that the former denotes "the collection of notions a people has of how reality at base is put together," and the latter refers to "their general style of life, the way they do things and like to see things done." He goes on to describe the relationship in terms of cultural symbolism:

It is the office of symbols then, to link [worldview and ethos] in such a way that they mutually confirm one another. Such symbols render the world view believable and the ethos justifiable, and they do it by invoking each other in support of the other. The world view is believable because the ethos, which grows out of it, is felt to be authoritative; the ethos is justifiable because the world view, upon which it rests, is held to be true. . . .
Religious patterns . . . thus have a double aspect: they are frames of perception, symbolic screens through which experience is interpreted; and they are guides for action, blueprints for conduct.[30]

Other chapters in this and a companion volume describe in more detail the historical record of Muslim conflicts with others (for example, non-Muslims, apostate Muslims, enemies of the Truth) and how such conflicts are justified and processed in religious and legal frameworks. Here I should like to highlight an aspect of the Islamic ethos of conflict that receives scant attention in these other chapters: religious and juristic disputation. From the beginning, Islamic civilization included other confessional communities that it recognized as "protected" (in theory if not always in fact), and "orthodox" Islam itself comprised several partisan schools of interpretation (*madhahib*, singular *madhhab*) that in theory (but again not always in fact) agreed to disagree on interpretations of doctrine and the implementation of the *shariʿa* in everyday practice. Thus the conflict between Muslims and non-Muslims within *dar al-islam* (lands under Islamic rule and where the Islamic religion is properly established and in practice) and the conflicts between and among Shiʿite and Sunni partisan schools of interpretation generated an ethos of disputation, for which there exists a considerable textual record from the Middle Ages to the present. In the final section of this chapter, we will return to the significance of religious disputation for comparative scholarship on war, peace, and statecraft.

Pathos

The historian of religions encounters the pathos of a religious tradition in theological, juristic, artistic, and historical texts. What happens when worldview and ethos do not "fit" together as neatly as Geertz suggested, when religious symbols fail to create an orderly sense of what is happening and of what needs to be done in the world? Geertz himself expounded on this aspect of religion as follows:

There are at least three points where chaos—a tumult of events which lack not just interpretations but *interpretability*—threatens to break in upon man: at the limits of his analytic capacities, at the limits of his powers of endurance, and at the limits of his moral insight.[31]

Disaster, violence, and war are for Muslims, as for others, among the most threatening experiences of life to forbear, rationalize, and interpret. Although the points at issue between confessional communities and among the partisan schools of doctrinal and juristic interpretation in Islamic civilization have often been resolved or kept in control through the rituals of polemical debate and public disputation, the ideal sometimes broke down in reality, and confessional/partisan zeal led to violence and bloodshed.[32] In these circumstances pathos became interwoven with ethos and worldview in interpretive struggles.[33] While many in the West, including some scholars, believe that they have discovered an ethos of war and violence in Islam, it can be argued alternatively that textual criticism demonstrates in some cases a hermeneutical pathos—a continuing struggle to overcome suppression, alienation, and intense feelings of otherness, in short, to construct and maintain on religious principles the social boundaries between order and disorder and to avert the attending threat of social disintegration.

A central claim made in this analysis is that social and cultural identities are manifested in conceptions of otherness. In monotheistic systems, such as Islam, Christianity, and Judaism, the divine is predominantly conceived of as totally other than human. On the plane of human existence, social structure within the community and the boundaries that separate insiders from outsiders to the community are constructed in reference to injunctions in the divine text that are continually in need of cultural affirmation. The struggle to exert and/or to resist power is one meaning of *jihad* and is rooted in the problem of otherness. Religious self-identity turns on processes of "othering" that operate in the rituals and cultural practices of polemics, textual hermeneutics, law, expulsion and excommunication, and, in the most extreme cases, violence and war. The question of construing, justifying, and exercising power over others on religious grounds is a fundamental aspect of religion—some would say of the "sacred"—and thus an analysis of moral traditions must come to terms with the religious appropriation of power and the relationship of violence to religion.[34]

Hermeneutical problems inevitably occur in analyzing the interrelationship of cosmology, worldview, ethos, and pathos. How constant and "fixed" is the meaning of a term such as *jihad* in the analysis of Muslim conceptions of justified war with enemies? Despite the common acceptance within a religious community of scriptural *loci probantes* and legal definitions of justified causes and conditions for war, the careful scholar must always suspect interruptions and displacements in the relationship between the words that signify something, the thing(s) signified, and the ranges of social and semantic significance that interpreters may attach to them. At the level of determining significance, one needs to ask: Do texts that seem to say the same thing always mean the same thing?[35]

Language philosophers and sociolinguists have constructed theories and methods for the analysis of discursive texts and performative speech acts of the kind we encounter in the Islamic tradition.[36] One way to look at a textual (written or oral) discussion of the grounds for Muslim conflict with enemies is to analyze the locution itself as a grammatical and intelligible statement on its own terms. In this regard many ethicists analyze moral traditions in terms of what texts qua texts say propositionally. Another level or dimension of meaning that the textual critic must consider is what the speaker, writer, or reciter of a text wanted to do by offering the text—perhaps something barely alluded to, or even suppressed, in the text but indicated in the context in which it is produced or recited or interpreted. A third area of meaning lies in the significance of the text for the reader or auditor—meanings, feelings, and results that might lie beyond the intentions and anticipations of the writer/speaker.

The importance of understanding how religious cosmologies and worldviews figure in cultural organizations of experience is suggested in Erving Goffman's analysis of "primary frameworks," of which there are two basic types, the natural and the social.[37] Night and day, the seasons, climates, and terrain are natural frameworks of human experience. Religious symbols and rituals belong to what Goffman defines as social frameworks.[38] Goffman puts it this way: "One must try to form an image of a group's framework or frameworks—its belief system, its 'cosmology'—even though this is a domain that close students of contemporary social life have been happy to give over to others."[39] Expanding on Goffman's argument, the historian of religion emphasizes that in traditional religions, cosmological systems—which are usually presented didactically if not always systematically in authoritative scriptural narratives (written and/or performed texts)—contain semantic fields that are woven into the written texts, oral performances, and ethos of that tradition. Moreover, primary frames are composed of discrete segments (for example, Qur'anic passages, narratives about the Prophet, hadiths, and so on) that are hermeneutically perceived as what, in Goffman's language, are "strips" in everyday life. The textual record of the Islamic ethos, which includes recorded discussions of the ikhtilaf (differences) among jurists, written Islamic legal opinions (fatwas), sermons (khutbas), and more recent ethnographic materials, illustrate that Muslims often see their lives as "strips" of moral and ritual situations that were established as paradigms in Qur'anic cosmology and exemplified in the Sunna of the Prophet.

In "frame" analysis the problem is to identify the kinds of transformative "keying" of strips, where something serves as a model for something else. "Keying" is defined as "a set of conventions by which a given activity, one already meaningful in terms of some primary framework, is transformed into something patterned on this activity but seen by the participants to be something quite else."[40] One example would be a prizefight, which is keyed on actual fisticuffs, but which means something else to participants and observers. An Islamic example would be making a *hijra*, "emigration," to establish a community of followers, as the Prophet did. To outsiders such an action may look like rebellion or subterfuge, but to participants the action means something more than that. Marilyn Waldman has shown how African Muslim reformers transformed this aspect of the Prophet Muhammad's biography and incorporated these "strips" into anticolonial projects.[41] In similar fashion we might regard contemporary expressions of *jihad* or striving in the path of God against enemies as semiotic "strips"; again, this is modeled on the prophetic example but takes place under quite different circumstances than those of Arabia in 624–28.

Frame analysis of the phenomena of ethos and pathos in Islam requires more research and explanation than is possible for this chapter. Nonetheless, it is clear that the analysis of semiotic links between cosmology, worldview, ethos, and pathos can be served by such interpretive strategies as frame analysis. That notions and enactments of peace, war, and statecraft in Islamic history have been consciously (and unconsciously) modeled on Qur'anic and prophetic paradigms is no longer at issue. The problem for research becomes one of explaining and interpreting these semiotic transformations. Finally, it should be emphasized that traditional religious cosmologies provide an analytical framework for understanding social and self-identity and hence also provide frameworks for defining others (outsiders). This process of "othering" is particularly subject to semiotic reversals and denials in universal, missionary religions, such as Christianity and Islam. At the general, utopian, cosmological level, such traditions seek to convert and incorporate outsiders—the whole of the rest of humankind—into insiders. At the particular, social level of experience, the reverse is often the case, when religious discourse functions to turn opponent insiders into outsiders, a phenomenon that is well documented, for example, in Islamic heresiographical literature.

Moral Dilemmas and Ritual Dimensions of Violent Conflict

I have argued that the cosmology that informs traditional Muslim worldviews and the Islamic ethos calls for striving in the Path of God against those who act as enemies of the kind of religious and social order that God enjoins upon humankind. It is a cosmology that calls for the pragmatic ordering of submission and service to God within an *umma* (community) founded by the Prophet (or prophets) and thereafter modeled on his (their) recollected examples. With Muhammad, the Seal of the Prophets, the Muslim *umma* is divinely ordained to Islamize the whole of humankind. The potential pathos of Muslim societies living under this worldview is that ultimate peace can only come when the *umma* has overcome all opposition, when *dar al-harb* is subsumed within *dar al-islam*, and/or humankind is brought before God in final judgment on the record of its service to the divine will. Conflict seems inevitable in such a world, but the religious impetus is always to get on with the task of obedience and effort in the Straight Path.

For the historian of religion, conflict and violence should not be regarded simply as aporias within the social order, but as part of a religious system of signification that is encoded in cultural myths and rituals. In scholarship on the history of religion, violence forms a subfield of critical studies, where the question is asked: What are religious communities doing when they ritually encode and/or respond to a semantics of violence or its suppression? How fundamental is violence to most if not all religious systems? Before taking up the matters of criticism and ritual studies, it is important to recognize that war and violence present moral dilemmas and always, at some level, involve questions of conscience.[42]

That war is a moral dilemma for Muslims and a problem in the study of Islam was noted by Marshall Hodgson.[43] The passage is worth quoting at length, for it has drawn some criticism from Muslim and non-Muslim scholars.

It is not just a Christian squeamishness, I think, that points to Muhammad's military measures as a central problem in his prophethood. Every virtue carries with it its own characteristic defects, every perception of truth is accompanied by its own temptations to falsehood. . . . Christianity has its own pitfalls. A peculiar test of Islam lies in how Muslims can meet the question of war. . . . Muhammad's prophethood, in fulfilling the monotheistic tendency toward a total religious community, at the same time left his community confronted with that temptation to a spirit of exclusivity that went with any vision of a total community and that received appropriate expression in warfare. The resulting problems came to form a persistent theme of Muslim history.[44]

Critics sometimes dismiss Hodgson's concerns on this point, on the grounds that Hodgson was a Quaker and a pacifist. Thus Hodgson's perception of war as a problem for Muslims is said to be a value judgment rather than a scholarly one. The criticism, however, is gratuitous and ad hominem. It would not work against atheists or Hindu nationalists, who might also advance the argument that morally problematic (because violent) consequences follow from the Islamic worldview. Hodgson's critics must direct their refutations toward his argument and not his religious background. In the language established earlier in this chapter, we might say that Hodgson saw war—or some historical instances of religiously motivated wars—as part of the pathos of Islam, as a tradition that established war, under certain conditions, as a religious duty. Unlike the duties to believe in the One God, pray to him, make the pilgrimage, marry, and raise a family, this duty of *jihad* raises complex ethical issues. Muslims are hardly oblivious to this.

Views such as Hodgson's are also challenged, of course, by many Muslims, who claim that ethical action is founded on establishing and extending the divinely commanded moral human order (*umma*). This requires personal and group efforts "in the Path of God," including the use of force, provided other means fail in dealing with backsliders from and resisters to God's truth.[45] The difference between Hodgson and Muslim critics, such as Fazlur Rahman, is not whether Muslims who follow their code have ethical intentions. Rather, the question is what constitutes a moral act. Hodgson saw pathos in blindly following an authoritative moral code into carnage. The difference between Hodgson and many of his Western Islamicist critics is that Hodgson dared to believe that moral issues do not disappear when a scholar takes up the study of a civilization other than his or her own. Indeed, Hodgson was a humanist in the classic sense.

Is Islam, then, a "religion of the sword," a tradition whose statecraft is guided by an ethic of conversion, coercion, and even war as an ultimate means to achieve its ends? Certainly, modern media coverage of Islam and many Western attempts to characterize the Arab or Muslim "mind" have often come to the conclusion that there is a discernible ethos of violence in Islamic society, not a pathos of ideals leading to tragic consequences but a conscious ethos of violence.

Less visible to Western students of just war theory, perhaps, is the considerable literary debate among Muslim intellectuals over whether or not *jihad* (the only justifiable war) is restricted by the *shari'a* to defensive purposes. Abdulaziz Sachedina follows the majority of contemporary Muslim jurists who restrict *jihad* as it applies to modern Muslim nation-states to defense against outside attack and/or internal subversion.[46] Thus, insofar as we choose to accept the preponderance of recent judgments by Muslim scholars on this issue, offensive war is not sanctioned by Islam.

It seems more helpful to agree with Fred Donner, who, following Quincy Wright, distinguishes between war as a "condition" and war as an "activity."[47] That which was referred to earlier as the "cosmological problem" of lying, deception, and leading astray can be seen as a condition of conflict—a pervasive condition of the Islamic superstructure of reality. This condition does not necessarily cause war as such; rather, it places war and all of the attendant problems of reasons for going to war, proper conduct in war, and treatment of one's enemies after war in a distinctively Muslim perspective. In this respect Islam entered the stage of history with a decidedly more developed perspective on the actualities of war than did Christianity, for example.

Examining another strand of this chapter, we might ask in what sense war and actual human violence toward others (non-Muslim groups and states, Muslim dissidents) are more properly thought of as the pathos of Islamic civilization. Are the wars and rebellions of Islamic history examples of what Geertz would regard as the lack of fit between the Islamic worldview and ethos, on the one side, and the sociopolitical realities in which Muslims have found themselves at particular times and in particular places, on the other? War in this sense would indicate historical failure in negotiating an appropriate resolution of the conditions of conflict and in coming to terms with the other in (nonviolent) ways that are enjoined by the *shari'a*.

For all that, we might still ask: Where in Islam do we find the equivalent of Arjuna in the Bhagavadgita, wrestling with the moral dilemma of cultural distaste for violence (*ahimsa*) versus the social duty (*dharma*) of his cosmologically mandated warrior caste? Again, where do we find anything like the pacifist tone of the Sermon on the Mount? In my opinion, the closest (though certainly not a direct) parallel is found in the discussions of theodicy in Islamic speculative theology, where the great debate over divine versus human responsibility for evil was waged.[48] The dilemma of human versus divine responsibility for evil is especially characteristic of the monotheistic religions and a major problem in comparative religious ethics. At a more fundamental level of this kind of study, however, is the problem of violence and religion—the uneasy sense that religion often begets violence and that violence often begets religion.

In chapter 3 of this volume, John Langan notes that in the modern age an ethics of human responsibility (versus divine absolutism) "transforms the problem of war from an issue of theodicy to an item in the agenda of social reform. . . . The problem ceases to be a problem about God and history and becomes a problem about ourselves and our failure to do what our situation requires."[49] Characteristic of this problem for Christians, Langan suggests, is the painful dilemma between the cosmological notion of a "god of the victors" (Christian nationalism) and a "God of the poor and oppressed" (liberation theology).[50] Like Hodgson, Langan wants to take the responsibility for war and violence off God's shoulders and place it on humanity—that is, on the shoulders of those in confessional communities who act in the name of God. Beyond "Christian squeamishness," there is a problem in scholarship of how to account for violence in religious systems. In the case of Islam, the probability of violence seems to follow from the absolute thrust and the eschatological promise of total Islamization of human society as the only divinely ordained, just, and moral (and humane) society.

Here it is worth asking: How did Islam historically implement its mission to Islamize and pacify the cosmological other, the unbelieving and satanic forces described earlier? Again, in comparison to early Christianity, Islamic theology appears to have been more aggressive in seeking to impose its worldview, but it often sought to do so by verbal persuasion and polemics. The earliest spokesmen for Islam on the frontiers of the conquests were Qur'an reciters, after all. There is growing evidence, moreover, that during the Abbasid revolution in the second quarter of the eighth century Muslim religious disputants—known as *mutakallimun*—were sent with (or ahead of) troops to preach the Islamic *da'wa*, the invitation to accept Islam.[51] Again, conversion was primarily by verbal coercion and attending economic and political inducements. Enforcing the vision of a just and God-fearing society was often a matter of persuasion through disputation with adversaries. Conflict over otherness and the various categories of being non-Muslim was normatively waged in speech acts, *kalam*. Local and regional social stature among the religious elites (*ulama*) was determined in part by the ability of a *mutakallim* (dialectical theologian) or *faqih* (jurist) to defeat an opponent in debate over a religious or legal point.

These debates were sometimes intraconfessional within Islam, that is, among the *madhahib*, the highly partisan schools of theology and law, but they were also interconfessional, involving Christians, Jews, philosophers, atheists, and others. In a work now in preparation on the development of Islamic theological discourse in the ninth to eleventh centuries, I attempt to show that interconfessional and interschool violence and bloodshed, such as between the Hanafites and Shafi'ites in eleventh-century Khurasan, tended to occur at those moments when the ritual of disputation broke down.[52] Those groups that more readily took to the streets than to entering into rule-bound debate, such as the Hanbalites and often the Shi'a—whether forced to do so or not—would seem to emphasize the possibility that the ethos of disputation in traditional Islamic society was not the cause, but rather the cultural alternative to violence and bloodshed. The latter marked the pathos of violence that Islamic law, religious thought, and cultural forms conspired in various ways to avoid, but not always successfully.

The fundamental problem for the historian of religion in dealing with the issues of war, peace, and statecraft ultimately comes down to the relationship of religion to violence. If we shift the question from the Islamic cosmological vision of God, as Langan suggests we must in the case of Christianity, to what the historian of religion would regard as the human problem of intra- and intercultural strategies for dealing with violence, then the history of Islamic legal and theological disputation deserves much closer study. In a religious tradition that claims the divine mandate to pacify human society, the goal is ultimately eschatological, to be realized on the Day of Judgment. How could such sharp and intractable religious visions as those that divided Muslims from their opponents within the realm of Islam as well as their enemies and those they conquered be negotiated without further violence?

Religious disputation (*munazara*) or "warring with words" became a powerful mode of discourse for constructing and maintaining those sectarian and political boundaries that would ideally have to be overcome for Muslims to realize their eschatological vision of world order and peace. René Girard's impressive and controversial study of *Violence and the Sacred*[53] is concerned primarily with the origins of violence in the ancient blood rituals of sacrifice; he wants to know if primitive ritual was a necessary mode of social formation that functioned to reencode and thus suppress from social memory the primal act (or state) of violence. In this regard Girard's analyses might be applied to Islam. Rituals of blood sacrifice in Islam are associated primarily with the end of Ramadan, the month of fasting in which the revelation of the Qur'an had its origins, and with the end of the pilgrimage to Mecca, the universal obligatory ingathering of Muslims for spiritual renewal amidst the symbols of their communal origins at Mecca.

There is more to ritual than blood sacrifice, however, especially among expansive universal religions such as Buddhism, Christianity, and Islam. Girard's project does not yet help us much to understand the reencoding of violence in the pious rituals of these three great religions. I would suggest that religious disputation can be seen as a form of linguistic ritual that evolved in most literate traditions, and certainly to a high degree of sophistication in medieval Islam. The public rituals of disputation and polemical discourse were set in a semantics of power, defeating the enemy, destroying his possessions (premises, arguments), and claiming victory (Truth). The vindication of those who were in possession of Truth, if not immediately translated into political power against the other, could be interpreted eschatologically. The posture of political ascendancy, by the same token, required the justification of a Truth that governed one's opponents. Demonstrating this thesis will require more research than has presently been done. Nonetheless, such a thesis suggests that the shift in focus from theodicy to ritual is indeed a move from the problem of God acting in history, as Langan suggests, to one of human beings acting to cope with powerful forces of disruption through the rituals of language and cultural boundary maintenance.

This is not to suggest that arguing about religion is a prophylactic against violence; indeed, unstructured argument without cultural rules may often lead to violence. Nonetheless, religious disputation was and still is a highly polished social performance in Hinduism, Buddhism, and Islam, one that has required training and years of apprenticeship under the master of one's school. It is a form of arbitration between contending religious individuals, groups, or communities over issues that may divide them deeply and can easily lead to bloodshed. Recent research illumines the violence that is both explicit and implicit in the myths and symbols of the major world religions.[54] What we should find interesting about Islam is not just that its cosmology and worldview envisioned conflict and the exercise of power, however, but also that the divisive stuff of social conflict and violence was regularly enunciated and enacted in the ritual framework of religious disputation, where the rules for judging success and performance belonged to the public cultural domain.

Such an approach may seem to divert the study of just war theory from the kinds of texts that specialists normally admit in evidence. The counterclaim made here is that for the historian of religion, at least, the problem of war entails the more fundamental problem of violence. The symbolism and semantics of violence in religion in turn require a much greater and more complex interpretation of the religious experience than the issues of *jus ad bellum* and *jus in bello* comprehend.

NOTES

1. The term "Islam" is notoriously broad, ranging from an essentialist notion of ordained religious beliefs and practices to a broad and variegated cultural, geographical, and political history of Muslim lands and peoples. I mean by "Islam" here the religion, not the entire civilization, but in the nonessentialist sense of religion as it is expressed in texts and symbolic acts that take place in historical contexts. I attempt to make this point more clearly in the third section of this chapter.

2. Earle H. Waugh, *Peace as Seen in the Qur'an*, Ecumenical Institute, Occasional Papers 3 (Tantur, Jerusalem: Ecumenical Institute, n.d.), 18.

3. Majid Khadduri, *The Islamic Law of Nations: Shaybani's Siyar* (Baltimore: Johns Hopkins Press, 1966), 17.

4. The semantic range of *jihad* is discussed in my article on "Islamic Violence in Islam: Towards an Understanding of the Discourse on *Jihad* in Modern Egypt," in *Contemporary Research on Terrorism*, ed. Paul Wilkinson and A. M. Stewart (Aberdeen: Aberdeen University Press, 1987), 55–71. See also Rudolph Peters, *Islam and Colonialism: The Doctrine of Jihad in Modern History* (The Hague: Mouton, 1979).

5. Qur'an 6:125–27; see Waugh, *Peace as Seen in the Qur'an*, 15.

6. Waugh, *Peace as Seen in the Qur'an*, 14. I discuss the social construction of worldviews that reflect situations in primal texts in the third section of this chapter, on methodology.

7. The Muslim Brotherhood, based in Egypt, is the oldest and perhaps best-established organization for the dissemination and implementation of resurgent

fundamentalist religious ideas and programs in the twentieth century. Sayyid Qutb's pamphlet on "World Peace and Islam" (*Al-Salam al-ʿalami wa-l-islam*) is discussed in Martin, "Islamic Violence in Islam."

8. These are human beings (*insan*) in a cosmic, generic sense, not historical beings.

9. The rest of this section is based on the suggestive analyses of Waugh, *Peace as Seen in the Qurʾan*.

10. Qurʾan 36:52–57, following Arberry's translation.

11. Fazlur Rahman, *Major Themes of the Qurʾan* (Chicago and Minneapolis: Bibliotheca Islamica, 1980), 28–29.

12. Ibid., 62–63. Emphasis in original.

13. The terms *islam* and *salam* are derived from the same Arabic root.

14. The phrase occurs at the following loci: 3:104, 110, 114; 5:79; 7:157; 9:67, 71, 112.

15. For a discussion of medieval Islamic treaties and other legal agreements and obligations among nation-states, see Majid Khadduri, *War and Peace in the Law of Islam* (Baltimore: Johns Hopkins Press, 1955).

16. On the Shuubiyya movement as expressed in Arabic literature, see Hamilton A. R. Gibb, "The Social Significance of the Shuubiya," in *Studies on the Civilization of Islam*, ed. Stanford J. Shaw and William R. Polk (London: Routledge and Kegan Paul, 1962), 62–73.

17. The Kharijites or "Seceders" were party to the dissent and strife of the civil wars of the first century of Islam. As such, Islamic law generally proscribed their views, and Muslim forces were often sent against them in their more remote retreats away from the more orthodox urban centers. In modern times "Kharijism" is often applied to fundamentalist dissidents. On the early period of the Kharijites, see Wilferd Madelung, *Religious Trends in Early Islamic Iran*, Columbia Lectures on Iranian Studies, no. 4 (Albany, N.Y.: Bibliotheca Persica, 1988), 54–76. On the modern significance of the term, see Johannes J. G. Jansen, *The Neglected Duty: The Creed of Sadat's Assassins and Islamic Resurgence in the Middle East* (New York, Macmillan, 1986), 59, 152, 179, and Gilles Kepel, *Muslim Extremism in Egypt: The Prophet and Pharaoh* (Berkeley: University of California Press, 1985), 58–60.

18. See Khadduri, *War and Peace*, 94–137, for a lengthy discussion of Muslim sources on these stages and terms. In addition, see John Kelsay, "Religion, Morality, and the Governance of War: The Case of Classical Islam," in *Journal of Religious Ethics*; 18, no. 2 (Fall 1990): 123–39; also Tamara Sonn, "Irregular Warfare and Terrorism in Islam," in *Cross, Crescent, and Sword: The Justification and Limitation of War in Western and Islamic Tradition*, ed. James Turner Johnson and John Kelsay (Westport, Conn.: Greenwood Press, 1990).

19. Worldview as "perception of the physical and social environment" is discussed by Michael Thompson, *Rubbish Theory: The Creation and Destruction of Value* (Oxford: Oxford University Press, 1979), 7. Thompson adds: "Inside our heads, in our thoughts, and in our language, we carry a more or less coherent model of the world—a world view—a way of making sense of our environment, social and physical"(57).

20. I am indebted to Clifford Geertz, "Religion as a Cultural System," in *Anthropological Approaches to the Study of Religion*, ed. Michael Banton, A.S.A.

Monographs, 3 (London: Tavistock Publications, 1966), 1–46, where he presents the rationale for this kind of schema. I have added the aspect of "cosmology" to account for the centrality of scripture and other foundational texts (e.g., texts on the Prophet as founder of the community) in history of religion analyses and the aspect of "pathos" to account for the cultural experience of tension and rupture between the normatively ideal and the historically actual. The burden now lies, as it does with Geertz's construction, in developing methods that interrelate the textual and social data comprehended by cosmology, worldview, ethos, and pathos. With Geertz, I believe that semiotic theory is a good place to look for viable supporting methods.

21. On the aspect of Qur'an recitation as ritual, see Kristina Nelson, *The Art of Reciting the Qur'an* (Austin: University of Texas Press, 1985); William A. Graham, *Beyond the Written Word: Oral Aspects of Scripture in the History of Religion* (Cambridge: Cambridge University Press, 1987); and Richard C. Martin, "Understanding the Qur'an in Text and Context," *History of Religions* 21, no. 4 (1982): 361–84. On the oral-heuristic methods of pedagogy in Islam, especially regarding *hadith* transmission, see Richard W. Bulliet, *The Patricians of Nishapur: A Study in Medieval Islamic Social History* (Cambridge, Mass.: Harvard University Press, 1972); and George Makdisi, *The Rise of Colleges: Institutions of Learning in Islam and the West* (Edinburgh: Edinburgh University Press, 1981).

22. Robert P. Scharlemann, "Theological Text," *Semeia* 39 (1987): 7.

23. This claim is not meant to preclude historical- and literary-critical studies of the Qur'anic text. Rather, it observes that beyond historicism, the historian of religions must account for the special role of scripture in the semiotic system of meanings that operate in a given tradition.

24. The concept of "textual community" is developed by medieval historian Brian Stock in order to account for the revival of literacy in eleventh-century Western Christendom and its historical impact. "What was essential to a textual community was not a written version of a text, although that was sometimes present, but an individual, who, having mastered it, then utilized it for a group's thought and action. . . . The outside world was looked upon as a universe beyond the revelatory text." Brian Stock, *The Implications of Literacy: Written Language and Models of Interpretation in the Eleventh and Twelfth Centuries* (Princeton: Princeton University Press, 1983), 90. In Islamic thought the "outside" world is represented as a legal/theological construct that lies within the cosmological purview of the text, as will be explained later.

25. Erich Auerbach, *Mimesis: The Representation of Reality in Western Literature*, trans. Willard R. Trask (Princeton: Princeton University Press, 1953), 14–15. Auerbach's literary analysis of the style of the Bible in contrast to the Homeric epics and subsequent European literary representations of reality (worldviews) needs to be done with respect to the Qur'an and the Islamic literary tradition. In this regard, see John Wansbrough, *Quranic Studies* (Oxford: Oxford University Press, 1977), 148–70.

26. See Bulliet, *Patricians of Nishapur*, and Makdisi, *Rise of Colleges*.

27. The claim is often made, especially by Muslims, that this system of deriving meanings from common sources (Qur'an, Sunna) and interpreting them according to commonly accepted principles has yielded stable meanings among jurists for such terms and concepts as *jihad*. Historically, this is represented in

the legal fiction of the "closing of the Gate of *ijtihad*" (independent or new interpretations) after the tenth century.

28. On this point, see Jonathan Z. Smith, *Imagining Religion: From Babylon to Jonestown* (Chicago: University of Chicago Press, 1982), 39–44.

29. That is to say, the focus here is on what people do, although in literate traditions the scholar relies, of course, to a considerable extent upon written sources.

30. Clifford Geertz, *Islam Observed: Religious Development in Morocco and Indonesia* (Chicago: University of Chicago Press, 1971), 97–98.

31. Geertz, "Religion as a Cultural System," 14. Emphasis in original.

32. Over the course of the Iran-Iraq War during the 1980s, many Muslims I met in Egypt, Pakistan, Malaysia, and Indonesia expressed extreme discouragement over the identification of Islamic causes with the tragic pursuit of the war, and a Lebanese Muslim intellectual has confided the opinion that the fatal factionalism among Lebanese Muslims is a failure of Islam itself. One need not concede these points in order to see the moral pathos, at least since the rise of nationalism, of striving in paths of God that are often cross-current and at cross-purposes with aspirations for Arab and Islamic nationalism.

33. This aspect of hermeneutics—the politics of interpretation—has been the preoccupation of many of Michel Foucault's writings on discourse and power and is described succinctly, though critically, by Edward W. Said, "Opponents, Audiences, Constituencies, and Community," in *The Politics of Interpretation*, ed. W.J.T. Mitchell (Chicago: University of Chicago Press, 1983), 7–32.

34. The seminal work on this topic is René Girard, *Violence and the Sacred*, trans. Patrick Gregory (Baltimore: Johns Hopkins University Press, 1977). For an excellent study of the issues raised by Girard's work and that of others on this topic, see R. G. Hamerton-Kelly, ed., *Violent Origins: Walter Burkert, Rene Girard, and Jonathan Z. Smith on Ritual Killing and Cultural Formation* (Stanford, Calif.: Stanford University Press, 1987).

35. In semiotic theory the problem is stated succinctly by Umberto Eco, *A Theory of Semiotics* (Bloomington. Indiana University Press, 1976), 7: "*Semiotics is in principle the discipline studying everything which can be used to tell a lie. If something cannot be used to tell a lie, conversely it cannot be used 'to tell' at all.*" (Emphasis in original.) A good demonstration of this principle at work in the analysis of a variety of modern Muslim social settings is found in Michael Gilsenan, *Recognizing Islam: Religion and Society in the Modern Arab World* (New York: Pantheon Books, 1982), especially 9–26.

36. Marilyn R. Waldman, *Toward a Theory of Historical Narrative: A Case Study in Perso-Islamicate Historiography* (Columbus: Ohio State University Press, 1980), applies speech-act theory to an eleventh-century Persian Islamic historical text.

37. Erving Goffman, *Frame Analysis: An Essay on the Organization of Experience* (Cambridge, Mass.: Harvard University Press, 1974). Natural frameworks are those that are thought to be the purely physical determinants of social behavior, such as the weather, geography, biology, and other areas formed by "fields" in the natural and life sciences. The study of natural frameworks is highlighted, for example, in the "geography of religion" subfield of religious studies (see, inter alia, Xavier de Planhol, *The World of Islam*, trans. Cornell University Press [Ithaca, N.Y.: Cornell University Press, 1959]). Primary social frameworks, on

the other side, are worldviews—Goffman calls them "special worlds"—in which the actor can become involved.

38. By social world, Goffman often seems to mean what I refer to as "worldview." Like Geertz, Goffman as a social scientist does not clearly distinguish between the primal, textual, abstract expression of a religious "world, cosmos" and the social occupation of that world by historical communities.

39. Goffman, *Frame Analysis*, 27.

40. Ibid., 43–44. Goffman states that keying is "one basic way in which a strip of activity can be transformed, that is, serve as an item-by-item model for something else." He goes on to add that "differently put, keyings are a basic way in which activity is vulnerable" (83).

41. For an analysis of this, see Marilyn R. Waldman, "The Popular Appeal of the Prophetic Paradigm in West Africa," *Contributions to Asian Studies* 17 (1982): 110–14.

42. For Palestinians and other Muslims caught up in the terror of incessant wars and destruction of the twentieth century, poetry has frequently been the venue for expressing the existential crises of having traditional values shattered by unending personal loss.

43. Marshall Hodgson, *The Venture of Islam: Conscience and History in a World Civilization*, 3 vols. (Chicago: University of Chicago Press, 1974), discusses the moral dilemma of war in Islam, significantly, at the end of his chapter on "Muhammad's Challenge, 570–624" in vol. 1.

44. Hodgson, *Venture of Islam*, 1:186.

45. For a Muslim counterpoint to the judgment that war is a problem for Muslims in particular, see Rahman, *Major Themes of the Qur'an*, 37–64, especially, 63–64.

46. Abdulaziz A. Sachedina, "The Development of *Jihad* in Islamic Revelation and History," in *Cross, Crescent, and Sword: The Justification and Limitation of War in Western and Islamic Tradition*, ed. James Turner Johnson and John Kelsay (Westport, Conn.: Greenwood Press, 1990). The minority view (which curiously has received wider circulation in the West than has the majority view) is that *jihad* is a religious and moral obligation to Islamize all of humankind, even with force, and is not restricted to the defense of Islamic states. On the latter see Jansen, *Neglected Duty*, and Kepel, *Muslim Extremism in Egypt*.

47. See Fred M. Donner, "The Sources of Islamic Conceptions of War," in this volume, especially n. 5.

48. For an excellent discussion of theodicy in Muslim (and Western) religious thought, see Eric L. Ormsby, *Theodicy in Islamic Thought: The Dispute over al-Ghazali's "Best of All Possible Worlds"* (Princeton: Princeton University Press, 1984), especially the introduction and first chapter.

49. John P. Langan, "The Western Moral Tradition on War: Christian Theology and Warfare," in this volume.

50. Ibid.

51. An interesting illustration of this is explored by Shlomo Pines, "A Note on an Early Meaning of the Term Mutakallim," *Israel Oriental Studies* 1 (1971): 224–40.

52. *Language, Truth, and Miracle: Religious Discourse and Power during the Renaissance of Islam* (book-length work currently in progress).

53. See note 34.

54. See James A. Aho, *Religious Mythology and the Art of War: Comparative Symbolisms of Military Violence*, Contributions to the Study of Religion, no. 3 (Westport, Conn.: Greenwood Press, 1981).

II

Holy War

5

"Holy War" Appeals and Western Christianity: A Reconsideration of Bainton's Approach

David Little

INTRODUCTION

If we define the use of force as the act of imposing confinement, suffering, or loss of property, sustenance, limb, or life upon human beings, it is a truism that religions, among other things, give serious and sustained attention to the problem of managing the use of force. Force has a natural way of commanding the interest of human beings, no doubt because it is related to what Peter Winch has called the "limiting notions" of human life—things like death and suffering, as well as birth and sexuality.[1]

It would be hard to read the Old Testament, the New Testament, or the Qur'an without encountering the questions of the legitimacy and limits of force. In each of these sacred books, and in the traditions that respectively flowed from them, the divine figure is extensively associated with efforts to restrict and regulate the use of force. Yahweh, God, and Allah are all predominantly characterized as exercising political and legal functions. They all perform these functions in such a way as to control certain illicit kinds of force, as well as other forms of disobedience, by themselves resorting to the use or threat of force, where necessary, as deterrence or punishment. Each deity, that is, is pictured as legitimating selected forms of force in the name of preventing or minimizing other kinds of "illegitimate" and "excessive" force.

Max Weber described the God of the Old Testament as a "God of Foreign Policy," though the term could, with some adjustment, be applied to the God of the Qur'an as well. The deity in both traditions is centrally preoccupied with the regulation and direction of force in international relations.

The New Testament generally reflects a different set of concerns; how-ever, serious and important attention is given there to restraining force. Much of Jesus' nonviolent counsel to his followers, together with the model of his martyrdom on the cross, is proposed as a means of subduing illicit force once and for all. Moreover, in the background of the events of the New Testament hangs the promise of severe punishment of the unrighteous by "forceful means" that are at least analogous to physical force.

What is surely clear is that for Judaism, Christianity, and Islam, con-trolling and channeling force is a subject of deep sacred significance. Central to the beliefs of each tradition is the conviction that God pos-sesses divine authority over force and establishes a divine or ideal stan-dard for its exercise. Obviously, the interpretation of that authority and standard varies among the traditions, but they all share this common concern.

Appeals to "holy war" or "religious crusade" in one or another tra-dition are one type of appeal to divine authority regarding the use of force. Not only is force undertaken for religious purposes and under direct religious authorization, but opponents in a holy war or crusade tend to regard each other as cosmic enemies with whom compromise is improbable.

As we shall detail shortly, this sort of appeal is manifest in the Old Testament, especially in the books of Deuteronomy, Joshua, and Judges; and it is variously present in the Christian tradition. There are strong traces, for example, in Augustine, in the medieval Crusades, among certain late medieval radical sects, and in the Puritan movement of seventeenth-century England. It is often claimed that modern ideological conflicts are but a contemporary adaptation of the holy war or crusading tradition.

In an effort to clarify the role and character of such appeals in Western Christianity,[2] I want to reexamine the way the idea of holy war or crusade has been understood and applied by some interpreters of the tradition. I shall do that by revisiting Roland Bainton's famous threefold typology concerning "Christian attitudes toward war and peace": pacifism, just war, and crusade (holy war is slightly different for him, as we shall see).[3]

I take up Bainton for two principal reasons: (1) Scholars such as James Turner Johnson and LeRoy Walters have proposed several interesting and important revisions of Bainton's typology, especially as it bears on the definition of a crusade or holy war.[4] Other scholars have taken issue with Bainton's historical judgments regarding the occurrence of holy war appeals, specifically in the Puritan Revolution.[5] Reviewing these revisions and criticisms will help, it is hoped, to sharpen our under-standing of the structure and function of crusade or holy war appeals. (2) While admitting that Bainton's specification of a holy war or crusade appeal was unrefined, and his application of the idea on occasion incorrect, we ought not to lose sight of the significance of the distinctions among holy war, just war, and pacificist appeals in Western Christianity. Bainton's views may need modification; they do not require rejection.

Accordingly, in addition to clarifying the role of holy war or crusading appeals, I shall proceed to defend two specific theses in respect to Bainton's work. First, the outlines of Bainton's typology, properly revised, are indispensable for understanding the complexity of Christian thinking concerning the use of force. It would appear that the Christian story is a story of shifting combinations of the three attitudes Bainton identifies. While pacifist and holy war or crusading appeals are undoubtedly mutually exclusive, the just war attitude serves to mediate between the two extremes. It affiliates at times with the holy warriors, at times with the pacifists.

Second, a careful reexamination of the evidence on which Bainton's discussion of Puritan justifications for the use of force, in particular, is based reveals that both proponents and opponents of holy war arguments existed in seventeenth-century England. Without ignoring it altogether, Bainton underestimates the significance of the effort to dissociate religious warrants from the use of force that was connected with the strong emphasis, especially among radical Puritans, upon "natural reason" and "natural rights," rather than religious revelation, as the basis for the organization and conduct of civil affairs. While the process of "desanctifying" or "secularizing" force, by which holy war or crusading appeals were undermined, was not restricted to this period, much occurred to reinforce that process.

CHRISTIAN ATTITUDES TOWARD WAR AND PEACE

For Bainton, pacifism, or the total renunciation of the use of force, was in general identified with the early Christian church to the time of Constantine, and later with many of the Christian sects that were established during and after the Reformation, such as the Mennonites, Quakers, and others. By contrast, both the just war and crusade or holy war positions developed after the Constantinian settlement in connection with the church's growing sense of civil responsibility. Both positions condone the use of force, though in different ways:

The advocates of the just war theory have taken the position that evil can be restrained by the coercive power of the state. The Church should support the state in this endeavor and individual Christians as citizens should fight under the auspices of the state. The crusade belongs to a theocratic view that the Church, even though it be a minority, should impose its will upon a recalcitrant world. Pacifism is thus often associated with withdrawal, the just war with qualified participation, and the crusade with dominance of the Church over the world.[6]

As Bainton recognizes, Christian Scripture includes references to all three forms of attitude, thus leaving the normative question in the air. Whether to resort to force was not an abstract or academic question for early Christians. They lived in close contact with the Zealots, who were a first-century insurrectionist group committed to hastening the age of the Jewish Messiah by acts of force against the Roman Empire.

In fact, the connections between the early Christians and the Zealots were so close that one scholar portrays Jesus as moderately sympathetic to the Zealot cause and therefore as being prepared to advocate the use of force against the Romans.[7] The key passage in support of this thesis is Luke 22:37, in which Jesus commands any disciple "who has no sword" to sell his cloak "and buy one." On the one hand, it is true that this passage does not confirm the image of Jesus as an uncompromising pacifist or absolute proponent of nonviolence. He does not here instruct his disciples to lay down their swords once and for all. On the other hand, the context in which this passage occurs conveys strong reservations about resorting to force, and thus it appears to distinguish Jesus from the Zealots. The disciples go on to inquire whether they should actually "strike with the sword." When one of them proceeds to do so, attacking a member of the party coming to apprehend Jesus, Jesus exhorts the disciple to stop and then promptly heals the man wounded by the disciple (Luke 22:49–51). It is, in fact, the deep sense of ambivalence about the use of force apparent in this passage that seems to pervade the entire message of the New Testament and thus to distinguish that message from the convictions of the Zealots, on the one side, and from absolute pacifism on the other.

There is no question that the Gospels abound with utterances linking Christian discipleship to a preference for nonviolent benevolence (for example, Matthew 5:38–40; Luke 6:27–29). At the same time, there are several famous passages that clearly authorize at least a restricted employment of force and thus provide a possible toehold for just war thinking. There is, for example, Romans 13:1–6. In the process of admonishing Christians to submit to the authority of the state, Paul goes out of his way to justify the state's use of the sword, doing so in familiar, if rather puzzling, terms. He does not rest his case with the simple assertion that existing political rulers "have been instituted by God." In addition, he contends that "rulers are not a terror to good conduct, but to bad. . . . Do what is good and you will receive [the ruler's] approval, for he is God's servant [literally, 'to you for the sake of good']. But if you do wrong, be afraid, for he does not bear the sword in vain."

These words have caused unending perplexity in the history of the

Christian church.[8] Does Paul mean by them that as a matter of fact all existing governments invariably do use force justly, and that therefore all governments should be submitted to? Or does he mean, as some have argued, that only those rulers who, in exercising their authority, in fact demonstrate conformity to independent standards of the just use of force are legitimate rulers and therefore to be obeyed? This second interpretation provides an especially plausible basis for just war thinking in the Christian tradition.[9]

Finally, there are in the Old Testament references to the use of force as specifically warranted and directed by God. Here, according to Bainton, is the basis for the "crusading idea." A typical example is Deuteronomy 7:

And when the Lord your God gives [your enemies] over to you and you defeat them; then you must utterly destroy them; you shall make no covenant with them, and show no mercy to them. . . . And you shall destroy all the peoples that the Lord your God will give over to you, your eye shall not pity them. (Deut. 7:2, 16)

Or, again, Deuteronomy 20:

In the cities . . . that the Lord your God gives you for an inheritance, you shall save alive nothing that breathes, but you shall utterly destroy them . . . as the Lord your God has commanded; that they may not teach you according to all their abominable practices. (Deut. 20:16–18)

According to Bainton, "The crusade stemmed out of the holy war" and "went beyond" it.[10] The holy war, strictly speaking, was a war fought with God's assistance, subsequent to the performance of cultic practices and ritualistic efforts at determining a favorable response from Yahweh. By contrast, the crusade "was fought not so much with God's help as on God's behalf, not for a human goal which God might bless but for a divine cause which God might command." Booty from such a war would be dedicated to Yahweh, and divine leadership would likely be manifested in victory despite overwhelming odds against it.[11]

On Bainton's account, then, the crusade is something more than a holy war, or a war that is religiously sanctioned. The authority and cause for fighting a crusade, together with the attitudes of the crusaders and the means of combat, are shaped exclusively and peculiarly by religious considerations.[12] A crusade is fought "under the authority of God or of His representatives on earth." "The cause is more than just, it is holy. The object is the vindication of religion or of something invested with the sanctity of religion."[13] The crusaders regard themselves as "godly and their opponents [as] . . . ungodly" for espousing blasphemous beliefs or "abominable practices."[14] In executing the crusade, it is permissible to employ force indiscriminately and with the objective of totally exterminating the enemy.[15]

It should be emphasized that along with pacifist and just war arguments, crusading appeals, in Bainton's sense, recur with some frequency throughout the Christian tradition. At a fairly early stage in the church's development, St. Augustine, for example, showed some of the marks of the crusader, despite his well-known concern to temper the excesses of armed conflict. One author captures those marks as follows:

Any violation of God's laws, and by easy extension, any violation of Christian doctrine, could be seen [by Augustine] as an injustice warranting unlimited violent punishment. Further, the . . . guilt of the enemy merited punishment of the enemy population without regard to the distinction between soldiers and civilians. Motivated by righteous [religiously inspired] wrath, the just warriors could kill with impunity even those who were morally innocent.[16]

In a similar spirit the church, during the Middle Ages, arrogated to itself the authority to settle disputes among Christian civil rulers and to pass final judgment regarding the legitimacy of the use of force. That authority was understood to include the right to initiate and supervise armed action against unbelievers, most prominently in the Crusades.[17] When Pope Urban II inaugurated the Crusades against the Holy Land in 1095, he declared that the "Holy Sepulchre of our Lord is polluted by the filthiness of an unclean nation. . . . Therefore go forward in happiness and confidence and attack the enemies of God."[18] Soldiers engaging in such a crusade performed not homicide, but "malicide," and any who died in battle thereby earned eternal salvation.

The standard restraints on the use of force were consistently set aside during the Crusades. As Bainton writes:

Crucifixion, ripping open those who had swallowed coins, mutilation—Bohemond of Antioch sent to the Greek Emperor a whole cargo of noses and thumbs sliced from the Saracens—such exploits the chroniclers of the crusades recount without qualm. A favorite text was a verse in Jeremiah, "cursed be he that keepeth back his hand from blood." There was no residue here of Augustinian mournfulness in combat. The mood was strangely compounded of barbarian lust for combat and Christian zeal for the faith.[19]

Very little heed was paid to noncombatant immunity.

[In the capture of Jerusalem] some of our men (and this was more merciful) cut off the heads of their enemies; . . . others tortured them longer by casting them into the flames. . . . But these were small matters compared to what happened at the temple of Solomon, a place where religious services are ordinarily chanted.

... [I]n the temple and portico of Solomon, men rode in blood up to their knees and the bridle reins. Indeed, it was a just and splendid judgement of God, that this place should be filled with the blood of the unbelievers, when it had suffered so long from their blasphemies.[20]

Together with these more familiar cases, there are important instances of crusading mentality within the Christian sectarian tradition. The Adamites, a late medieval radical sect in Bohemia, are such an example.

The Adamites regarded themselves as avenging angels [called upon by God] to wield the sword throughout the world until all the unclean had been cut down. Blood, they declared, must flood the world to the height of a horse's head.... From their island stronghold they constantly made nocturnal sorties—which they called Holy War—against neighboring villages.... [T]hey set the villages on fire and cut down or burnt alive every man, woman and child whom they could find; this too they justified with a quotation from Scriptures: "And at midnight there was a cry made—Behold, the Bridegroom cometh."[21]

EVALUATING BAINTON'S "CRUSADE TYPE"

It is necessary to decide whether we ought to follow Bainton's preference for "crusade" over "holy war" in designating the third type of attitude toward the use of force in Christian history. To begin with, recent scholarship suggests that there are some reasons for dropping the words "holy war" altogether as a means for describing religious wars in the Old Testament, since the term as such does not appear and seems to be drawn from Greek sources. "[A scholarly] consensus seems to be emerging that the wars of ancient Israel should not be called 'holy war,' but 'Yahweh war' [or 'wars of the Lord']."[22]

However, whatever this substitution accomplishes so far as the refined understanding of the Old Testament goes, it sacrifices in regard to comparative study. The category "holy war" has the advantage of potentially encompassing religious wars in traditions beyond the Old Testament, whereas the categories "Yahweh war" or "war of the Lord" do not. It would simply remain to specify the defining characteristics of a holy war as a generic term (wherever it came from) in order then to determine, for comparative purposes, whether examples can be found in different traditions. The more serious problem is whether it is useful for apprehending Christian beliefs about war to follow Bainton in construing all religiously oriented wars as "crusades" in his narrowly defined sense of the term, and, as a consequence, to drop the notion of holy war.

There is, in fact, strong evidence that Bainton's proposal is too narrow. For Bainton, Christian attitudes toward the use of force favor either a crusade, which is religious and unrestrained, or a just war, which is secular and restrained. That is, the authority and cause of war must either be religious or secular, the attitudes of the combatants either uncontrolled or disciplined, and the means of warfare either indiscriminate or moderate.[23]

But Walters and Johnson have both demonstrated that this dichotomy is too sharp to accommodate actual Christian attitudes. "Holy war doctrine," in Johnson's words, "is fundamentally a form of just war doctrine inherited from the late Middle Ages, and it takes its bearings from the idea, at least as old as Augustine, that God himself inspires and commands some wars."[24] It seems clear, as Walters has demonstrated, that medieval and late medieval holy war theory was analogous, rather than antithetical, to just war thinking. Wars initiated by papal authority and conducted to protect the Christian religion were simply an additional aspect, alongside temporal authority and secular causes, of what was considered the "just" use of force. Nor did the theorists discussing these matters advocate undisciplined attitudes or "the use of unrestrained violence in the prosecution of religious war. In fact, one searches in vain for any principled distinction in the theorists' prescriptions for the conduct of justifiable political and religious wars."[25] In short, Bainton's emphasis on the crusading idea to the exclusion of all other forms of religious war ignores prominent types of religiously sanctioned use of force in the Christian tradition.

Bainton's preoccupation with the crusade may also be responsible for a certain amount of neglect and distortion on his part concerning attitudes toward force prior to and during the Puritan Revolution in seventeenth-century England. In the first place, he overlooks figures like Francis Bacon, whose book, *Considerations Touching a Warre with Spaine* (1624), refers explicitly to religious reasons for waging war that "presuppose . . . the content of late medieval just war doctrine; . . . and may be read conservatively as tending only to broaden the reasons for justifiably going to war."[26] Johnson continues:

The relation between classic just war doctrine and holy war thought in England at this time is obscured if they are conceived as two ideal types quite distinct from each other. Rather they interpenetrate each other, with holy war ideas emerging as redefinitions of certain of the categories of the just war tradition. Without the habits of thought created by the just war tradition, holy war thought in England in the sixteenth and seventeenth centuries would have been much different—if indeed it had come to exist at all.[27]

It is of interest that Bacon expressly favored defensive over offensive religious wars.[28] However, his readiness to expand the category of preemptive defense against perceived threats to the Christian religion served in effect to blur the line between defensive and offensive wars. For example, Spain, simply by establishing and undertaking to advance the cause of Catholicism against England, represented for Bacon a threat to English Christianity that constituted an actionable cause for preemptive war against Spain.[29]

The crucial point is that in the premodern period, when Bacon was writing, religion, at least on the dominant view, "was a matter of state" in a way that was anticipated by medieval society.[30] The state, or civil society, came to understand itself as, at bottom, a religious entity. Therefore, national security, or the "just" defense of the state, was fundamentally a matter of the protection of religious orthodoxy, by force, if need be. It followed that the "extension" of the just war categories to include religious considerations was perfectly natural, and it was done without necessarily falling under Bainton's description of a crusade. In the interest, then, of accommodating widespread attitudes toward religious justification for the use of force that are nevertheless not of Bainton's "crusade type," it seems fitting to retain a broader category like "holy war." In respect to such a category, a crusade would be a subtype of holy war, still defined by Bainton's indicia, but it would not exhaust the possible types of religious war.

Not only is Bainton's understanding of his third type of Christian attitude toward force too restricted to account for thinkers like Francis Bacon, but he also has failed, possibly because of his exclusive fascination with the crusade, to appreciate the complexity of attitudes toward force within religious movements like Puritanism, a movement that for him clearly manifests "a [oneway] shift from the just war to the crusade."[31]

It is true, Bainton admits, that the Puritans toyed for a time with attempts to keep their revolution against Charles I within just war terms. Various arguments were voiced to the effect that Charles had transgressed the proper limits of his authority and therefore had become an "arbitrary" ruler whom the citizens had a right to "discipline" in the name of the just exercise of force. Together with such arguments, it was also frequently contended that the Parliament, and in some cases the Puritan army, as "lesser magistrates," were justified in taking up arms against an unjust authority in order to restore legitimacy to the English government.[32] Bainton might, for example, have quoted Oliver Cromwell's statement of 1644 in this regard: "I profess I could never satisfy myself of the justness of this War, but from the authority of Parliament to maintain itself in its rights; and in this Cause I hope to approve myself an honest man and single-hearted."[33]

However, Bainton points out that sustaining these arguments was difficult when Parliament, "dominated by the Presbyterians, recoiled from [the] extreme measures against the king" that were being advocated by Cromwell and his Independent and radical Puritan followers.[34] For Bainton, it was the self-evident inadequacy of these arguments that drove the Puritan revolutionaries to invoke the crusade theory as "the final answer" to why their insurrection was justified. In my judgment, Bainton is partly right about the emergence of the crusading idea at this point.

Herbert Palmer, as early as 1643, saw that it might come to this. "If it should ever happen," he wrote, "that Parliament should joyne with a King to cast out the true Religion, and bring in Popery, yet might we resist." Oliver Cromwell grew impatient with the quest for the authority of the prince as a guarantee for the justice of the cause. How can the prince determine the justice of a holy war? If it is holy, it is holy no matter what prince, parliament or people may say to the contrary. All of these quibbles about the seat of authority may be but "fleshly reasonings." The Lord Himself has given the answer. "Let us look unto providences; surely they mean somewhat. They hang so together; they being so constant, so clear and unclouded." ["Malice, swollen malice [is] against God's people, now called Saints, to root out their name; and yet [the Saints], by providence, having arms, [are] therein blessed with defence and more."] The crusading theory in these words is complete.[35]

Bainton alludes to the celebration by Puritan preachers of the famous massacre at Drogheda in 1649 during Cromwell's Irish campaign (1649–50). For example, Hugh Peters wrote:

Sir, the truth is Drogheda is taken, 3,352 of the enemy slain, and 64 of ours. . . . Ashton the governor killed, none spared. . . . I came now from giving thanks in the great church. . . . Dublin, September 15, 1649. Similarly Peter Sterry preached a Thanksgiving sermon before parliament entitled, The Coming forth of Christ . . . being a publicke Thanksgiving for the Victories obtained by the Parliaments Forces in IRELAND, especially for taking of Drogheda.[36]

Cromwell's own justification went like this:

I am persuaded that this is a righteous judgment of God upon these barbarous wretches, who have imbrued their hands in so much innocent blood; and that it will tend to prevent the effusion of blood for the future, which are the satisfactory grounds to such actions, which otherwise cannot but work remorse and regret.[37]

Johnson contends that Bainton overstates the case. In general, he says, Cromwell's forces were quite restrained in the battles that took place on English soil, as well as those that occurred during the Irish expedition. Cromwell typically attempted to "fight against armies, not against the populace; his terms when besieging towns were, though firm, not unusual for wars of the period, and even the massacre at Drogheda upon which Bainton places so much weight was the result of a loss of communication between commander and troops."[38]

However, in the case of the Drogheda massacre, I am forced to side with Bainton against Johnson. There is strong evidence here, it seems to me, of an out-and-out crusading mentality. It is true that overall, Cromwell's record of restraint in battle was exemplary. But whatever the circumstances in which the massacre took place, it is, in my view, indisputable, as the citation from Cromwell demonstrates, that Cromwell himself "sanctioned a holocaust" in this case, "thereby blackening the name for justice tempered with mercy which up to that point had been deservedly his."[39]

There are additional hints of a "crusading tone" to some other aspects of the use of force by Puritans. For example, after his remarkable victory at Dunbar in 1650, during the Scottish campaign, Cromwell wrote:

Because of their numbers, because of their advantages, because of their confidence, because of our weakness, because of our strait, we were in the Mount, and in the Mount of the Lord would be seen; and . . . He would find out a way of deliverance and salvation for us—and indeed we had our consolations and our hopes.[40]

An eyewitness reported that before the battle, "Oliver was carried on with a divine impulse; he did laugh so excessively as if he had been drunk; his eyes sparkled with spirits."[41]

Finally, Johnson himself provides abundant evidence that some Puritans, at least, qualified as full-fledged crusaders on Bainton's terms. In the 1620s and 1630s certain Puritans began either to stretch the just war categories beyond recognition or to abandon them altogether. Specifically, there emerged the ideas that God directly commands certain wars, which become obligatory for Christians, and that "holy war has no limits, but is an unrestrained, all-out struggle of good against evil."[42]

William Gouge and Thomas Barnes were two such Puritan divines. Gouge explicitly opened the door to an offensive war undertaken to maintain the truth and purity of religion. Johnson continues:

Though Gouge relies verbally on the received doctrine of just warfare, his meaning clearly supports a theory advocating holy war. For example, in his arguments for the lawfulness of war for Christians, Gouge is concerned not with depicting war as the lesser of evils, the conclusion toward which just war doctrine tends, but rather with showing that, far from forbidding war, God actually urges his people into battle.

In all [his] lengthy and repetitive listing of reasons proving war lawful for Christians, Gouge looks only once to the New Testament, and then only for a supporting reference to Israelite experiences in war. Though the just war doctrine has its base in Augustine's concern for the showing of Christian charity to enemies as well as neighbors, Gouge nowhere includes even a reference to charity; yet he is deeply concerned with righteousness. . . . It is not the manifestation of God's love in limiting the cruelties of war with which Gouge concerns himself; it is rather the upholding of a narrowly conceived personal righteousness on the part of the soldiers on his own side. These are the only ones to whom God's love extends, and to them only so long as they keep free from sin. Gouge concludes the . . . exhortation by calling the sort of war of which he speaks "the worke of the Lord, . . . his warre," and by terming soldiers who die in battle "martyrs."[43]

While Gouge did not pay particular attention to the conduct of war, Thomas Barnes did:

Barnes places no restrictions on cruelty in war. Once commanded, cruelty, wickedness, and inhumanity follow inexorably. The only restraint possible is in the decision whether to begin war; yet even here the decision rests with God. Barnes's rather bloodthirsty stance is concisely expressed in this statement: "The stretching out of the sword to bloud, requires the putting on of a kinde of cruelty; as wee see in Samuell, who hewed Agag in pieces without any shew of compassion; as wee see in Joshua, who hanged up the five heathenish kings without any compassion." This sentiment is as far as possible from Augustine's mournful warrior who kills only because it is the more just choice. [Though Christians must be merciful, according to Barnes, the special] implication [he draws] is inescapable: blood-lust and cruelty remain in a holy war but are sanctified by the cause and by God's command. Having a godly call to war is for Barnes essential, for once in a war there can be no limits to its ravages.[44]

Bainton is thus correct about the emergence of the crusading form of holy war during this period. On the other hand, he is incorrect in overplaying the importance of the crusade during the Puritan Revolution. This is true not only because, as we saw, he disregards noncrusading forms of holy war that are manifest prior to and during the Puritan Revolution, but also because he underplays references to "secular" just war theory at the time. These references are of the greatest importance in drawing the proper distinctions between the holy war category (understood, now, more broadly than Bainton defines it) and the other attitudes in the Christian tradition, namely, the just war and pacifist attitudes.

Interestingly, in his essay on the Puritan Revolution, Bainton does admit at one point that when Parliament itself made it impossible any longer to argue a "lesser magistrate" defense of the revolution, Puritan thinkers "began to veer in two directions. Some abandoned any Christian theory whatsoever and moved straight over into a secular war."[45] However, in his eagerness to take up the second—the crusading—direction, he unfortunately minimizes this maneuver. He mentions in passing individuals like the Leveller leader, John Lilburne, who contended that "when the army defied parliament by seizing the person of the king, England *was then dissolved into a state of nature in which the army could make a fresh start at the constitution of a government by choosing its own representatives.*" Moreover, Jeremiah Burroughes also sought "secular grounds" for the war, "and went so far as to claim that *the war was not for religion but only for the civil right which guaranteed religion.*"

For wee have not onley a right to our Religion, by the Law of God, but wee have a Civill right to this our Religion, that other Christians have not had, and therefore there can be no scruple in this.[46]

To begin with, Bainton neglects similar passages embedded in Cromwell's writings as well as in the writings of many other Puritans, passages that coexist inconsistently with the crusading emphasis.[47] More important, Bainton ignores another highly significant "shift," alongside the development of crusading ideas, that took place during this period, namely, a shift to a belief in "natural rights" and "natural reason" as the basis of civil authority and the just administration of force. It is this shift that is attested to by the references to the Leveller Lilburne and to Burroughes.

To espouse natural right as the proper basis for civil order, as did radical Puritan sects like the Levellers and others, is, at bottom, to take a radical stand regarding which reasons for the use of force are acceptable. In the first place, such a belief implies that anyone, including a magistrate, bears the burden of proof for using force—that is, for imposing confinement, suffering, or loss of property, sustenance, limb, or life—upon anyone. That is because force invariably inflicts at least some undesirable effects. It is also because, given the "nature" of human beings, force is readily subject to abuse and arbitrariness.

In the second place, only those reasons for using force are acceptable that appeal to what human beings hold in common "by nature," rather than to what distinguishes or differentiates them one from another. Not all human beings hold the same religious beliefs, nor possess the same amount of wealth and property, nor have the same education, nor are born in the same ethnic or cultural tradition, nor have the same race or sex. It is therefore utterly inappropriate to invoke as a reason for using force against another any of these considerations.

By contrast, all human beings commonly experience the pain and distress of arbitrary confinement, of severe suffering, or of being deprived of property, sustenance, limb, or life. Therefore, force may be justified, and may only be justified, "by nature," at least, if it is undertaken in the service of preventing or rectifying the object of any of these common human aversions. Force, that is, may legitimately be used for two basic reasons: first, it may be used as a countermeasure against

arbitrary force or injury, or against being arbitrarily "deprived of human
subsistence," as another Leveller, Richard Overton, put it.[48] Second,
understood as the infliction of suffering or disablement, force may be
used as a therapeutic measure against injury or disease. Thus does
natural or common right circumscribe the use of force according to the
dictates of natural or common reason.[49]

We need to emphasize that the Levellers and kindred spirits, like
Roger Williams, inferred from these beliefs a radical doctrine of the
separation of church and state, as is suggested by Burroughes's remarks.
As Overton put it:

As for matters of conscience or opinion about religion or worship, with which
human society, cohabitation and safety may freely subsist and stand together—
[they do] not fall under the power of the magisterial sword. . . . For the limits
of magistracy extend no further than humanity or human subsistence, not to
spirituality or spiritual being.[50]

On this view, the "sword of steel" is radically set apart from the "sword
of the spirit." The Word of God, like all spiritual messages, might legitimately be communicated and tested only by peaceful means, only
by the "law of the spirit," and not by the means of coercion. Part of the
pacifist message, at least, is here reasserting itself: True religion cannot
be compelled. On the other hand, the conviction that one side of human
activity—the "outward side"—could still legitimately be subjected to
coercive control, albeit secular control, was of course the point at which
just war thinking and pacifist thinking continued to diverge.

The implication of all this for Christian attitudes toward the use of
force is that right in the midst of considerable "holy war talk," certain
Christian groups and individuals (not always consistently) were, in the
name both of reason and of the proper understanding of the message
of the New Testament, resolutely and systematically turning their backs
on all forms of holy war argument, the more restrained, just war–related
version as well as the crusade version. Instead, there emerge here the
foundations for a "secularized just war doctrine" that conforms to similar
developments beginning to take place in the late medieval and early
modern thought associated with the names of Suarez, Victoria, Ames,
and Grotius, and somewhat later with Locke and Vattel.[51]

By embracing the notion that the licit grounds for the initiation and
exercise of force are not religious but "natural," the just war position
came explicitly to abjure the holy war attitude altogether and, in fact,
to form a partial association with the pacifists. By grounding the standards of the legitimate administration of force in natural reason rather
than in religious revelation, secular just war proponents took up a more
absolutist position than had many of their medieval or Reformation

forebears. That concerned their unconditional agreement with the pacifists on one thing: Religious warrants ought to be thoroughly dissociated
from the use of force. Force might neither be invoked to regulate religious
belief, nor might religious belief be invoked to regulate force. This conviction had momentous consequences not only for just war doctrine ever
after, but for the whole question of the foundations of civil order. Clearly,
the modern doctrine of the secular state with its indispensable commitment to religious liberty and freedom of conscience followed from it.
Bainton, then, misdescribes the Puritan movement not only by overlooking subtleties about holy war thinking but, equally seriously, by all
but ignoring the emergence of a secular just war theory of force during
this period whereby the legitimation of force is completely disconnected
from religious belief and practice.

CONCLUSION

However unrefined Bainton's notion of crusade was, and however in
need of historical amendment his discussion of the Puritan movement
turned out to be, his tripartite typology, when properly revised, is still
deeply illuminating of "Christian attitudes toward war and peace." One
thing is clear: The Christian story is a story of shifting combinations
among these three essentially irreconcilable attitudes.

So long as there was no Constantinian settlement, the pacifist incli-
nations of the early church made sense. However, after the settlement,
so long as the civil regulation of religious belief and practice was regarded
as more or less "natural," as it was in much medieval and mainline
Reformation thought, then both the extension of just war categories to
include religious considerations (following the analyses of Johnson and
Walters) and the more extreme form of religious crusade followed in-
telligibly and even predictably from central Christian doctrines.

But when such an arrangement came to be regarded as thoroughly
"unnatural," as it was increasingly thought to be in the premodern
period, all that changed. Then the just war tradition drifted away from
its uneasy alliance with holy war thinking and tended toward a new, if
still-uneasy, alliance with the pacifist preference for dissociating religious
conviction from the use of force. In that new alliance holy war thinking
became the "odd person out."

NOTES

1. Peter Winch, "Understanding a Primitive Society," in *Rationality*, ed.
Bryan Wilson (New York: Harper and Row, 1970), 107.

2. Although my original topic referred to "ideological" as well as "religious"
reasons for resort to force, I shall refrain from any discussion of the former

because I am not clear about the meaning of "ideology" as distinguished from "religion." I do not doubt that we make distinctions, but I am just not clear on exactly how the lines are to be drawn. I am ready to be instructed by others. In any case, I have a sufficiently broad topic in simply trying to sort out the more standard theological discussions of resort to force in the Western Christian tradition.

3. Roland Bainton, *Christian Attitudes toward War and Peace: A Historical Survey and Critical Re-evaluation* (Nashville, Tenn.: Abingdon Press, 1960).

4. James Turner Johnson, *Ideology, Reason, and the Limitation of War* (Princeton: Princeton University Press, 1975), esp. chap. 2, "From Just War to Crusade," and app. 1, "Puritan Revolution as Crusade"; LeRoy Walters, "The Just War and the Crusade: Antitheses or Analogies?," *Monist* 57, no. 4 (October 1973), 584–94; cf. Walters, "Five Classic Just-War Theories: A Study in the Thought of Aquinas, Vitoria, Suarez, Gentili, and Grotius" (Ph.D. diss., Yale University, 1971).

5. David Little, "Some Justifications for Violence in the Puritan Revolution," *Harvard Theological Review* 65 (1972): 577–89. "It has been clear for some time, then, that one way to study the Puritan Revolution is to examine it as an exercise in moral and religious argumentation over the use of violence. But while scholars of the period understood that, they have not, for the most part, satisfactorily executed the examination. For example, Michael Walzer in his volume, *Revolution of the Saints* (Cambridge, Mass.: Harvard University Press, 1965), adopts some doubtful suggestions made by Roland H. Bainton, and argues as follows: In their attempts to justify a resort to violence, the Puritan agitators, and most particularly individuals like Oliver Cromwell, finally left the categories of the just-war behind, and appealed instead to the tradition of the holy-war or the crusade. Indeed, both Walzer and Bainton come close to contending that the very notion of a political revolution precludes an appeal to just-war categories. . . . While there is some truth in this account, . . . the general conclusion that the sorts of justification for violence offered during the Puritan Revolution demonstrate 'a shift from the just-war to the crusade,' strikes me as extraordinarily misleading" (578–79). I shall rehearse some of the particulars at the appropriate point later on. Cf. Johnson, *Ideology, Reason, and the Limitation of War*, 143–44, where my response to Bainton and Walzer is supported.

6. Bainton, *Christian Attitudes toward War and Peace*, 15. So far as the prevalence of pacifism in the early church goes, Bainton admits that the matter is complicated: "The evidence, then, for Christians in the armed forces before the time of Constantine adds up to this: until the decade A.D. 170–80 we are devoid of evidence; from then on the references to Christian soldiers increase. The numbers cannot be computed. The greatest objection to military service appears to have been in the Hellenistic East. The Christians in northern Africa were divided. The Roman church in the late second and third centuries did not forbid epitaphs recording the military profession. The eastern frontier reveals the most extensive Christian participation in warfare, though concurrently we find there a protest against it among groups tending to ascetic and monastic ideals" (71–72). According to Bainton, until the time of Constantine, the church fathers more or less explicitly condemned military service. There remains some uncertainty as to whether the grounds for the prohibition were exclusively Christian rejection

of the use of force or whether they also included the fear of idolatry, since soldiers were required to worship the emperor. Bainton does, though, express some doubt regarding the importance of idolatry (72–74).

7. S.G.F. Brandon, *Jesus and the Zealots: A Study of the Political Factor in Primitive Christianity* (New York: Charles Scribner's Sons, 1967). Cf. the criticisms by George R. Edwards, *Jesus and the Politics of Violence* (New York: Harper and Row, 1972). Edwards's criticisms render doubtful much of Brandon's interpretation. Still, Luke 22:35–38 remains, as Bainton admits, "puzzling" (*Christian Attitudes toward War and Peace*, 56–57). Bainton deals with the question of Jesus' relation to the Zealots at 58–59; "We may infer that Jesus was traduced before the Romans as a Zealot, otherwise they would not have crucified him; but equally we may assume that he was not a Zealot, for otherwise his countrymen would not have preferred Barabbas."

8. See Bainton, *Christian Attitudes toward War and Peace*, 59–61 for a discussion of the diversity of interpretations of Romans 13.

9. Bainton mentions Romans 13 as a textual basis for just war thinking (ibid., 59), but he does not attend specifically to this suggestion of independent standards for the legitimate use of force as the relevant point of contact.

10. Ibid., 44–45.

11. Ibid.

12. Walters, "Just War and the Crusade," 584, usefully organizes Bainton's criteria of the crusade according to authority, cause, attitudes, and means of combat, and he undertakes to compare Bainton's understanding of the crusade with his notion of the just war. We shall turn to that comparison later.

13. Roland Bainton, "Congregationalism and the Puritan Revolution from the Just War to the Crusade," in *Studies on the Reformation* (Boston: Beacon Press, 1963), 250. Cf. *Christian Attitudes toward War and Peace*, 47.

14. Bainton, "Congregationalism and the Puritan Revolution," 270.

15. Bainton, *Christian Attitudes toward War and Peace*, 48–49.

16. Frederick H. Russell, *The Just War in the Middle Ages* (Cambridge: Cambridge University Press, 1975), 19–20.

17. Ibid., 194.

18. Bainton, *Christian Attitudes toward War and Peace*, 112.

19. Ibid.

20. Ibid., 112–13.

21. Norman Cohn, *The Pursuit of the Millennium* (New York: Oxford University Press, 1970), pp. 220–21.

22. See Peter C. Craigie, *The Problem of War in the Old Testament* (Grand Rapids, Mich.: Eerdmans, 1978), 49–50. Craigie indicates that von Rad's view that war in ancient Israel was uniformly a cultic act engaged in by the amphictyony has been widely modified by scholars like R. Smend, *Yahweh War and Tribal Confederation*, trans. Max Gray Rogers (Nashville, Tenn.: Abingdon Press, 1970); see nn. 8, 49. "While the war was religious by association, it was no more a cultic and holy act than was sheep shearing" (G. Fohrer, *Geschichte der israelitischen Religion* [Berlin: De Gruyter, 1969], 109).

23. See Walters, "Just War and the Crusade," 584.

24. Johnson, *Ideology, Reason, and the Limitation of War*, 81.

25. Walters, "Just War and the Crusade," 587–91. For example, Walters cites

an arresting instance from the writing of Thomas Aquinas of the parallels between just war criteria and criteria for a valid crusade indulgence. Thomas's
three just war criteria are (1) authority of the prince, (2) just cause, and (3) right
intention. "In order," he writes, "for a [crusade] indulgence to be valid, three
things are required: first, a cause pertaining to the honor of God; second authority in him who grants it, for it is principally the Pope who can grant an
indulgence . . . ; third, it is required that whoever wants to receive an indulgence
must be in a state of charity. . . . A suitable cause is designated when 'the support
of the holy land' is specified; a proper authority is designated when the authority
of the Apostles Peter and Paul and of the Pope himself are mentioned; and
charity in the recipients is designated when the papal letter speaks of 'all who
are truly penitent and confess [their sins]' " (*Quodlibitem* II, 16, cited in Walters,
"Just War and the Crusade," 587).

26. Johnson, *Ideology, Reason, and the Limitation of War,* 87–88. As Johnson
points out, Bacon mentions as permissible causes for war such things as follows,
things of the sort mentioned by Aquinas and late medieval just war thinkers:
propagation of the faith, liberation of Christians from servitude to infidels, recovering of countries once Christian, recovering and purging consecrated places
profaned by infidels, revenge against blasphemy, and "anti-Christian cruelties
and bloodshed" (cited ibid., 86–87).

27. Ibid., 88.

28. Ibid., 90.

29. Ibid., 92.

30. Ibid., 90. (Emphasis in original.) While I emphatically agree with Johnson
that it was the deep interconnection between religion and civil order in the
premodern period that made so natural the extension of just war categories to
include religious considerations, I believe that Johnson puts it too categorically
when he contends that such "had not been the case when just war doctrine
was being codified in the twelfth and thirteenth centuries." It is of course true
that the sort of nationalistic religion Bacon had in mind was missing in the
Middle Ages. However, the hierarchic coordination of spiritual and temporal
power, as, for example, in Thomas's thought, made equally "natural" the extension of just war categories to include religious considerations, as Thomas
held (see note 25). When religion is regarded as directly connected to the domain
of coercive power, as it was among the dominant groups, at least, in both the
Middle Ages and the premodern period, then the "extended" view of just war
thinking makes perfectly good sense in either case.

31. Bainton, "Congregationalism and the Puritan Revolution," 251.

32. Ibid., 263–64.

33. From *The Writings and Speeches of Oliver Cromwell,* ed. W. C. Abbott, 4 vols.
(Cambridge, Mass.: Harvard University Press, 1937–47), 1:292; cited in Little,
"Some Justifications for Violence," 581.

34. Bainton, "Congregationalism and the Puritan Revolution," 263.

35. Ibid., 266–67. It seems appropriate to add the further comments of Cromwell (in brackets) to Bainton's quotation. Cromwell's statement is found at *Writings and Speeches,* 1:697.

36. Bainton, "Congregationalism and the Puritan Revolution," 269.

37. Cited in Robert S. Paul, *Lord Protector: Religion and Politics in the Life of Oliver Cromwell* (Grand Rapids, Mich.: Eerdmans, 1964), 226.

38. Johnson, *Ideology, Reason, and the Limitation of War*, 144–45.

39. Paul, *Lord Protector*, 210. As Paul suggests, Cromwell may in part have justified the slaughter as retribution for massacres of Protestants that had taken place in Ireland eight years before. However, in the first place, such a "justification" would not pass muster as a just war argument, and second, he appears to have been seriously mistaken about his facts: "Cromwell seems to have held all Ireland responsible for the massacres of eight years before. There can have been few—if any—at Drogheda who had taken part in them; certainly not the officers, certainly not the English soldiers, and almost certainly not Ormand's own regiment, raised in his ancestral domains around Kilkenny" (210, n. 2).

40. Ibid., 226.

41. Ibid.

42. Johnson, *Ideology, Reason, and the Limitation of War*, 104.

43. Ibid., 121–23.

44. Ibid., 128.

45. Bainton, "Congregationalism and the Puritan Revolution," 266.

46. Cited at ibid., 266. Emphasis added.

47. See Little, "Some Justifications for Violence," 587. "In 1645, Cromwell made a striking appeal for religious toleration on the ground that 'in the things of the mind we look for no compulsion, but that of light and reason' (Abbott, 1,377). The general tendency of many of his contemporaries, of course, was to argue that 'freedom of religion' derived not only from a true understanding of the Christian faith, but also from the principle of the universal right to consent 'in the things of the mind,' a principle based . . . on a belief in 'right reason.' It was concluded from this belief that all religions were tolerable to the extent they conformed to the principle of toleration. As Paul shows, Cromwell actually went remarkably far in espousing and allowing for this principle. His specific objection to Anglicanism and Roman Catholicism was that they did not, in his judgment, clearly conform to the standard of liberty of conscience" (ibid., 588 n. 28). See Paul, *Lord Protector*, 325–33, for a persuasive discussion of Cromwell's concern, as an "Independent," for liberty of conscience.

48. Richard Overton, "An Appeal to the People," in *Puritanism and Liberty*, ed. A.S.P. Woodhouse (Chicago: University of Chicago Press, 1974), 333. See also 324–325 for Overton's discussion of the "just use of force" based upon "this natural radical principle of reason."

49. I have borrowed this summary by and large from a recent paper of mine, "Are There Universal Standards? Israel and the Problem of Human Rights."

50. Overton, "Appeal to the People," 332.

51. See Johnson, *Ideology, Reason, and the Limitation of War*, chaps. 3 and 4, for an able and illuminating discussion of the rise of "secular natural law." It is now fairly clear that Locke, for one, is, at bottom, doing little more than extending basic Leveller ideas on political obligation, the use of force, and so on. See Richard Ashcraft's monumental study, *Revolutionary Politics and Locke's Two Treatises of Government* (Princeton: Princeton University Press, 1986), especially, 150–66.

6

Holy War (*Jihad*) in Islamic Religion and Nation-State Ideologies

Bruce Lawrence

FORETHOUGHTS ABOUT LANGUAGE AND LABOR

The interface between ideology and religion has specific nuances in an Islamic context. Theirs is a dialectically charged relation, and it is difficult to avert the danger of seeming to privilege one above the other. *Jihad* requires attention to both words. Within the annals of Muslim history there are no ideological motives for invoking the call to *jihad* that are not at the same time cloaked in religious language, and yet every religious term has, at least in the modern period, an ideological valorization. An explanation is in order.

To separate religion from ideology by seeming to privilege the former and debunk the latter becomes problematic as a strategy for analyzing Islamic evidence. All proponents of *jihad*, whether writers or actors, intellectuals or politicians, are ideologues. At the same time, they are religious ideologues, since, despite the history of the critique of ideology, religion and ideology merge for them, as for others, during the modern or technical age.[1]

Muslims, like Christians and Jews, are inescapably moderns. They experience modernity even while not fully embracing modernism. One of the most radical consequences of modernity is to transform every theology or philosophy into a species of ideology. This happens implicitly in the conceptual reflections of present-day Sunni theorists; it is made explicit by their Shi'i counterparts, whether one looks to a "secular" Iranian ideologue such as Ali Shari'ati or a clerical theoretician such as the late Ayatollah Murtaza Mutahhari.[2]

Our goal is to compare. We strive to make valid comparisons, yet if our labors are to succeed, we must first situate the categories of our comparison within historical contexts that make clear the dissimilarity of that for which we are claiming some measure of correspondence or similarity. There is no exact equivalent in Islamic vocabulary for what is meant by "holy war" in Western Christendom. To use *jihad* as the Muslim equivalent of "holy war," we must begin by mapping its distinctiveness, that is to say, we must trace its ideological construction as well as its religious reference.

Jihad is an especially complex category: not only does it have scriptural and juridical usages, but its invocation as a Muslim duty has been contested within Islam. Moreover, those who contest have equal claim to being devout Muslims, whether Sunni or Shiʿi or Sufi in their filiations. Still more complex is the translation of *jihad* as "holy war" and its use as the pivotal term in comparing Muslim and Christian concepts of "holy war." When we speak of holy war, we immediately infer a series of historical asymmetries. They must be exposed before we can proceed to the analysis of particular cases. Otherwise our labor is wasted; it becomes a futile exercise leading to the reproduction of cross-cultural, intercreedal stereotypes.

Three asymmetries deserve mention. The first asymmetry between Christian and Muslim holy wars is existential; it applies to us as citizens of the technical age. We speak from a moment in world history during which Christian, or at least residually Christian, polities—whether democratic (United States) or Communist (USSR)—dominate the discourse about global hegemony. From a Muslim perspective, American and Russian worldviews are naturally, necessarily conjoined, since neither the United States nor the USSR projects an agenda that depends upon, or considers, Muslim interests. Moreover, it is we, not they, who hold conferences about war and peace in comparative perspectives, they being any of the more than thirty nation-state polities that are majoritarian Muslim and represent some 600 million believers in Allah and his last prophet, Muhammad. Americans, even more than Russians, are "present-minded," to use R. L. Schuyler's phrase as developed by J. H. Hexter,[3] in the sense that we are aware of, and engaged by, our unique role as world actors. Despite other differences, we elites of the Euro-American West have a common destiny: we share the legacy as well as the benefits of globally diffuse, multinational capitalism. Not Russians but Afro-Asian Muslims, elites and nonelites alike, are the other to us; they are also, despite our best efforts at constructing, maintaining, and advocating parity, the lesser, because now the weaker, other. How else can we interpret the cultural faultline attendant upon the publication and then hyped-up promotion of Salman Rushdie's *The Satanic Verses* in fall 1988 to spring 1989? This was not an equal contest between competing worldviews. Rather, it confirmed what has been evident since World War II: Muslim sensibilities do not register, except negatively, among Euro-American opinion setters, or, as one wag put it, we love to hate the ayatollah and all his fanatic followers.

A second asymmetry informing discussion of Muslim and Christian holy wars is scriptural. The prism of canon formation helps to particularize the radical separation of Muslim from Christian notions of authority. Within two decades after the death of the Prophet (632 A.D.), a standard recension of the Qur'an was fixed and enforced by the third Caliph 'Uthman (ca. 650A.D.); it remains the same Arabic text used by all Muslims till the present day. It is a scriptural standard supplemented by collections of sayings/deeds (*hadith*) attributed to the Prophet Muhammad. While Muslims differ among themselves about the significance of *hadith*, the Qur'an remains the bedrock of scriptural authority in Islam. By contrast, the distinctively Christian Scripture, those twenty-seven books taken to be the "new" testament, never achieved canonical status till the sixteenth century, when an internal dispute between Protestants and Catholics required a conciliar decree by the Roman church at Trent. Although regional bishops and councils had earlier adopted those books now known collectively as the New Testament, "it had no strictly official status in the church at large. Its authority, rather, was de facto, resting upon a consensus which had emerged through centuries of experience with a much larger body of scriptures than that limited number which attained canonical standing."[4] In effect, the Bible, prior to the Reformation, was much less a fixed point of authoritative reference for Christians than the Qur'an had been, and continues to be, for Muslims.

The third, and for our purposes the most important, asymmetry is historical. It must be traced to originary moments. As Abdulaziz Sachedina has often noted, power, far from being alien to the first Muslims, was integral to their self-identity.[5] Since the era of the Prophet Muhammad and his initial followers, Islam has had to deal with power—political and military, economic and social, cultural and religious. The Qur'an, as the foundational text inscribing Muslim self-identity, was inextricably linked with power. Its genesis, as also its preservation, coincided with the earliest and most explosive period of Islamic expansionism. Christianity, by contrast, only harnessed scriptural authority to the exigencies of political life when it became a state religion. Ethical norms construed by the first, urban Christians did not engage Roman institutions of statecraft and warfare except oppositionally. While the Constantinian phase of the early church augured the constructive use of power by Christians, this use did not begin till the fourth century. The interlude between Christ's death and Constantine's conversion produced other influences—Gnostic and Stoic, Greek and Roman—that implicitly shaped Christian efforts to appropriate power, just as they complicated the strategy of Christian rulers and theorists in justifying war.

All three of these Christian-Muslim asymmetries, from present status in world history to scriptural formation and authority to engagement with power, inform our discussion of Christian and Muslim holy war. They cannot be ignored, but they also have to be weighed against other considerations. For despite these three asymmetries, there is a sense in which the experience of both communities is identical vis-à-vis the issue of waging war. Neither Christians nor Muslims could fight and kill, at least collectively, without contradicting the "clear intent" of Scripture. For Muslims the dilemma is framed admirably by Abdulaziz Sachedina in his distinction between an expanding Muslim polity that did not "make the world safe for Islam" and the Qur'anic requirement that all "holy war" be waged to propagate Islam, not merely to subjugate and rule non-Muslims. Similarly, Fred Donner has graphically pointed out that it was Byzantine precedents, not Qur'anic ideals, that informed early Islamic conquests. For Christians, on the other hand, the distance between scriptural idealism and historical reality was measured by the juxtaposition of New Testament injunctions to refrain from killing alongside the necessity of Christian polities to wage war. Either way, both observant Muslims and practicing Christians could not avoid the radical severance between scripturally mandated norms and historically expedient practices. In failing to be consistent with foundational markings, Christians and Muslims stand equally condemned, symmetric in their flaws if not in their virtues.

Yet in trying to understand Muslim and Christian advocacy of holy war, one must rely on diachronic asymmetries more than moral symmetries between the two communities. The asymmetries explain, for instance, the variant responses that Muslims and Christians adopt as they attempt to reconcile experiential demands to revelatory dictates. Islamic theorists perceive warfare as intrinsic to history. They never advocate that human beings should expect a cessation of warfare. Consider Ibn Khaldun, the late fourteenth-century Maghribi historian, often lauded as the Thucydides of Islam. In his view the problem facing Muslims was not whether to fight but how best to fight. Ibn Khaldun extols both Muhammad and Ali as exemplary warriors and also sophisticated military strategists.[6] For Christians, by contrast, warfare remains a nefarious by-product of historical circumstances that thrust devout believers into positions of power. It is only intrinsic to history as a result of human sinfulness, not divine mandate. To the extent that Jesus is reconceived as a model warrior, he is fighting against human nature rather than against other humans. Despite the best efforts of just war theorists, with a strong assist from hymnodists ("Onward, Christian Soldiers"), warfare is an incidental *mythomoteur* for Christians, while it has been, and will continue to be, a foundational *mythomoteur* for Muslims of every generation.

How then can one keep in check the tendency to see the Islamic engagement with warfare as either (*a*) a systemic flaw of Islam as a universal religion or (*b*) a uniform characteristic of all Muslims in all circumstances? The only safety valve is constant vigilance, looking at Islamic norms as specific cultural constructs and the modern world as a further set of sociopolitical constructs. Both contribute to the worldview formation of particular Muslims, and neither can be neglected in examining the question of holy war in Islam. Despite journalistic assertions to the contrary, often recycled and reinforced by "respectable" academics, there is no such entity as Islamic essentialism; every statement that begins "Islam is" or "Muslims say" has to be qualified with contextual referents. The same is true a fortiori with assertions about holy war.

Ideology is the crucial category for informing discussion about Islamic notions of warfare, and before turning our attention to particular instances of *jihad*, we ought to indicate just how differently Muslim holy war appears when interpreted through the template of ideology. Like every artifact in the spectrum of ideologies, discourse about war must be related to the subcategories of gender, class, and race. To the extent that war remains definitionally confined to "armed violence between sovereign states," it already reflects both a gender and a class bias. Just war theorists in Christendom restrict the scope of what war can be by seeing it only as armed struggle between male elites who fight by the same rules. That point cannot be either ignored or dismissed because it entails other qualifications of just war theory. For instance, how can just war theory account for expressions of violence the agents of which lie outside, or act against the custodians of, a sovereign state? By enthroning the view of one gender and one class, does just war theory implicitly disenfranchise or delegitimate other forms of protest that may be private and domestic, as also other kinds of armed insurgence that may be rural and centrifugal rather than urban and centripetal?

However one meets the objection of gender/class bias, one must also highlight the race-specific character of just war theory. It tends to preoccupy Euro-American Caucasians rather than Asian browns or African blacks. It also tends to spin out tangents of discourse that tack back and forth between two ideological poles, often labeled capitalist and Communist or, more recently, First and Second worlds. Moreover, the dominant discourse too often pits capitalist against Communist without a recognition of the influence that Marxist-Leninist terminology has had on the global debate about just war theory. In particular, those African blacks and Asian browns who are too often pigeonholed as "Third World" seem to respond more to Marxist-Leninist notions of revolution than to Euro-American musings about just war.[7]

Even though preformed biases of gender, class, and race are inscribed into the "universal" theory of just war, they do not negate our task; rather, they complicate its performance by underscoring just how necessary it is. Having admitted that the study of *jihad*, like *jihad* itself, is informed by ideological considerations, we can scan several historical contexts without imputing Islam-specific traits to them. Only in the comparative endeavor may we permit ourselves to isolate aspects of an Afro-Asian Islamic experience that differ from Euro-American Christian warfare. While we cannot erase our own ideological formation, we can at least stretch its parameters by conversing with ourselves as well as about those others whom we are endeavoring to understand.

SPECIFIC ISLAMIC INSTANCES OF HOLY WAR OR JIHAD

Jihad is a multivalent category of reference within the Islamic symbol system. It is not limited to holy war, nor is it decisive to the Qur'an if one considers all the themes and counterthemes of that book of revelation on its own terms. A crucial principle, internal to the Qur'an, is that of abrogation (*naskh*). The Qur'an provides the basis for its own continuously revised interpretation (2:106, 13:37, 16:101, 22:52). God's transcendence above humanity's knowing and God's sovereignty beyond human attempts to appropriate, and so limit, his power extend even to his final self-disclosure in prophecy, the Qur'an. The Qur'an ended prophecy but not divine intervention in human affairs. While Muhammad lived, the book remained open; it could always be updated. With his death in 632 A.D., the question of leadership for his community also raised the related question: what would be the nature and the limits of ongoing divine intervention? Sunnis and Shi'is have responded to these twin problems in opposite ways. The Sunnis have closed the book, applying its "clear" directives to juridical legislation. They have also closed ranks around a discrete set of leaders who defend the book and the will of the majority. They are caliphs, their shibboleth is order, their fear is sedition/discord/disbelief.[8] The Shi'is accepted the book but often located decisive meanings within the ambiguous or allegorical verses (3:7) at the same time that they posited a continuing source of oral revelation in a set of leaders who are related to the Prophet Muhammad both by kinship and by piety. They are imams, their shibboleth is justice, their fear is tyranny/oppression/disbelief.

While belief in the Qur'an and rejection of disbelief are traits common to both Sunni and Shi'i Muslims, that commonality does not allow the construction of a theory of either just war or revolution that would bracket them together under one umbrella rubric labeled "the Muslim view of *jihad*." Rather, we will pursue an alternate strategy. We will discuss *jihad* as a leitmotif of Islamic ideology that has variant expressions among Sunni and Shi'i theorists as well as Sunni and Shi'i activists.

Typically, Orientalists who assess *jihad* leap into the annals of Muslim history by either downplaying the Shi'i difference or else ignoring its significance. The former approach characterizes the author of the article on "Djihad" in *The Encyclopaedia of Islam* (new edition). He rehearses all the standard references from Sunni sources and appears to give a comprehensive picture from etymological to apologetic usages of *jihad*. The only sop to Shi'i sensibilities is brief reference to the general doctrine of the Shi'a: "Due . . . [to] their dogma concerning 'the absence of the Imam', who alone has the necessary competence to order war, the practise of the *jihad* is necessarily suspended until the re-appearance of the Imam or the ad hoc appointment of a vicar designated by him for this task."[9] The Dutch Arabist Rudolph Peters, though his book is entitled *Islam and Colonialism: The Doctrine of Jihad in Modern History*, excludes any consideration of Shi'i evidence. He presumes both Shi'ite conformity to the Sunni pattern and their nonadvocacy of *jihad* till the return of the hidden Imam.[10]

Yet there is a marked Shi'ite difference. For Imami or Twelver Shi'is, who comprise the majority of the Shi'ite community, *jihad* is not indefinitely deferred, nor is it held in abeyance till the return of the hidden Imam. *Jihad* is constantly extolled, and it can be waged not only by the hidden Imam but by one who has been chosen by the Imam, an individual whose scholarship and piety ensure that he has been commissioned by the Imam, that is, a Shi'i cleric. Also, the enemy against whom *jihad* must be waged is not merely the outsider "infidel" or non-Muslim. It is also those Muslims who have not accepted true Islam. Since true Islam can only be Imami Shi'i Islam, there are many enemies who are other "Muslims." As one student of the classical Imami juridical sources has noted, the classification of enemy encompasses "the entire hateful Sunni world, a world held responsible for all the harassment and persecution to which the Shi'is were subjected throughout the ages."[11]

While the legal position of Imami jurists has seldom translated into day-to-day action, it is foolhardy, as well as wrong, to deny that there is a Shi'i difference on the issue of holy war in Islam. The Shi'i difference is not only real, it is also pervasive. To highlight that difference and bring it into discussion at the level that it merits, we will give four case instances: one historical, one contemporary, one theoretical, and one ethnographic. The first two are Sunni, the second two are Shi'i. At least within the Islamic tradition we will strive for some surface parity of the disparate approaches to just war theory, which is also just revolution theory.

Case One

It was July 1912 in southern Morocco. The French Protectorate had been formally established in northern Morocco (Fez) three months earlier. Far from consolidating their power, the French feared that Moroccan tribes might coalesce around a local leader who would challenge the authority of the Alawite dynast whom they continued to recognize as sultan even while stripping him of effective power. It was from Tafilalet in the lower range of the Atlas Mountains that other Muslim warriors had emerged to shape and reshape the course of Moroccan history. Now in summer 1912 history seemed about to repeat itself. A new pretender to the Moroccan throne arose from the south. His name was el Hiba.

Tall, bearded, swathed in the blue cloth of the Sahara nomads, el Hiba's credentials as a resistance leader were impeccable. His father, Ma el Ainin, had achieved legendary status among his people for opposing the French in Mauritania. When Ma el Ainin died in October 1910, el Hiba had succeeded to his father's *baraka*. Once again it seemed that the duty of the people of the trans-Atlas was to purify Dar el-Islam—to expel corrupt functionaries, annul taxes not sanctioned by the Qur'an and drive out the infidel. Few of the men who streamed out of the desert to proclaim el Hiba sultan at Tiznit in summer 1912 had ever seen a European. They certainly did not possess the remotest notion of modern firepower; ivory-encrusted muskets made up the bulk of their weaponry. They trusted to the sanctity of their cause and the *baraka* of their chief.[12]

His followers could also accept el Hiba as an initiator of *jihad* because he was, for them, the sultan. At the same time, however, the puppet Alawite sultan was threatening to escape from French containment and to assume leadership of his own *jihad* movement. In order to solidify his claim to royalty, el Hiba had to move quickly, and he did. His strategy was to capture Marrakesh, the most important commercial/military/strategic city in southern Morocco, and to secure it as his new capital. Before the French could mobilize a counteroffensive, el Hiba succeeded in entering Marrakesh. Overcoming minimal local resistance, by late August his camel-mounted warriors controlled the city. The French command was alert to the danger that el Hiba might consolidate his newly won position and become a truly formidable foe. A career colonial officer, Colonel Charles Mangin, nicknamed the Butcher, notable for his success in recruiting Senegalese troops into the French army, was dispatched to deal with el Hiba.

Mangin had five thousand troops under his command when he marched to face el Hiba's army of ten to fifteen thousand men. Yet it was an unequal contest because Mangin possessed far superior firepower. On the fateful morning of September 6, 1912, when the two armies closed to within half a mile of one another, Mangin

opened up with the full force of his twelve 75s, eight machine guns and 1,200 Gras rifles. The effect was catastrophic. The Moroccans, many of whom were armed only with sticks and stones, reeled but, incredibly, kept their cohesion. Their line folded like a crescent around the now-halted French square. Mangin redistributed his artillery, and the carnage continued. The 75s tore bloody gaps in the Moroccan lines while el Hiba's antique guns, served by a Spanish renegade, fired too high or else drove their shells into the parched earth without exploding. By nine o'clock, the Moroccans had had enough. They crawled away, leaving two thousand dead on the plain and thousands more wounded in what was the worst single defeat during the history of the French conquest of Morocco. Mangin sent his four hundred horse toward el Hiba's camp, virtually deserted as the remnants of his army fell back on Marrakech. Mangin counted two dead and twenty-three wounded.[13]

This brief bloodletting smashed the threat of el Hiba to the French bid for control in southern Morocco. More importantly, the battlefield slaughter of el Hiba's followers undercut his claim to *baraka*, as also the legitimacy of his call to *jihad*.

The case of el Hiba demonstrates several of the features about *jihad* that deserve attention when discussing its relevance to just war theories. From a Sunni Muslim perspective the presence of the infidel, in this case the French, on Muslim soil provoked the desire for a defensive war. The war could not be fought without a leader, one who mobilized resources and planned strategies but, above all, motivated others to fight and possibly to die. According to the conditions required by the Sunni perception of *jihad*, el Hiba was a legally authorized *mujahid*, or holy warrior, as would have been the Alawite sultan had he not been restrained by the French in Fez.

But the significance of this episode goes beyond its formal compliance with the conditions needed to wage *jihad*. Its real importance lies in the disparity of potential to make war and win war that existed for the two combatants. Not only were el Hiba's troops unfamiliar with the West, they did not possess what were then modern armaments, and they knew nothing of modern tactics of ground warfare. They outnumbered the enemy, but the enemy enjoyed a firepower advantage that defied numerical superiority: the final ratio of dead, two thousand to two, would sound like hyperbole in any premodern account of pitched battles.

Numerous other instances of *jihad* movements against colonial powers could be cited. Rudolph Peters, though his book is conceptually flawed, does give a summary recapitulation of seven historical moments when indigenous Muslim leaders, through appeal to *baraka* and in compliance with Sunni conditions for *jihad*, fought against colonial forces invading their territory. All lost. They lost battles and more; they lost countless lives of their countrymen and coreligionists. Rather than glorify that record, it seems more fitting to reflect on the significance of those losses for the subsequent history of the countries from which not only *jihad* but other violent protests against the colonial order were waged. No judgment is more balanced than that offered by the historian Michael Adas:

The grim toll of human lives lost in these unequal contests and their pronounced tendencies toward self-destruction must be set against the widely touted claims by Franz Fanon that violence has served as a source of renewal, uplift, and solidarity among colonized peoples. Fanon's own evidence contradicts these assertions, and his propositions do not hold up under empirical testing. Though oppressed groups may come to consider force essential to relieve their degradation and deprivation, the great cost in human lives of violent social protest should not be minimized nor its physical or psychological ravages mistaken for agencies of moral regeneration. These cautions seem particularly relevant in situations . . . where the gaps between the force that incumbents and protesters can bring to bear on each other in conflict situations is [*sic*] so overwhelmingly unequal.[14]

The disproportionate advantages of modern firepower and modern warfare tactics have reduced the realistic claims that can be made on behalf of *jihad* in the technical age. It is no longer possible for any Muslim oppositional party or resistance group to overthrow a modern nation-state through the invocation of *jihad*. Agents of the nation-state have access to a panoply of instruments of power, not the least of which is the modern army. To the extent that the modern army becomes a microcosm of the state as a whole, as Anthony Giddens has pointed out,[15] *jihad* cannot succeed except by co-opting the armed forces. Unless one accounts the Iranian Revolution as a *jihad* movement, which Khomeini never did,[16] *jihad* has not, nor will it, become the leitmotif for any successful Muslim resistance movement. Afghanistan, rather than being the exception to this generalization, proves its validity on two counts. First, the government that has ruled in Kabul since the Soviet invasion of 1979 lacks the degree of internal administrative coordination that would qualify it as a nation-state. Instead, the Afghan polity of the past decade has functioned more as a state-nation, to use Richard Falk's felicitous term, a state marked by independent borders yet lacking the operational mechanisms for self-perpetuation. Second, those who oppose the Soviet-backed regime and deny it legitimacy call themselves *mujahidin*, but they suffer from inveterate divisions, claiming absolute loyalty to factional leaders while relying on outside aid for the modern weaponry without which they would fare no better than el Hiba's troops against Mangin's 75s. Far from demonstrating the persistence of *jihad* as a viable form of contemporary warfare, Afghanistan may well illustrate its ultimate futility.[17]

Those who wish to claim for *jihad* a central, pivotal role in contemporary Muslim polities will undoubtedly point to the case of a dissident group in Egypt (appropriately named al-Jihad) that not only plotted against the pharaoh but killed him. President Sadat fell to assassins' bullets in October 1981. Those who killed him invoked *jihad* as their cause; an ideologue who supported the same cause wrote a short tract

titled *Al-Farida al-Gha'iba* (The missing precept), which pointedly referred
to *jihad*. Both the group and its ideology have been the subject of intensive scrutiny from many quarters. Yet none of the vast and still-growing
literature about them challenges the conclusions reached here: *jihad* does
not succeed in mobilizing an ideology that could replace the modern
nation-state with an alternate polity. Those who advocate *jihad* have
been reduced to the role of terrorists; they are not counterrevolution-
aries. The anachronism of what Sadat's assassins tried to do may be
deduced from scanning contemporary *jihad* groups in Egypt.

Case Two

Instead of doing a social scientific survey, which has already been
tried by others, let me offer as the second case an anecdotal *aperçu*.

In December 1988, after the first meeting of the Rutgers/USIP Project,
I was heading home to Durham, North Carolina. My mind was less
filled with Santa Claus or reindeer than holy war and crusaders. Waiting
for my plane in the Newark airport, I began to read the Sunday *New
York Times*. The headlines spoke of stranded Armenians and Panamanian
quandaries, but finally on page 27 I found a news item about the Middle
East—my part of the world. It was titled "Islamic Militancy Again Roils
Egypt." On the preceding Thursday, it seemed, an Egyptian security
agent had been killed in a suburb of Cairo. Why? He was part of a recent
police raid to round up Islamic fundamentalists. The day before,
Wednesday, the police, entering a local mosque, had arrested sixty Islamic fundamentalists. The zealousness of the police provoked mosque
goers. " 'Entering the mosque upset people who wouldn't normally have
any sympathy for the jihad,' he [an anonymous witness] said, using the
Arabic word for holy war that is the generic term here for clandestine
Islamic activists."

As interesting as the *Times* article was up to this point, it still did not
prepare me for the sequel to the police action:

> After the initial roundup, residents said, an unidentified attacker reached into
> a car and slashed lethally at the 38-year-old plainclothesman, setting off another
> spate of detentions as the police hunted down the killer. . . .
>
> Today [Saturday], in apparent calm, police riot trucks were parked at inter-
> sections with helmeted guards brandishing shotguns and assault rifles with fixed
> bayonets.
>
> In August [four months earlier], five people were killed in clashes with police
> in Ein Shams in demonstrations that worried the authorities because the protes-
> ters included ordinary citizens not affiliated with extremist groups.
>
> The prevalent view among Egyptian intellectuals and Western diplomats is
> that the fundamentalists do not have mass support and are not able to challenge
> the security forces militarily. However, in this volatile and generally religious

society, they are able to turn economic and other grievances, including those against the police, to their favor, these analysts say.[18]

The second part of this article made two valuable points, both of them by inadvertence. One is that the incident that erupted in Cairo was at once sporadic and low-level. It involved one dead plainclothesman, killed by spontaneous anger at an overreactive police action. To fit it into a recurrent pattern, the reporter had to reach back into the August files to find a comparable incident. The major point of both incidents, however, was only brought out in the conclusion: those who invoke *jihad* have neither mass support nor the military firepower to challenge the omnipresent, and nearly omnipotent, Egyptian security forces.

Why does *jihad* no longer generate popular appeal nor pose a threat to nation-state polities in the Sunni Muslim world? Fouad Ajami has provided an answer at once simple and grim. *Jihad* advocates function as terrorists, with all the hope and fear that the enterprise of terrorism evokes. "When terrorism becomes commonplace, as David Apter noted, it can be accepted. What begins as a challenge to the state ends up confirming its rationality. . . . The state is said to be (by its custodians, by its many, many spokesmen) the only dike against great upheaval and disorder [read *fitna*]. This is a game that all states play; this also happens to be a game at which the Egyptian state is particularly skilled."[19]

While further eruptions of *jihad*-coded violence will take place in the Sunni Muslim world, they will be minor irritations rather than large-scale threats to the authoritarian regimes who continue to control all the instruments of state power, not only military and political, not only social and economic, but also religious and ideological. "There is substantial evidence," notes the historian Emmanuel Sivan, "of a long-standing and conscious effort on the part of territorial states to create a network of symbol-laden, stylized and repetitive social activities to define a meaningful focus of group loyalty, i.e., the national entity." As a result, Sunni fundamentalists "seem quite pessimistic as to their own chances. Most of their work takes place in the private sphere (e.g., in mosques that are privately-owned and not state-controlled, or in voluntary and welfare associations). They see the public sphere dominated by the state and its 'secular religion.' "[20]

Among Shi'i Muslims, however, there is a different canon for measuring state power and also for projecting the ideological role of *jihad*. We will look at one theoretical and one ethnographic account of the Shi'i appropriation of *jihad*.

Case Three

The theoretician whose writings we will examine is Ayatollah Murtaza Mutahhari. Mutahhari was among the foremost Iranian clerics, a man whom Khomeini once described as "the fruit of my life" and "a part of my flesh." Although he was killed in 1979 at the outset of the Iranian Revolution, Mutahhari's numerous speeches, articles, and pamphlets are still widely quoted, and several, including a small pamphlet titled *Jihad: The Holy War of Islam and Its Legitimacy in the Quran*, have been translated into English. The pamphlet itself consists of a series of four lectures, all of which were delivered in the early 1960s, long before the Iranian Revolution and probably as part of a monthly debating colloquium (*quftar-i mah*), attended by secularists as well as clerics. We are less concerned to look at the Qur'anic justifications for *jihad* that Mutahhari adduces than to delineate what stands out as an approach at once distinctively Shi'ite in method and characteristically modern in tone. Distinctively Shi'ite is the subtlety of exegetical techniques, so subtle that an entire lecture (#4) is dedicated to the question of abrogated verses. Earlier in Lectures #1 and 2, Mutahhari had emphasized that abrogation is not merely a chronological procedure, that is, determining which revelatory dicta (*ayat*) came first, which later, and then preferring the second to the first. Instead, in his view, abrogation requires always interpeting the unconditional as the conditional, so that a general injunction about *jihad* (e.g., 9:73 "O Prophet! Fight the *kuffar* [disbelievers] and hypocrites and be stern against them) must be qualified by the following, more complete *aya* (2:190): "And fight in the path of God with those who are fighting with you and do not transgress, God loves not those who transgress." While Sunni *fuqaha* or jurists use a variety of *hadiths* or Prophetic traditions to justify what would be called *jus in bello*, Mutahhari is able to set forth specific guidelines solely with reference to an inferential reading of Surah 2:190. Here is his exhortation:

O You of Faith! Fight those who are fighting you—i.e., fight them because they are fighting you—but do not violate the limit. What does this mean, not to violate the limit? Not to be the transgressor? Naturally its obvious meaning is that it is those who are fighting us that *we* are to fight and not anyone else, and that it is on the battleground that we are to fight, meaning that we are to fight with a certain group of people and *that group is the soldiers* that the other side have sent, the men of war whom they prepared for war with us and who are fighting us. These it is we are to fight, and, in every day language, we are not to turn chicken on the battlefield, we are not to run away. We must cross swords, exchange bullets, and fight. But with people who are not men of war, who are not soldiers, who are not in a state of combat, such as old men, old women— in fact all women, whether they are old or not—and children, we must not interfere and we must not do any of the other things that are counted as transgression. We must not do these things. We must not cut down their trees (i.e., ruin their economic resources). We must not fill their canals. Such things we must not do. These are all transgressions.[21]

As interesting and suggestive as this passage is, still more compelling is the tone of all four lectures. They demonstrate a single point, that *jihad* is always defensive, and hence the second lecture provides the thematic key to the pamphlet. It is titled "Defense or Aggression." Aggression, for Mutahhari, is an absolute, unmitigated evil. He excoriates aggression yet quickly adds, "All war, on all sides, is not always aggression. War can be aggression but it can also be a reply to aggression, for sometimes the reply to aggression must be given by force."[22] Since only defensive war is justified, one is obliged to delineate what it is that must be defended. On this point, again using the exegetical principle of interpreting the unconditional through the conditional, Mutahhari reasons that all oppressed Muslims can be defended, including especially the Palestinians. "We may be in a situation," he suggests, "whereby a party has not transgressed against us but has committed some type of injustice against a group from another people, who may be Muslims, or who may be non-Muslims. If they are Muslims—like today's plight of the Palestinians who have been exiled from their homes, whose wealth has been seized, who have been subjected to all kinds of transgression— while, for the moment, the transgressor has no intentions against us, is it permissible for us in such circumstances to hurry to the help of those oppressed Muslims and deliver them or is this not permissible? Certainly (it is)."[23]

Defensive war can have a still larger frame of reference. While it may refer to self-defense, fighting against transgression that afflicts one's rights as an individual or a tribe or a nation, it may also refer to something more. According to Mutahhari:

There exists something superior to the rights of the individual or nation. Something more holy, more sacred, the defense of which in accordance to the human conscience is higher than the defense of individual rights. And that something is the rights of humanity. [He goes on to detail what is meant by such rights, and then concludes:] I do not think that anyone has any doubts that the holiest form of *jihad* and the holiest form of war is that which is fought in defense of humanity and of humanity's rights.

Such a paean to idealism demands a practical illustration of its feasibility, and Mutahhari goes on to provide it:

During the period in which the Algerians were at war with the French colonialists, a group of Europeans helped them in their war and the *jihad* of such people was holier than the *jihad* of the Algerians, because the Algerians were defending the cause of their own rights, while the cause of the others was more ethical and more sacred than that of the Algerians.[24]

For the remainder of the third lecture Mutahhari elaborates the genesis of the new interpretive stance he has begun in this passage. Any group of people who are fighting for freedom of belief or freedom of thought deserve support from outsiders, and those who offer such support, even if they are non-Muslims supporting other non-Muslims, are waging the greatest *jihad*, a *jihad* on behalf of the universal rights of humanity.

Few contemporary Muslim ideologues rival Mutahhari in expanding and redefining *jihad*. Within a Shi'i frame of reference, the renowned spokesman for the Shi'i community of southern Lebanon, Shaykh Muhammad Husayn Fadlallah, has signalled some new directions to *jihad* as *da'wa*. Unlike classical jurists, he does not argue that *da'wa* or calling the world to Islam can be implemented apart from *jihad*, nor does he concur with them that in the absence of the Hidden Imam, the Muslim community is restricted to reactive or defensive *jihad*. Rather, Shaykh Fadlallah establishes power (*quwwa*) as a generic, foundational quality of human life and then explores how the urge to secure power takes on a distinctly Islamic expression. *Jihad*, in his estimate, becomes a subcategory of *quwwa* that is inseparable from *da'wa*. It is at once required and legalized by the Islamic need for power.[25] Unlike Mutahhari, however, Shaykh Fadlallah does not project the scope of *jihad* beyond the boundaries of the Muslim community (*dar al-islam*), nor does he suggest that non-Muslims can wage *jihad*, much less the best of all *jihads* (that waged on behalf of humankind).

The imaginative thrust of Mutahhari's rhetoric has thus far not translated into ground-level tactical successes for the fledgling Islamic Republic of Iran. What has happened, instead, has been a practical reexamination of *jihad* precisely because of its widespread invocation to justify not just waging the war against Iraq but using very young, untrained combatants to face a professional army furnished with modern weapons, both legal and illegal. Iranian reactions to the *jihad* against Iraq provide us with the fourth case in our survey of Muslim instantiations of holy war.

Case Four

It would be impossible to gauge the reaction of Iranians to the Iran-Iraq War in religious/ideological terms were it not for the publication of an extraordinary anthropological study. Because he was an Austrian national, Reinhold Loeffler was granted access to Iranians in a southern, tribal village both before and after the Revolution. In his book, *Islam in Practice: Religious Beliefs in a Persian Village*, he recorded some poignant voices of outrage against the dominant ideology of the Islamic Republic of Iran. Some of his informants criticized the regime largely in secular terms, such as the following:

Now, young men with no proper training go to the front and are senselessly killed. I don't believe they are martyrs going to paradise. Who knows how many young men have been killed. If there had been a strong army, as there was under the Shah, this would not have happened. Also, when this reverend sir came to power, he immediately started to attack the whole world, made every-body his enemy. He should first have set the affairs of the country right, and then, like the Prophet, worked to gradually establish Islam and to create an example of true Islamic life. Then the world would have said, "Look, how truly human that society is," and come toward Islam all by itself.[26]

Others, however, faulted Khomeini for identifying too closely with the Last Imam:

He also claims to be the representative of the Last Imam, that is, that he came to prepare the way for the coming of the Last Imam. I know this cannot be true because the Last Imam himself does not know when God will order him to come. [The speaker goes on to enumerate what he perceives to be Khomeini's principal shortcomings, for example, his flamboyance, haughtiness, and venge-fulness. But what most distances Khomeini from "the great ones," in his view, is lack of compassion.] Finally, the prophets and Imams were kind and com-passionate. Before his final battle the Imam Husayn exempted his followers from the obligation of *jihad* so that they might save their lives. Khomeini, however, pitilessly incites people to go to their deaths. All these things showed and show that his claims are unjustified. He is not what he pretends to be.[27]

The hardest moments for many Iranians have been those when family members quarreled among themselves about whether or not the Iran-Iraq War was a holy war. A father-son dispute went like this:

My son now is telling me about the true Islam; they have to fight a holy war (he says) and of necessity get killed. I tell him there is no holy war in the absence of the Last Imam. He shouts at me saying I do not understand a thing. These young ones are like unfledged birds. When they try to fly, they fall from the tree and a cat eats them. They cannot discern the right road. I tell him to stay out of everything, to mind his own business, and do his studies; it's not the right time. But he won't listen. He will get hurt.[28]

The bitterest lament of all conjoined despair about the war dead with despair about betrayal of the deepest ideals of Shi'ism, to strive for justice, that is to say, freedom and humanity:

Some of the clergy wore their garb to gather people around themselves and make them devoted to themselves. But they did not pursue the essence of religion, that is, freedom and humanity. The Imam Husayn whom they are flaunting so much now—again only outwardly, not in truth—fought for that freedom and humanity and in this struggle sacrificed himself and his family. The Muharram celebration should be a remembrance of this and a reminder for us to follow his order to do the same, that is, not to submit to oppression but to fight it. But the mullahs never taught us that. . . . They were right when they called for a revolution against the Shah because he was an oppressor. But I don't think that this was a real revolution. The clergy do not allow it that those basic principles, freedom and humanity, become established. . . . In the past it was repression by the Shah, now it is repression by the clergy.

They refuse to stop this war in which our young men are being killed for no reason. They simply tell them that if they get killed, they will go to paradise. This is a very cheap thing to say. Is there a proof of it? Of course we believe in the after-world. But in a matter of such gravity, when thousands and thousands of young men are sent to their deaths in this belief, one should have especially strong evidence. We are seeing what is going on and we know they are telling lies, but we cannot say it. If we open up our mouths, they shut them by force. Like our former landlords, they have gathered a bunch of illiterate youngsters around themselves by giving them much more money than they could otherwise earn and telling them to suppress us.[29]

These are admittedly random voices, taken from but one village by a single anthropologist. They do not include women's voices, nor do they record the same voice over a span of years, except in rare instances. Yet the sample is reflective of a range of popular sentiments about Islam and the current regime, as well as attitudes toward the Iran-Iraq War and values about war in general and holy war in particular.

COMPARATIVE ASSESSMENTS

One could cite many more examples of *jihad*, "holy war," than these, but I do not believe that they would modify or reverse the major points of our investigation. It becomes much clearer what *jihad* is and is not when one places the rhetoric of holy war into the actual circumstances, either historical or actual, of present-day Muslim polities. Above all, one cannot trace just war theory in an Islamic context without first delineating differences between Sunni and Shi'i norms. For Sunni Muslims, the invocation of *jihad* is framed by the hegemonic strictures of the modern nation-state. No rival group within the boundaries of a majoritarian Muslim country has the power to wage war on a transregional, much less international, scale. *Jihad* has become little more than a pejorative code word for random protest against excesses committed by the regime in power.

For Shi'i Muslims, the situation seems to be more favorable, at least initially. One nation-state has adopted an explicit religious ideology and under the guise of *jihad* has waged war over a protracted period of time, with great cost of life and pain to the families of both martyrs and survivors. That nation, of course, is the Islamic Republic of Iran, and the war it waged for eight years was against the avowedly secular, Ba'athist regime of Iraq. Yet the *jihad* invoked in the name of Islam by Ayatollah Khomeini failed to attain its goals. The opponent was not defeated, the hated enemy was not deposed. Even had Iranian forces been militarily successful, there would have been many devout Shi'is who would have continued to question the appropriateness of such a war: can there be any invocation of *jihad* in the absence of the Hidden Imam? Can anyone, even a learned, pious cleric, convince others that he has been designated as the Hidden Imam's vicar? For many, especially illiterate or semiliterate Iranian peasants, the answer to that question was and remains No.

However, *jihad* retains its symbolic valence as more than a battlecry for both Sunni and Shi'i Muslims, but especially for Shi'is. The major *mythomoteur* for Shi'is remains the call to justice, symbolized by the injustice perpetrated against Husayn on the plain of Karbala, Iraq, in the late seventh century. One may reasonably doubt that the pragmatic limits to political/military *jihad* will curtail or deplete the spiritual elan that motivates those for whom history has still to disclose the will of a just God.[30]

NOTES

1. I am using these terms in the sense that they are introduced and refined by Marshall Hodgson, following Karl Jaspers. See *The Venture of Islam*, 3 vols. (Chicago: University of Chicago Press, 1974), 1:50–52.

2. On Mutahhari's contribution to the Shi'ite reformulation of ideology, see my recent study of fundamentalism, *Defenders of God: The Fundamentalist Revolt against the Modern Age* (San Francisco: Harper and Row, 1989), 221–24.

3. See J. Hexter, "The Historian and His Day," in *Reappraisals in History* (New York: Harper and Row, 1961), 1–13. I am indebted to Douglas Streusand for this reference and also its implications for Islamic historiography.

4. Harry Gamble, Jr., "Christianity: Scripture and Canon," in *The Holy Book in Comparative Perspective*, ed. Frederick M. Denny and Rodney L. Taylor (Columbia: University of South Carolina Press, 1985), p. 44.

5. See, for example, "The Development of *Jihad* in Islamic History and Revelation," in James Turner Johnson and John Kelsay, eds., *Cross, Crescent, and Sword: The Justification and Limitation of War in Western and Islamic Tradition* (Westport, Conn: Greenwood Press, 1990).

6. Ibn Khaldun, *The Muqaddimah: An Introduction to History*, trans. by Franz Rosenthal (Princeton: Princeton University Press, 1967), 161, 228.

7. For the inversion in usage that has attended the concept "Third World," see Carl E. Pletsch, "The Three Worlds, or the Division of Social Scientific Labor, circa 1950–1975," *Comparative Studies in Society and History* 23, no. 4 (October 1981): 565–90. Like "development theory," "third world" has been attacked without so far being supplanted, yet its heuristic benefit for comparative analysis can never be allowed to erase its hieratic, even myopic, implications.

8. For the range of homologies that apply to Arabic *fitna*, usually rendered into English as "sedition" or "disorder," see the lexical display mounted by E.

W. Lane, *Arabic-English Lexicon*, vol. 2 (reprint, Cambridge: Islamic Texts Society, 1974), 2335–36.

9. *Encyclopaedia of Islam*, 1st ed. (Leiden: E. J. Brill, 1954–), 2:538–40. The reference to "an ad hoc vicar appointed by the hidden Imam in his absence" for the purpose of waging *jihad* suggests that *jihad* continues to have importance for Imami Shi'is, but the author never pursues the implications of this reference, as does Kohlberg; see note 11.

10. The relevant passage is as terse as it is dimissory: "The Twelver Shi'ites have fundamentally the same notions as the Sunnites, except that they hold that the jihad-obligation is conditional upon the manifest presence of the Imam. Thus the doctrine of jihad has lost its practical consequence since the last Shi'ite Imam went into Concealment in the year 873 AD. Armed defence against attacks against Moslem lives and properties, however, remains obligatory, but this is not to be called jihad." Rudolph Peters, *Islam and Colonialism: The Doctrine of Jihad in Modern History* (The Hague: Mouton, 1979), 13.

11. Etan Kohlberg, "The Development of the Imami Shi'i Doctrine of Jihad," *Zeitschrift der Deutschen Morgenlaendischen Gesellschaft* 126 (1976):68. Peters, *Islam and Colonialism*, cites Kohlberg's article in his bibliography but seems to have ignored its content otherwise.

12. Douglas Porch, *The Conquest of Morocco* (New York: Alfred A. Knopf, 1983), 258. N.b. *baraka* equals "spiritual power" linked to "charismatic authority."

13. Ibid., 266–67.

14. Michael Adas, *Prophets of Rebellion: Millenarian Protest Movements against the European Colonial Order* (Chapel Hill: University of North Carolina Press, 1979), 189. Even though Adas's subject groups were non-Muslim and their protest movements uninformed by the ideology of *jihad*, his conclusions still provide a sober look at the rhetoric of both Islamic combatants and contemporary Muslim apologists.

15. See Anthony Giddens, *The Nation-State and Violence* (Berkeley: University of California Press, 1987), 250–51.

16. While in exile, Khomeini was very conscious of secular opposition to the Pahlavi regime, and before his triumphal return in early 1979, he used to speak of his mission in either general religious terms (to form an Islamic government) or quasi-secular terms (to launch an Islamic republic). See Ervand Abrahamian, *Iran between Two Revolutions* (Princeton: Princeton University Press, 1982), 520, 532–36. It was the language of Third World protest, linked to Franz Fanon and Ali Shari'ati, that characterized Khomeini's speeches; reference to *jihad* came from another ayatollah, Murtaza Mutahhari.

17. Wilhelm Dietl, *Holy War*, trans. Martha Humphreys (New York: Macmillan, 1984), chap. 22, attempts to portray Afghanistan as a cauldron of religious fervor that will eventually spew up a consensually sanctioned, politically independent charismatic ruler. His favorite candidate is Golbuddin Hekmatyar. Yet his account relies more on journalistic narrative than comprehensive analysis. On Afghanistan, as on virtually every other part of the Muslim world where he examines holy war or *jihad*, he is more eager to record his own impressions than to give a balanced account. The chapter on Pakistan, a curt 12 pages (in a 350-page book), is obsessed with the figure of Zia al-Haqq. The chapter is

even entitled "Allah and His General." Benazir Bhutto is never mentioned. Yellow journalism, here as elsewhere, fails.

18. Alan Cowell, "Islamic Militancy Again Roils Egypt," *New York Times*, Sunday, December 11, 1988, 27.

19. Fouad Ajami, "In the Pharaoh's Shadow: Religion and Authority in Egypt," in James Piscatori, ed., *Islam and the Political Process* (New York: Cambridge University Press, 1983), 34.

20. See Emmanuel Sivan, "The Arab Nation-State: In Search of a Usable Past," *Middle East Review* 19/3 (Spring 1987): 29.

21. Murtaza Mutahhari, *Jihad: The Holy War of Islam and Its Legitimacy in the Quran*, trans. Mohammad S. Tawheedi (Albany, Calif.: Moslem Student Association [Persian Speaking Group], n.d.), 35. Emphasis added.

22. Ibid., 32.

23. Ibid., 36–37.

24. Ibid., 52–53.

25. *Jihad*, for Shaykh Fadlallah, is directly linked to *da'wa*, and the crucial discussion of *jihad* in his book takes place in the subchapter titled "The Instrumentality of *Jihad* in *Da'wa*." Since *jihad*, like *da'wa*, is linked to the requirements of actualizing power, its invocation becomes justified, or legalized, by the quest for power. Hence Shaykh Fadlallah declares that "the legalization of *jihad* emanates from the need of Islam for power" (*wa-hiya inna tashri'a 'l-jihad intalaqa min hajati 'l-Islam ila quwwat*). Yet the actual steps by which this gambit is deployed are not spelled out. See Muhammad Husayn Fadlallah, *Al-Islam wa-mantiq al-quwwat* (Beirut: Dar al-Islamiya, 1981), 204.

26. Reinhold Loeffler, *Islam in Practice: Religious Beliefs in a Persian Village* (Albany: State University of New York Press, 1988), 229.

27. Ibid., 235.

28. Ibid., 237.

29. Ibid., 240.

30. Space precludes elaboration on the theme of striving for justice as a modern ideological appeal that goes far beyond its traditional formulations, even while also connoting *jihad* to the Imami Shi'is of Iran. For instance, the influential anti-Pahlavi pamphleteer, Ali Shari'ati, formulated an "order of unity" (*nezam-i tawhid*) that harked back to the martyrdom of Imam Husayn. Husayn's sacred sacrifice became, in Shari'ati's view, not only the historical model for continuous opposition to persistent evils but also the existential catalyst for "striving toward justice, equity, human brotherhood, public ownership of wealth, and, most important of all, a classless society" (Abrahamian, *Iran between Two Revolutions*, 466).

III

International Law

7

The International Law of War as Related to the Western Just War Tradition

William V. O'Brien

The positive international law of war, the *just in bello* or war-conduct law, is the product of several interrelated sources. These sources may best be understood in terms of the classic distinction between *jus naturale*, natural law as understood in two broad traditions, the Aristotelian-Thomistic-Scholastic and the state-of-nature–Stoic-Hobbesian-Grotian-Lockean-Rousseauan versions of natural law, and the *jus gentium*.[1] The *jus gentium* was originally a kind of private international law or conflict of laws in imperial Roman practice. It was designed to deal with legal disputes between nationals of different Roman dependencies who were not eligible to invoke Roman civil law, for example, a commercial dispute between an Athenian and a resident of Alexandria. After the fall of Rome, European scholars kept the legacy of Roman civilization alive, particularly the legacy of Roman law. The *jus gentium* gradually became more of a *jus inter gentes*, a law between peoples—later nations—rather than between nationals of different jurisdictions, public rather than private international law. Thus, when modern nation-states emerged and developed an international legal system, international law was first known as "the law of nations," *droit des gens, Voelkerrecht*.[2]

The *jus naturale–jus gentium* concepts assumed that reasonable persons had access through "right reason" to a universal natural law, *jus gentium*. The precepts of *jus naturale*, it was believed, were confirmed and applied in the laws and practices of diverse peoples, later nations, revealing common values, basic legal principles, and prescriptions of domestic and international law, for example, *pacta sunt servanda*.

It is important to be aware of the relationship between *jus naturale* and *jus gentium* because both have contributed to the development of the modern law of war. However, as James Turner Johnson has demonstrated persuasively, a European *jus gentium* going back to the medieval age of chivalry was more influential than natural-law just war arguments in the evolution of the positive war-conduct law.[3] Nevertheless, there are war-conduct prescriptions in classical just war doctrine, mainly in the writings of the later Scholastics.[4] In the first part of this chapter I will trace the contributions of just war doctrine to the early positive law of war as it developed roughly from the Middle Ages to the time of the Thirty Years' War and the publication of Hugo Grotius's *De Jure Belli ac Pacis* (1625).

Classic just war doctrine, grounded in but not limited to the Thomistic-Scholastic natural-law tradition, did not develop much after the time of Suarez in the early seventeenth century. While state-of-nature writers after Grotius continued to debate *jus ad bellum* issues of just war, the divisions of centuries of putatively religious conflict followed by the dominance of secular philosophies in the eighteenth century discouraged interest in the justice of recourse to war. Writers such as Grotius, Locke, and Vattel continued to be concerned with *jus in bello* issues, but with an increasing recognition of the growth of a customary war-conduct law, *jus gentium*.[5] Armies became almost entirely professional, and the practice of belligerents was regulated by a growing law of war in which military law concerned with internal administration and discipline merged with international law.[6] By the time of the American Revolution there was a well-developed law of war that the American armies were eager to abide by as a demonstration of American responsibility.[7]

In the years between the American Revolution and World War I the positive international law continued to develop, first as customary law and then through the codification efforts of the 1899 and 1907 Hague Conferences and other international conventional initiatives. This development was greatly invigorated and expanded by the secular concept of "humanity," which was closely related to the concept of "civilization" as implying a source of legal and moral standards.[8] International-law writers emphasized the restraints enjoined on the conduct of war waged by "civilized," that is, European, nations as compared to the barbarism of lesser breeds without the law.[9] The idea of "humanity" inspired the Red Cross movement to succor the wounded and sick and, later, prisoners of war and civilian victims of war.[10] Humanity was also invoked in various efforts to ban weapons and means of warfare causing "superfluous suffering."[11]

Actually, "humanity" seems to have been a substitute for discredited natural-law sources of normative guidance, spurned in the nineteenth and twentieth centuries because of their suspicious religious connections and "unscientific" character. This has only changed with the age of Nuremberg and Hiroshima, wherein there has been a revival of natural-law approaches. Clearly, then, classic just war doctrine did not contribute much to the law of war during the main period of its development, 1648–1914. However, as just war doctrines have developed based on a variety of religious and/or philosophical approaches and have achieved respectability in the contemporary era, I will evaluate in the second part of this chapter their contributions to current war-conduct law. To this I will add a brief account of the contributions of the Catholic church through papal, conciliar, and episcopal pronouncements to the modern law of war.

SOURCES OF JUST WAR JUS IN BELLO IN CLASSIC JUST WAR DOCTRINE

The chief sources of classic just war doctrine are of three sorts:

1. The theological tradition, represented by the writings of St. Augustine, St. Thomas Aquinas, and the late Scholastics. From this last group I will consider Victoria and Suarez, although there are many other important contributors.[12]

2. The canonists and ecclesiastic councils.

3. Customary *jus gentium* incorporated into just war doctrine, mainly by later Scholastics.

I accept Johnson's view that classic just war doctrine must include all three of these sources and that Alfred Vanderpol was wrong in limiting his study of the doctrine to the Scholastic writers.[13] However, I intend to rely mainly on Victoria and Suarez as writers who produced classic just war doctrine in its most comprehensive form. I will not attempt to review the literature on the customary *jus gentium*; this would be a major task in itself. I will rely on Johnson for the contributions of the canonists.[14]

The diverse writings of St. Augustine deal mainly with *jus ad bellum* issues, although Augustine's insistence on avoidance of "evil intention" forms the basis for St. Thomas Aquinas's development of the requirement of "right intention."[15] Paul Ramsey's claim that the principle of discrimination or noncombatant immunity has its roots in Augustinian thought has not been widely accepted.[16] St. Thomas's contribution to just war doctrine is structured almost entirely in terms of the *jus ad bellum*. However, as will be argued later, Thomas's insistence on right intention is clearly an important contribution to the *jus in bello*.[17] Meanwhile, a war-conduct law was being developed in the medieval world, primarily because of the influence of chivalry and also because of the pronouncements of the canonists and some ecclesiastical councils, as Johnson demonstrates.[18] By the sixteenth century Victoria and other Scholastic writers were presenting an eclectic mixture of just war Scholastic natural law and customary *jus gentium* sources in their treatment of war conduct. When Hugo Grotius wrote *De Jure Belli ac Pacis* in 1625, he drew on this work of the late Scholastics as well as precedents from classical antiquity.[19]

Rather than list the contributions to the positive law of war of just war writers individually, I will proceed through the main chapters of the *jus in bello* as we know it today and indicate what, if any, evidence there is of contributions from classic just war doctrine and/or influences on, and recognition and encouragement of, the emerging war-conduct law.

JUST WAR DOCTRINE AND THE EMERGING LAW OF WAR

I will limit this discussion to the law of land warfare. An outline of this body of law as it is treated by publicists, military manuals, and international conventions is as follows:

1. Basic principles: military necessity, humanity, and chivalry
2. Combatant and noncombatant status
3. Limitation on means and methods of warfare
4. Prisoners of war
5. Treatment of wounded and sick
6. Belligerent occupation—treatment of civilians
7. Communications and agreements between belligerents
8. Sanctions

Basic Principles of the Law of War

There are many definitions of the principle of military necessity, and I will submit my own later. To begin the discussion, I will use the definition of this and the other two basic principles in the U.S. Air Force's 1976 pamphlet AFP 110-31, *International Law: The Conduct of Armed Conflict and Air Operations.*[20] The Air Force pamphlet continues a tradition of reiterating these three basic principles that was unfortunately discontinued by the Army's 1956 manual FM 27-10.[21] Moreover, the Air Force definitions and discussions are more comprehensive and relevant to our inquiries than any others with which I am familiar. AFP 110-31 states:

Military necessity is the principle which justifies measures of regulated force not forbidden by international law which are indispensable for securing the prompt submission of the enemy, with the least possible expenditures of economic and human resources. This concept has four basic elements: (i) that the force used is capable of being and is in fact regulated by the user; (ii) that the use of force is necessary to achieve as quickly as possible the partial or complete submission of the adversary; (iii) that the force used is no greater in effect on the enemy's personnel or property than needed to achieve his prompt submission (economy of force); and (iv) that the force used is not otherwise prohibited. ... Armed conflict must be carried on within the limits of the prohibitions of international law, including the restraints inherent in the principle of "necessity." However, the legitimacy of any particular act cannot be judged without reference to all the principles which govern armed conflict including reciprocity as discussed in Chapter 10.[22]

In terms of just war principles, the heart of the principle of military necessity is the principle of proportion.

AFP 110-31 then discusses the principle of humanity as follows:

Complementing the principle of necessity and implicitly contained within it is the principle of humanity, which forbids the infliction of suffering, injury or destruction not actually necessary for the accomplishment of legitimate military purposes. This principle of humanity results in a specific prohibition against unnecessary suffering, a requirement of proportionality, and a variety of more specific rules examined later. The principle of humanity also confirms the basic immunity of civilian populations and civilians from being objects of attack during armed conflict. This immunity does not preclude unavoidable incidental civilian casualties which may occur during the course of attacks against military objectives, and which are not excessive in relation to the concrete and direct military advantage anticipated.[23]

Finally, AFP 110-31 states:

Although difficult to define, chivalry refers to the conduct of armed conflict in accord with well-recognized formalities and courtesies. During the Middle Ages, chivalry embraced the notion that combatants belonged to a caste, that their combat in arms was ceremonial, that the opponent was entitled to respect and honor, and that the enemy was a brother in the fraternity of knights in arms. Modern technological and industrialized armed conflict has made war less a gentlemanly contest. Nevertheless, the principle of chivalry remains in specific prohibitions such as those against poison, dishonorable or treacherous misconduct, misuse of enemy flags, uniforms, and flags of truce. The principle of chivalry makes armed conflict less savage and more civilized for the individual combatant.[24]

St. Thomas, drawing upon St. Augustine, requires right intention as a *jus ad bellum* condition for just war. This condition obviously has *jus in bello* implications. Right intention requires that nothing be done that is not necessary to the success of the just cause. Moreover, nothing should be done that impairs the prospect for just and lasting peace. To use military terms, right intention lays down a grand strategic limit on the strategic and tactical conduct of war. Strategic or tactical necessity should not overrule the limits set by right intention.

The later Scholastics continued to insist on right intention, although Suarez replaced that term with "the proper manner of making war," suggestive of an even more explicit relationship between the *jus ad bellum* category and the *jus in bello*.[25] Suarez insists that "it is not permitted to multiply without reason the damages imposed on enemies."[26] Similarly, Article 22 of Hague Convention IV (1907) states that "the rights of belligerents to adopt means of injuring the enemy is not unlimited."[27]

Thus far the point has been made by the Scholastics that nothing that is not necessary to the success of just ends should be permitted. Victoria is noteworthy for the extent to which he justified the doing of all that is necessary for the just cause. Answering the question, "What is permitted to do against enemies in a just war?" Victoria states:

In a just war, one has the right to do all that is necessary for the defense of the public good. That is clear since the end of war is the defense and the conservation of the State. It is, moreover, what an individual has when he defends himself, as we have shown;—a fortiori, the State and the prince possess this right.[28]

On this subject Suarez states:

War once commenced, and until it has won victory, it is permitted to cause to the enemy any damage that appears necessary, either to obtain satisfaction or to achieve victory, provided that they [the just belligerents] themselves do not violate the rights of the innocents, which would be an evil in itself.

The reason is that, if an end is permitted, all the means necessary to reach this end are equally permitted. As a consequence, throughout all the course and time of war, everything that is done against the enemy, except murder of innocents, is not contrary to justice; for ordinarily all other damages are considered as necessary to the end of the war.[29]

Classic just war doctrine, then, coincides with the modern war-conduct law principles of military necessity and humanity. It holds that everything truly necessary to the just end should be permitted, short of violations of the principle of noncombatant immunity (without mention of other violations of the law of war), with the provision that nothing not truly necessary should be permitted. This generous definition of military necessity, however, should be interpreted in the light of the requirement of right intention. The just war definition of military necessity includes, without using the terms, the principles of proportion and discrimination or noncombatant immunity.

As indicated, the modern principle of humanity includes the principle of avoidance of superfluous suffering and the principle of discrimination or noncombatant immunity. Otherwise, it simply reiterates the principle of military necessity, insisting that no unnecessary damage be done. I will address the issue of unnecessary suffering under the category of the prohibition of cruel means. Note that discrimination or noncombatant immunity is considered so important in the mature classic just war doctrine that it is the sole specified restraint on military necessity. Generally speaking, the principle of humanity is supported by the *jus ad bellum* requirement of right intention.

Classic just war doctrine does not deal with most of the issues of chivalry raised by the modern interpretation of AFP 110-31. Perhaps it would have seemed superfluous for moralists to write about the chivalric code. The principal issue discussed in just war doctrine is that of good faith in communication and agreements. To this point, St. Thomas Aquinas has an interesting discussion of the morality of ambushes. As against arguments that good faith must always be maintained between enemies and that ambushes are therefore immoral violations of good faith (an exaggerated view, to be sure), St. Thomas argues that ambushes are morally permissible. He distinguishes immoral violation of promises to the enemy, for example, in a truce, from situations in which one conceals one's intentions and capabilities from the enemy, as in an ambush. Clearly, falsehoods and broken promises between enemies are considered immoral and would seem to fall into the category of violations of the principle of chivalry as later understood.[30]

Combatant and Noncombatant Status

The issue of determining combatant and noncombatant status for purposes of the law of war is complicated in classic just war doctrine by the underlying distinction between just and unjust belligerents. There appears to be a propensity or temptation to treat all members of the society waging an unjust war as "guilty." However, as Johnson brings out:

For these writers "innocence" means lack of any direct contribution to the war effort, and it disregards the fact of citizenship in the nation with which one's own is at war. Guilt means just the opposite: direct involvement in the war, whether one is a citizen of the enemy state or not.[31]

Johnson cites Victoria's definition of innocent persons as including children, women (except for individual cases of guilt), clerics, religious, foreigners, guests of the enemy country, "harmless agricultural folk and also . . . the rest of the peaceable civilian population."[32]Suarez states:

The *innocents* are, and this by virtue, one can say, of natural law, children, women, and all those who are incapable of carrying arms, ambassadors, by virtue of the law of nations, and according to positive law among Christians: religious, priests, etc. Cajetan thinks that this results from a custom to which it is necessary to conform.[33]

The positive law of war developed customary rules regarding combatant status that were codified in the 1907 Hague Convention IV. Article 1 of this convention requires combatants

1. To be commanded by a person responsible for his subordinates;
2. To have a fixed distinctive emblem recognizable at a distance;
3. To carry arms openly; and
4. To conduct their operations in accordance with the laws and customs of war.[34]

Johnson rightly points out that throughout most of the period of the development of classic just war doctrine the weapons and means of war permitted discriminate fighting, but that by Suarez's time more indiscriminate weapons were becoming more common.[35] This point should be emphasized because of the long interval between the culmination of classic just war doctrine in the early seventeenth century and the revival of modern just war doctrine after World War II. Obviously, modern weaponry and strategies, for example, starvation blockades, rendered discriminate warfare difficult if not impossible. Moreover, the phenomenon of total war, elements of which appeared in the Napoleonic Wars and the American Civil War, changed the definition of functional relationships to the "war effort" and encouraged practices such as saturation countervalue city bombing.[36] I will not develop this point since chapters in a companion volume deal with the issues of combatancy and noncombatant immunity.[37] However, I think that credit should be given to the classic just war doctrine for overcoming the propensity toward indiscriminate warfare latent in some versions of the just/guilty dichotomy.

Limitation on Means and Methods of Warfare

I will not discuss efforts to mitigate medieval wars by limiting the days when fighting was permitted by the Church, for example, the truce of God, promulgated by the Council of Clermont in 1095 A.D. Just war writers appear to have raised no objections to weapons of the time. It was the Second Lateran Council of 1139 A.D. that sought to ban the crossbow, the *arbalest*. The Second Lateran Council's canon condemned the crossbow as "a deadly and God-detested" weapon and decreed that those who used it against "Christians and Catholics" should be anathema.[38] Unlike the rationale of "superfluous suffering" that has supported modern bans on weapons and means of warfare, the real rationale for the ban on the crossbow seems to have been political and social. Apparently it was feared that this new weapon could be used by common men to challenge the near monopoly of armed force of the knightly class.

Grotius devotes considerable space to various aspects of the use of poison and poisoned weapons.[39] In my limited review of classic just war writers I have found no such discussions.

While the classic just war writers have little or nothing to say about weapons, they are very interested in questions of property. Three categories relating to property can be distinguished in the contemporary international law of war: wanton destruction, pillage, and confiscation of property.

Wanton destruction is prohibited by Article 23(g) of the 1907 Hague Convention IV, which especially forbids belligerents "to destroy or seize the enemy's property, unless such destruction or seizure be imperatively demanded by the necessities of war."[40] This means that destruction incidental to combat operations is permitted but that widespread destruction of property not immediately necessary to such operations is prohibited.

Classic just war doctrine appears to be less restrictive than the law of war that was codified in the 1907 Hague Convention IV. While the lives of the innocent were to be spared, their property was fair game for the just belligerent. Victoria answers the question "Is it permitted in a just war to despoil the innocents?" as follows:

It is certain that one can take from innocents the goods and things which the enemy could use against us, such as arms, ships, machines of war. It is evident that otherwise one could not achieve victory, which is the goal of the war. Moreover, one may take from the innocents their money, burn or destroy their wheat, kill their horses, if that is necessary to weaken the enemy forces. The corollary of this is that if there is a perpetual war one can despoil indiscriminately the innocent as well as the guilty among the enemy, for their resources serve to sustain an unjust war, and, on the contrary, one can weaken their forces and despoil the inhabitants of their country.[41]

Wanton destruction results from organized military operations. Pillage is the work of combatants acting individually in seizing private property. Article 28 of the 1907 Hague Convention IV states, "The pillage of a town or place, even when taken by assault, is prohibited,"[42] However, in the wars of the Middle Ages and Renaissance, armies were sustained in considerable measure by pillage. Moreover, as Article 28 suggests, the practice of encouraging troops to attack a strongly held place by promising them opportunities for pillage was commonplace.

Victoria supports the practice of pillage:

Can one permit soldiers to pillage a town? That in itself is not prohibited, if it is necessary to make war, terrorize the enemy, or raise the courage of soldiers.

This is also the opinion of Sylvester. By the same token, it is permitted to burn down a town for a reasonable cause. However, as such authorizations entail many acts of cruelty, of savagery, unworthy of a man, but which are committed by barbaric soldiers: massacres of innocents, corporal punishment, rapes and dishonor of women, pillage of temples, it is without doubt a very great iniquity to hand over to pillage a town, above all a Christian town, except in case of absolute necessity. But if military necessity requires, that is not prohibited, even though it is to be feared that the soldiers might commit some of these hideous excesses that the commanders are obliged to forbid and, if they can, prevent.

... Notwithstanding all that has been said, soldiers are never permitted to pillage or burn without the authorization of their prince or commander, for they are not the judges but the executioners; otherwise, they will be liable for restitution.[43]

Since so much of medieval and Renaissance warfare was siege warfare, it is remarkable that the classic just war writers do not discuss it. There are serious moral questions in siege warfare. Are there any limits to indiscriminate starvation tactics? Should innocents caught in a siege be permitted to depart? Is it permissible to use catapults to cast boulders or inflammable materials into the fortified place indiscriminately? Is it permissible to declare that failure to surrender will mean denial of quarter and pillage of the town if and when it falls? None of these questions appears to be addressed in the sources consulted.

Prisoners of War

The positive war-conduct law requires that quarter be given, that prisoners of war be removed from combat areas, that they be well treated, and that they be exchanged at the end of the war or earlier by agreement. The customary law was codified and developed further in the 1899 Hague Convention II and 1907 Hague Convention IV and in numerous Red Cross conventions, culminating in the 1949 Geneva Convention Relative to the Treatment of Prisoners of War.[44] Based on the monitoring and support functions of the International Committee of the Red Cross, the international law concerning prisoners of war is comprehensive and detailed.

I do not find any discussion of treatment of prisoners of war in the sources consulted. Victoria discusses the question whether prisoners of war may be put to death. His answer is interesting because it reflects his awareness of developments in the positive law of war:

Is it permitted to kill those who surrender or prisoners, recognizing that they are guilty? It can be answered that, properly speaking, there is no reason why, in a just war, prisoners or those who surrender, if they are guilty, could not be put to death, without, properly speaking, violating justice. *But in war, there are many customs established by the law of nations, and it appears agreed by the habits and usages of war that, once the victory is won and all danger averted, prisoners, if they have not taken flight, are not put to death; and it is necessary to the law of nations to the extent that good men are accustomed. As to those who surrender, I have never heard of a parallel custom existing; moreover, in the surrender of strong places or towns, those who surrender usually stipulate that their lives will be saved and that they need not fear for their heads.*[45]

I need not attempt to discuss the positive law of war concerning care for the wounded and sick. Serious efforts to assure their care did not develop until the middle of the nineteenth century.[46]

Belligerent Occupation—Treatment of Civilians

The point has already been made that while the lives of innocents were protected by just war doctrine, their property was highly vulnerable. The permissibility of wanton destruction and pillage when required by military necessity has already been discussed. The rationales varied, but they all added up to open season on the property of the occupied population. In addition to the requirements of immediate military necessity, we have seen the argument that preventive seizure or destruction of anything that might help the enemy was permitted.[47] Given the cast of just war doctrine at that time, when righting wrongs was paramount just cause, there was a tendency to fall back on the concept of just restitution and "satisfaction" in order to justify keeping war booty, broadly interpreted. It is interesting that Victoria's treatment of pillage comes just after his discussion of war booty in answer to the seventh question of the third part: "Do all those things taken from the enemy become the property of those who took them?"[48]

Needless to say, the provisions for maintaining law, order, and basic governmental functions under belligerent occupation that developed in the customary law as codified in the 1907 Hague Convention IV and as further elaborated in the 1949 Geneva Convention Relative to the Protection of Civilian Persons in Time of War were not remotely contemplated by the classic just war writers. Many of these provisions, of course, were necessary because of the great increase in the role of government in the centuries after Suarez. However, one has the impression that there was comparatively little concern for the fate of the occupied populations in war except to protect their lives. Needless to say, by the time a just belligerent had destroyed or taken all that was required by immediate as well as preventive military necessity, as well as all that could be considered war booty, or that fell to pillage, or that could be written off as just restitution by the guilty, there might be very little left for the population to live for.

The propensity of the classic just war writers to discriminate against the active belligerents on the putatively unjust side is reflected in Victoria's brief handling of the question of hostages. This was to be a major issue in the modern Franco-Prussian War as well as World Wars I and II. On executing hostages, Victoria says:

May one put to death hostages who, either at the time of truces, or when the war is ended, are turned over by the enemy, if the latter break their word and do not carry out the agreements made?

"Proposition Unique." If the hostages were among the guilty, that is to say, those who took up arms, one has, in that case, the right to them to death. But if they are among the innocents, as stated earlier, they cannot be put to death: this is the case of children, women, and other innocent persons.[49]

Thus Victoria justifies killing such prisoners of war as "guilty," a position quite contrary to the emerging positive law of war.

It is unnecessary to repeat the opinions of just war writers with respect to communication between belligerents. I take it that the "ambassadors" mentioned in Suarez's definition of innocents include a variety of envoys and pages who communicated between belligerents.[50] The obligations to respect the maxim *pacta sunt servanda* is clear in St. Thomas Aquinas's discussion of the cases in which the enemy may be misled.[51]

Sanctions

The modern law of war considers that the sanctions for its observance are reprisals against lawbreakers and war-crimes proceedings.[52] Neither is satisfactory. Reprisals tend to lead to spirals of reprisals and counterreprisals that simply erode the standards of legal or moral conduct. War-crimes proceedings depend on the fortunes of war and can be drastically subjective and unfair. The law of war is supposedly based on the hope and expectation of reciprocity; yet the question arises as to what to do if the enemy violates the law. Does this warrant comparable violations by the injured party?

It seems to me that there are two implicit attitudes regarding sanctions within the *jus in bello* in classic just war doctrine. First, the always-present tendency to distinguish the just from the guilty encourages punishment in a variety of ways for behavior violative of the norms of *jus in bello*. The putatively unjust party is already "guilty" because of its *jus ad bellum* position. If, in addition, it egregiously violates war-conduct standards, it can be punished. Second, as far as the putatively just belligerent is concerned, the sanction for this moral—as distinguished from legal—body of prescriptions is the conscience of the nation, its authoritative decision makers, and individual commanders and soldiers. In this respect, in my opinion, we have come full circle. Today we know that reprisals are not an adequate sanction for the law of war, that legitimate war-crimes proceedings depend upon whether the fortunes of war produce a more or less just victor, and that reciprocity is seldom a reasonable expectation, for example, treatment of prisoners of war in the Korean and Vietnam wars. In my view the conscience of the belligerent nation, its authoritative decision makers, and its individual commanders provides the sanction for the law of war. Moral nations, men and women, fight for fundamental values, not the least of which is the value of the moral and legal tradition of restraint in war.

MODERN JUST WAR DOCTRINE AND THE LAW OF WAR

Modern just war doctrine takes a variety of forms. Just war writers usually use the same general concepts and categories but often place different emphases and interpretations on them. Several generalizations can be made about modern just war writers, however:

1. They tend to concentrate on the moral dilemmas of nuclear deterrence and defense.

2. They are inclined to concentrate on theoretical theological or ethical issues such as the origins and rationales for the principle of discrimination and the meaning of "intention," as in the debate over the use of the principle of double effect.

3. Modern just war writers have not given much attention to the law of war issues of conventional, revolutionary, and counterinsurgency warfare, that is, the kinds of warfare that have flourished since World War II under the umbrella of the nuclear balance of terror.

The principal exceptions to (1) and (3) appear to be Michael Walzer and myself. This raises a problem in structuring the second part of this chapter. If I proceed through the chapters of the law of war as outlined in the discussion of the contributions of the classic just war writers, I may have to sing an uncomfortable duet with Walzer backed by a seldom-heard chorus of leading modern just war writers whose interests were not particularly focused on the law of war except for the principle of discrimination, the subject of other chapters in the companion volume to this book.[53]

I propose, instead, to change my organization and methodology in the second part of this chapter and to comment briefly on those contributions of modern just war writers that are relevant to the modern positive law of war, again prescinding from detailed discussions of the principle of discrimination. I will then conclude with a brief account of Catholic official pronouncements relevant to the law of war.

As in the discussion of classic just war doctrine, I will concentrate on a few major figures, fully recognizing that there are many important contributors to modern just war doctrine. In making my selection I exclude writers who are essentially recording the history and content of just war thought. The writers I have selected all combine elements of recovery of the just war tradition with their own creative interpretations of and extrapolations from basic just war concepts as they apply them to the practical security dilemmas of the contemporary world.

I would consider Father John Courtney Murray, S. J., as the first major modern just war theorist.[54] However, I will defer reference to his contributions to the discussion of official Catholic thought on war, since much of Murray's analysis is related to the teaching of Pope Pius XII. This means that in point of time and, certainly, the weight of his contribution, I will start with Paul Ramsey. I will then review material relevant to the law of war as treated in this chapter from the works of James Turner Johnson and Michael Walzer. I will conclude this survey with a summary of my own work.

Paul Ramsey

I have suggested that the basic principles of the laws of war laid down by military manuals and publicists incorporate the two basic principles of just war *jus in bello* by including proportion in military necessity and discrimination in humanity. The order of these principles is important. The order in field manuals that places military necessity first and humanity second implies that one starts with the positive authorization to use armed force and then applies a limit to that force in the principle of discrimination. This, however, is not the way that Paul Ramsey structures his just war doctrine.

For Ramsey, all discussions of the morality of war must begin with the establishment of the primacy of the principle of discrimination or noncombatant immunity from direct, intentional attack. Every act of war must pass the test of discrimination before it submits to the test of proportionality. Most of Ramsey's writing on war was focused on nuclear deterrence and defense. He did, however, make a foray into the subject of revolutionary war and counterinsurgency at a critical time (1966) in the Vietnam War. I will quote a key passage on this subject demonstrating the relation between the principles of discrimination and proportion in Ramsey's thought:

The relation between the tests [discrimination and proportion] seems to be as follows: the ends justify the means, since nothing else can; but they do not justify any means. The means which no ends can justify have to be determined by the principle of discrimination. The statement that only the ends justify the means is a statement falling under the principle of proportion; so understood, it is unquestionably correct. The statement that the ends do not justify the means (or are not capable of justifying any and all means) is a statement falling under the principle of discrimination; so understood, it too is unquestionably correct. The principle of proportion is regulative of all actions that are finally *to be done*; prudence governs in determining the effects or consequences that ought ever to be let loose in the world. Especially in politics, only the ends justify the means.[55]

After this restatement of his basic position, Ramsey evaluates the morality of revolutionary warfare (guerrilla warfare and terror), as in Vietnam, and counterinsurgency tactics such as air and land attacks on insurgent forces who deliberately shield themselves with the civilian population. Ramsey comes to the sweeping conclusion that such wars of national liberation are intrinsically immoral if, as is usually the case, the insurgents employ strategies and tactics that are overwhelmingly countervalue rather than counterforce, hence indiscriminate.[56] On the other hand, Ramsey thinks that counterinsurgent attacks on mixed targets wherein the insurgents had intermingled with the population may be moral in the same way that use of catapults in sieges in the Middle Ages against mixed military-civilian targets was permissible.[57] Needless to say, the reception of this paper, originally presented to the annual meeting of the American Society of Christian Ethics in Evanston, Illinois, January 21–22, 1966, was not entirely enthusiastic.

However, while Ramsey did not specifically condemn the American involvement in Vietnam, he did apply the principle of proportion to suggest that a military power such as the United States would tend almost inevitably to employ disproportionate means in such a war:

[A] chief lesson to be drawn from Vietnam is that, when an industrial power like the United States gets involved in counter-insurgency in a traditional and preindustrial society, *disproportionate violence is bound to be done*. Indeed, that is the one proper way to condemn the U.S. involvement.[58]

In another important reaction to events in Vietnam, Ramsey evaluated the arguments for and against the U.S. use of nonlethal incapacitating gases in that war. Ramsey found that such chemical means may pass the test of discrimination and, indeed, be more humane than many other means of war. He pointed to the use of such means by police forces around the world. Still, Ramsey recognized that chemical warfare has been banned by international law. The question, then, is whether it is proportionate to override this ban in order to carry out military operations in a more humane, discriminate manner than would otherwise be possible. Ramsey asks:

Is the first act of using incapacitants already an act that is out of control[?] If it is, it is inordinate and ought never to be done no matter how humane it may be in the first instant. Would our self-imposed limitation of gas warfare to the more humane means be a rule that could be enforced (and transgressions of this punished) by means that themselves are still limited and capable of being kept graduated? Have our military planners played out enough scenarios to know that there are obvious boundaries at which to agree to stop, once the nonrational boundary that at present prohibits chemical-biological-radiological warfare has been replaced by even a more rational rule humanizing warfare in the immediate areas over which incapacitating gases might first be used effectively?

If not, then, the step better not be taken. Still, it is important that in reaching this negative conclusion we be clear from which test we reached it.[59]

Ramsey's own view was that future belligerents would not be able to resist the temptation to use chemical warfare, a prediction that seems to be borne out in recent developments.[60]

Again, it must be said that Ramsey's greatest contribution to the *jus in bello* is in his insistence on the primacy of the principle of discrimination and in his unrelenting efforts to reconcile that principle with nuclear deterrence and defense. Since the issue of discrimination is not my subject and since the moral/legal issues of nuclear deterrence and defense are really moral, not legal, I will not evaluate Ramsey's treatment of them.

James Turner Johnson

James Turner Johnson has not undertaken a comprehensive and systematic presentation of the laws of war. However, he has made a number of extremely important contributions to the understanding of it. I would consider the following to be Johnson's principal contributions to the understanding and support of war-conduct law:

1. The point that the law of war is *lex lata*; that its future lies with the *lex ferenda*; and that between the two is customary international law.[61]

2. Ramsey's insistence on the priority of the principle of discrimination over the principle of proportion need not be accepted, with major consequences for the definition of the principle of military necessity.[62]

3. Any concept of just and legally permissible war rests on the assumption that the theories and practices of limited war have validity in reality.[63]

4. An effective law of war must be intercultural, transcending the Western origins of positive international law.[64]

5. International law has not sufficiently dealt with the problems of internal and/or mixed internal/international interventionary wars.[65]

Having recognized the importance of the conventional international law of war, Johnson observes:

Lex ferenda, because of its definition by the idea of "ought," is clearly a realm in which moralists can feel at home. In fact, when the international lawyer enters the region of *lex ferenda*, it might be argued that he puts off his legal mantle and takes on that of the moral philosopher or theologian. His mode of discourse, instead of depending on precedents, treaties, and court decisions interpreting them, tends rather in the direction of the language of moral analysis and has to do with values, obligations flowing from them, principles incorporating them, and so on.[66]

This is a concise and valid statement of the relationship that ought to obtain between just war theorists and the positive law of war.

In addressing the issue of the priorities between the principle of proportion and that of discrimination, Johnson attacks the questions from perspectives of limited war and asserts:

In the context of the limited war idea, the principle of proportion emerges as logically prior to that of discrimination in its special limited sense, since the two characteristics that express the former, limitation by resources and overall aims, must be considered logically prior to those that express the latter: limitation by means, geography and targets. This priority is heightened by the further observation that proportionality in this context has implications both for the initiation of war and for its waging once begun—in traditional language, both *jus ad bellum* and *jus in bello* implications—while discrimination in the limited war context pertains only to the waging of war.[67]

This, of course, challenges Ramsey's contention that discrimination is the first test.[68]

Johnson's third principal contribution to the advancement of the law of war can be simply stated. He emphasizes that legal and moral restraint in war must be effected by limited, as opposed to total, war and, inter alia, demonstrates the relations between Francis Lieber's 1863 code for the Union armies and concepts of limited war.[69]

Johnson emphasizes a point central to the present enterprise, namely the need for the intercultural study of international law generally and the law of war in particular. Recognizing the limits of Western approaches to international law and of his own writing, he says:

The just war tradition of the West represents one culture's attempt to determine when and how violence is appropriate; at the same time, it is the tradition that historically gave birth to international law in the modern sense, and it remains apt to speak of international law as forming a part of this tradition as it exists in the contemporary world. Yet historically Western culture, no less than other cultures, has had a dual problem with regard to the regulation of violence: internal questions having to do with such matters as defining a legal monopoly of violent means and regulating single combat, and external questions having to do with the relevance of the internally directed restraints in wars with other cultures. . . . So we must recognize the particularity or cultural relativity of the ways just war tradition has devised to deal with these two problems, the internal and external regulation of violence. Still, what can be discovered about this effort has obvious implications for the development of both international law and modern moral doctrine on the justification and restraint of war. It is thus in order to ask what has been conceived within just war tradition as the form of appropriate cultural regulation of violence.[70]

The last point that I would emphasize in reviewing Johnson's contributions to the contemporary law of war is his recognition that this law remains focused on interstate hostilities and has yet to deal adequately with civil and/or mixed internal/international conflicts.[71] It should be added that Johnson's writings reflect a solid familiarity with the most important contemporary publicists on international war-conduct law.[72]

Michael Walzer

Michael Walzer's *Just and Unjust Wars* is arguably the most influential of the modern just war books. The format—brief case studies interspersed with moral arguments—and style make it more readable and interesting for a broader public than that which reads the other just war texts. The book is widely used in university courses and, significantly, at service academies and schools of higher military education, for example, the Army War College. While one may disagree with Walzer's reasoning and conclusions in many cases, there is no doubt that he has greatly increased interest in the law of war. Walzer himself states at the outset that his is a book of "practical morality" aimed at the ordinary citizen and/or soldier, expounded "in its philosophical form" as "a doctrine of human rights."[73]

Walzer criticizes international-law writers who attempt to perpetuate legal positivism in interpreting and applying black-letter law that is notoriously unreflective of belligerent practice and expectations.[74] He acknowledges the policy-oriented efforts of scholars such as Myers McDougal but rightly points out that they are really engaged in creative ethical thinking rather than legal interpretation.[75] Nevertheless, Walzer refers to positive international law when it serves his purpose, as he does to classic and modern just war doctrine. In effect, Walzer uses all resources he deems relevant to his enterprise.

Despite the independence of Walzer's approach from the structures and categories of the international law of war, he treats at one point or another most of the standard subjects discussed in the legal literature. Walzer's human-rights approach to war collides head-on with the traditional basic law of war principle of military necessity. Properly understood, the principle of military necessity is the source of authority to use armed coercion so long as it is proportionate to legitimate military ends and limited by the principle of humanity, notably including discrimination, and the laws of war.[76] In just war terms, as discussed in indicating the difference between Ramsey and Johnson, one begins with proportion and then turns to the limit of discrimination—and any other limits enjoined by morality or law.[77] Walzer is not uninterested in winning just wars; he refers in his preface to "the dilemma of winning and fighting well."[78] Still, Walzer's approach, similar in this regard to Ramsey's, is to start out with a firm moral roadblock against immoral means that violate human rights and then see if winning is possible.

From this perspective Walzer is contemptuous of the principle of military necessity, which he calls a "plea" rather than a principle. Referring to military necessity by the German term *Kriegsraison*, Walzer says:

In fact, it is not about necessity at all; it is a way of speaking in code, or a hyperbolical way of speaking, about probability and risk. . . .

"Reason of war" can only justify the killing of people we already have reason to think are liable to be killed.[79]

Walzer then proceeds to the discussion of noncombatant immunity and the definition of noncombatants, following which he introduces the first of several versions of the principle of double effect to be employed in interpreting the principle of discrimination or noncombatant immunity.[80] That discussion is beyond the scope of this chapter.

In the passage quoted here, Walzer manages to misrepresent the principle of military necessity as it has been understood in American, British, French, and other field manuals and scholarly texts. The definition of military necessity he quotes from Morris Greenspan's monograph on the law of war only refers to military utility.[81] It does not include the standard element found in U.S. military materials of compliance with the laws of war, for example, in the definition quoted from the Air Force's AFP 110-31 earlier.[82] It is, then, unfair and simply inaccurate to slip in reference to the German term *Kriegsraison*. *Kriegsraison* does not mean simply reason of war or military necessity in the sense of the French version, *raison de guerre*. *Kriegsraison* has a special historic meaning, namely, that military necessity is not limited by the laws of war. This interpretation has been explicitly condemned by official American, British, and French pronouncements and publications as well as by virtually all non-German publicists.[83] As the quotations from AFP 110-31 of the principles of military necessity and humanity indicate,[84] Walzer raises a false issue when he opposes "military necessity" to noncombatant immunity.

Walzer does not discuss the principle of humanity as such. Instead, it could be said that his whole approach is based on his own human-rights concept of humanity. Walzer considers that the historic concept of chivalry is dead, along with the socioeconomic structures within which it flourished, but that some lingering sense of honor may sometimes be found among professional soldiers.[85]

Walzer forcefully presents a very controversial approach to belligerent or combatant status. He brushes aside the law of war requirements outlined earlier[86] and claims that the test for combatant status should be identification with the rights of the people, particularly people attempting to throw off tyrannical rulers and foreign interveners. Walzer was part of the antiwar movement during the Vietnam War, and he clearly has Vietnam in mind when he discusses revolutionary war and counterinsurgency. His approach to the relation between revolutionary combatants and the people could be summarized in the proposition that where there is smoke there is fire. All presumptions are in favor of the proposition that revolutionary forces that achieve any significant success must be voluntarily supported by the people. He discounts arguments that the people very often may be either opposed or indifferent to the revolution but are coerced into support.[87]

While Walzer has a moral presumption for the rights of revolutionary guerrilla forces, he has a moral presumption against the entire enterprise of counterinsurgency in revolutionary wars. Since the insurgents, following Maoist revolutionary strategy, are the fish swimming in the sea of the people, they cannot be attacked without attacking the people along with the insurgents. Such attacks are inherently disproportionate and indiscriminate. Walzer concludes:

In the theory of war, as we have seen, considerations of *jus ad bellum* and *jus in bello* are logically independent, and the judgments we make in terms of one and the other are not necessarily the same. But here they come together. The war cannot be won, and it should not be won. It cannot be won, because the only available strategy involves a war against civilians; and it should not be won, because the degree of civilian support that rules out alternative strategies also makes the guerrillas the legitimate rulers of the country. The struggle against them is an unjust struggle as well as one that can only be carried on unjustly. Fought by foreigners, it is a war of aggression; if by a local regime alone, it is an act of tyranny. The position of the anti-guerrilla forces has become doubly untenable.[88]

One of Walzer's most notable contributions to the law of war is his chapter on "War against Civilians: Sieges and Blockades."[89] He evaluates the moral issues in sieges of particular places and then moves on to blockades, which, in effect, may be sieges of whole countries or even large parts of continents. Walzer's human-rights concern for noncombatant immunity obliges him to condemn such strategies. I may add that I have often wondered why there has not been greater recognition that sieges and blockades may be as much countervalue attacks on noncombatants as modern attacks with countervalue conventional, chemical, or nuclear means and strategies. Walzer concludes:

This principle [of noncombatant immunity] rules out the extended form of the naval blockade and every sort of strategic devastation, except in cases where adequate provision can be made, and is made, for noncombatants. It is not a principle that has been commonly accepted in war, at least not by the combatants. But it is consistent, I think, with other parts of the war convention, and it has gradually won acceptance, for political as much as moral reasons, with reference to a very important form of contemporary warfare.[90]

Walzer further extends this judgment to systematic destruction of crops and food supplies. At the end he raises an issue that overlaps the category of belligerent occupation and protection of civilians in war. The 1949 Geneva Convention Relative to the Protection of Civilian Persons in Time of War requires not only the feeding of civilians denied sustenance by enemy action but relief supplies of all necessities when circumstances require.[91]

I will not discuss Walzer's treatment of nuclear deterrence and defense. There is no realistic positive law of war on the subject. It challenges both the principles of proportion and discrimination to the point that Walzer seeks refuge in a doctrine of supreme emergency—which is, ironically, a version of German *Kriegsraison* that he has rejected in general.[92]

Walzer's treatment of chemical warfare is, unfortunately, very peremptory, appearing in his discussion of *jus in bello* reprisals. Walzer simply states: "The rule about poison gas is legally established, but it is not morally required."[93]

It will be recalled that the two sanctions for the law supposedly available are *jus in bello* reprisals and war-crimes proceedings.[94] Walzer holds that reprisals are not permitted except for the "lesser parts of the war convention."[95] Thus they are never permitted against noncombatants. However, as just indicated, Walzer does not consider use of poison gas to be a violation of the "war convention," but only of positive international law. Accordingly, retaliation in kind with chemical means would be morally and legally permissible. Finally, although Walzer discusses war-crimes proceedings at length, he sees the necessity to emphasize self-enforcement of the law of war through command responsibility and proper training in the military.[96]

William V. O'Brien

My work, *The Conduct of Just and Limited War*, differs from the other just war books referred to in at least two respects.[97] First, it incorporates positive international law into modern just war doctrine, not impressionistically and selectively as in the case of Walzer, but systematically. Second, the book attempts to demonstrate the relation of limited war, as discussed by Johnson,[98] to the just and legal conduct of war by chapter-long case studies of World War II, Korea, Vietnam, and the Yom Kippur War. The book also includes a chapter on the modes and channels of limitation of war. This chapter stresses the importance of planning and preparing for just and limited war by developing the strategies and capabilities that might make possible reconciliation of military necessity with moral and legal limits. It also stresses the importance of command responsibility for ensuring compliance with laws of war as well as with the *jus ad bellum* requirements of proportion and right intention.[99]

As to basic principles, I combine the principles of military necessity and humanity into the principle of legitimate military necessity. This principle authorizes the use of means that are truly necessary to the accomplishment of a legitimate military purpose, limited by the positive law of war and by the dictates of natural law. I add natural law—not "humanity"—because there are important aspects of warfare that are not adequately regulated by the law of war, notably with respect to the means of destruction. I also address the procedural aspect of decisions of military necessity and the need to acknowledge that such decisions must be subject to review within a commander's own chain of command, perhaps by supranational command structures, for example, NATO, and possibly by some kind of domestic or international tribunal. Accordingly, I define legitimate military necessity as follows:

Legitimate military necessity consists in all measures immediately indispensable and proportionate to a legitimate military end, provided that they are not prohibited by the laws of war or the natural law, when taken on the decision of a responsible commander subject to review.[100]

My treatment of the principle of chivalry is as follows:

It will be recalled that the chivalric code made major contributions to the development of the just-war *jus in bello*, notably in connection with the development of the principle of discrimination. While the subjects linked to the principle of chivalry today are not the most critical of the law of war, they are important. In particular, the relation of chivalry to recognition of enemies as honorable adversaries is important to the just conduct of war. Moreover, the emphasis on good faith enjoined by the principle of chivalry is fundamental to meeting the just-war requirement of reasonable negotiations to terminate a war once it has begun.[101]

My treatment of belligerent status rests on the positive law of war provisions of Article 1 of Hague Convention IV (1907)[102] and Article 4 of the 1949 Geneva Prisoner of War Convention. I also draw on Articles 43 and 44 of the 1977 Geneva Protocol I, which attempt to mitigate the requirements of wearing uniforms and carrying arms openly except in the attack.[103] However, these articles were subsequently objected to by the United States government, which feared that they encouraged terrorism. For this and other reasons the United States has refused to ratify the 1977 Geneva Protocol I, which it had signed.

My basic position is to extend at least some of the rights and duties of combatants to irregular forces, but as observed in my chapter on the *jus in bello* in revolutionary warfare, there are many obstacles to such a policy.[104] In my chapter on Vietnam I point to the solution of assuring prisoners taken from the revolutionary forces of minimal protection without recognizing them as bona fide prisoners of war. Such ad hoc arrangements have been possible with the cooperation of the International Committee of the Red Cross.[105]

The principal subjects discussed regarding weapons and means of warfare are as follows:

1. Strategic countervalue aerial bombardment
2. Tactical use of firepower
3. Weapons causing superfluous suffering
4. Chemical warfare
5. Crop destruction and starvation strategies

I condemn the U.S.-British strategic countervalue bombing of World War II:

> Taken together, standard area bombing and fire bombing constituted a major, if not the major, part of U.S. and British strategic bombing. They were, and were intended to be, a salient, characteristic component of the total war effort against Germany and Japan. Their violation of the basic *jus in bello* principles of proportion and discrimination was, therefore, sufficiently significant to jeopardize the claim of the Western Allies to be conducting a just war.[106]

Although there may well have been violations of proportion and discrimination in U.S. air attacks on North Korea, I am aware of nothing comparable to the "city busting" of World War II. As to bombing of North Vietnam, I have a decidedly different view from that held by antiwar critics and the media. My view is that most of the strategic bombing attacks against North Vietnam were on legitimate military targets. They were intended to be and largely were counterforce rather than countervalue. Their proportionality would have to be judged in the light not only of the objective of interdicting the flow of men, weapons, and materiel to the South, of destroying the military infrastructure, but also of compelling the North Vietnamese government to discontinue the war in the South. I point out that evaluation of the proportionality of the bombing of North Vietnam is complicated by the fact that in the end it was not successful in its purposes. Of course, one response from the hawks would be that the bombing was too controlled, proportionate, and discriminate, as well as too graduated; a disproportionate, indiscriminate aerial blitz might have knocked North Vietnam out of the war. I find the bombing proportionate as well as discriminate, particularly in contrast to that of World War II.

At this point the issue of overall moral evaluation of a war arises. Must a war be just in all the categories of *jus ad bellum* and *jus in bello*? My sense is that, notwithstanding regret over the excesses of strategic bombing, World War II is widely judged to be a just war. On the other hand, notwithstanding the significant improvement in attempts to respect proportionality and discrimination in the strategic air war in Vietnam, the bombing of the North is widely condemned as part of "our illegal and immoral war in Vietnam." Apparently, perception of just cause influences judgments about war conduct. It may also make a difference in whether you win or lose.[107]

A much better case can be made that, generally speaking, tactical use of firepower in Vietnam almost routinely violated the principle of proportion and frequently violated the principle of discrimination. The latter judgment is mitigated somewhat by the recognition that the enemy's systematic involvement of civilians and civilian population centers in the fighting (which Walzer admiringly commends)[108] made collateral damage inevitable.[109] This remains a major issue in virtually all modern wars because of the great increases in firepower and mobility. The answer is not in some ingenious new law of war rules but in encouragement of strategies and tactics emphasizing counterforce operations and in much more effective control of the use of firepower.

A number of charges were raised in the Vietnam War about weapons that allegedly caused superfluous suffering, for example, the bullets from the M-16 rifle. Clearly the most important charge was that napalm was such a means; indeed, it became a symbol for those condemning the war. My analysis was confined to the experience of international law. A means causes "superfluous suffering" when an international consensus says it does. In the past this has usually happened when a weapon was considered of low military utility.[110] Napalm was used extensively in World War II and Korea. It is in the arsenals of virtually all military powers. Efforts to ban it by convention in the 1970s failed. All that could be agreed to was the 1980 Geneva Weapons Convention, which provides that the direct, intentional use of napalm against civilians is illegal.[111] I do not find any just war concepts to deal with this subject other than proportion and discrimination, and napalm is not inherently a disproportionate and indiscriminate weapon.[112]

I disagree with both Ramsey and Walzer on the use of nonlethal incapacitating gases and other chemical means. I believe that a strong rule of customary international law had been developed by the time of the Vietnam War banning the use of chemical warfare. It was important to maintain the threshold against such warfare. The United States was wrong to break the chemical warfare threshold even though the non-lethal chemical means employed in themselves could certainly be used proportionally and discriminately. American abstention from the use of chemical means in Vietnam would not have influenced the Soviets, Iraqis, or others who have since employed chemical warfare, but the United States might now be in a stronger position to lead the struggle against proliferation and use of chemical means had it not used them in Vietnam.[113]

Crop destruction and starvation as a means of war raise difficult issues. First, as a matter of practice they have been employed by belligerents from earliest times. Second, crop destruction may now be effected by herbicides, which may be assimilated into chemical warfare. The United States specifically reserved the right to use herbicides when it finally ratified the 1925 Geneva Gas Protocol after the Vietnam War.[114] Article 14 of 1977 Geneva Protocol I now prohibits "starvation of civilians as a method of combat."[115] I was unable to reach a clear judgment: "Whether this attempt will be successful in light of the possible costs in terms of losses from alternative means and strategies remains to be seen."[116]

My treatment of the categories of prisoners of war, treatment of the wounded and sick, belligerent occupation and treatment of civilians, and communications among belligerents follows largely the guidelines of the positive law of war and does not represent much dependence on theoretical just war thinking. On the contrary, I take it that just war *jus in bello* has little to say beyond laying down the principles of proportion and discrimination, with perhaps a contribution here and there. The great bulk of the law of war has been hammered out by diplomats, lawyers, and soldiers with very little input that I can detect from modern just war doctrine. This is why I incorporate so much of the positive law of war into my just war framework.

Finally, on the subject of sanctions for the law of war, I reject both reprisals and war crimes as realistic remedies for the victim of violation of the law. Reprisals have failed in their supposed function of supporting the law and have often eroded it. By now a law-abiding belligerent cannot take reprisals against prisoners of war or civilians. There is little left except, as Walzer suggests, using some otherwise illegal weapon or means. Of course, I disagree with him that chemical warfare is such a means.[117]

Just war-crimes proceedings require just victors. Modern wars have often produced no victors and some unjust victors. The only judicial remedy I see for war crimes is self-imposed, as in the experiences of the cases—much more numerous than generally realized—of the U.S. military court-martials for actions that would be considered war crimes in Vietnam.[118]

There is little or no prospect of reciprocal respect for the law of war by prospective enemies. The just must observe the law because it is the right thing to do. It may also turn out to be the prudent thing to do. Certainly one does not win wars by specializing in war crimes.

The Catholic Church and the Law of War

The modern Catholic church has been a great supporter of international law, as well as international organization. Most of this support has been directed to development of machinery for pacific settlement of disputes and to the *jus ad bellum* of the League of Nations and the United Nations. The latter has greatly influenced Catholic teaching. In Father John Courtney Murray's 1959 just war analysis of the strategic situation, he emphasized Pope Pius XII's support for the United Nations Charter. Accordingly, in consonance with UN war-decision law, older warrants for offensive just war were eliminated, leaving only self-defense.[119] Murray's discussion of *jus ad bellum* proportionality deserves mention, since that proportionality should inform all decisions about *jus in bello* proportionality. He asserts:

Pius XII laid some stress on the fact that the comparison here must be between realities of the moral order, and not sheerly between two sets of material damage and loss. The standard is not a "eudaemonism and utilitarianism of materialist origin," which would avoid war merely because it is uncomfortable, or connive at injustice simply because its repression would be costly.[120]

As to weapons and means of war, I will not discuss nuclear weapons. The issues of Hiroshima and Nagasaki and of modern nuclear deterrence and defense are an immense and complex study beyond the scope of this chapter. Pope Pius XII and other high church officials have condemned chemical and biological warfare but in sweeping terms, lumping them with atomic weapons as weapons of mass destruction that escape control.[121]

Not surprisingly, papal, conciliar, and episcopal pronouncements have been addressed mainly to the nuclear dilemmas and pleas for arms control and disarmament. For example, the much-discussed 1983 pastoral letter, *The Challenge of Peace*, of the American Catholic Bishops says nothing about the law of war.[122] Yet I would assume that the National Conference of Catholic Bishops would strongly support any law of war convention under consideration for U.S. adhesion.

There is, however, one specific encouraging mention of the law of war in Vatican II's *Gaudium et Spes*, the Pastoral Constitution on the Church in the Modern World:

On the subject of war, quite a large number of nations have subscribed to various international agreements aimed at making military activity and its consequences less inhuman. Such are conventions concerning the handling of wounded or captured soldiers, and various similar agreements. Agreements of this sort must be honored. Indeed they should be improved upon so that they can better and more workably lead to restraining the frightfulness of war.

All men, especially government officials and experts in these matters, are bound to do everything they can to effect these improvements. Moreover, it seems right that laws make humane provisions for the case of those who for reasons of conscience refuse to bear arms, provided however, that they accept some other form of service to the human community.[123]

I will conclude by repeating that while nuclear dilemmas are naturally paramount in the minds of modern just war thinkers and authoritative Catholic spokesmen, the law of war as it pertains to conventional and, particularly, revolutionary war and counterinsurgency is the law that is being challenged constantly in the many armed conflicts being waged. The law governing these conflicts deserves more attention from modern just war doctrine.

NOTES

1. Heinrich A. Rommen, *The State in Catholic Thought* (St. Louis: Herder, 1945), 1–29, 153–83.

2. Ibid.; J. L. Brierly, *Law of Nations*, ed. Sir Humphrey Waldcock, 5th ed. (Oxford: Oxford University Press, 1963), 16–20.

3. James Turner Johnson, *Ideology, Reason, and the Limitation of War* (Princeton: Princeton University Press, 1975), 25, 27–33, 75. See Johnson's chart, app. 1.

4. See Ibid., 195–203.

5. Ibid., chap. 4.

6. James Turner Johnson, *Just War Tradition and the Restraint of War* (Princeton: Princeton University Press, 1981), 184–87; Geoffrey Best, *Humanity in Warfare* (New York: Columbia University Press, 1980), 59–62.

7. Martin J. Clancy, "Rules of Land Warfare during the War of the American Revolution," *World Polity* 2 (1960): 203–317.

8. Best, *Humanity in Warfare*, 141–43, 157–66.

9. For example, August Heffter states: "Civilized nations admit war as . . . an inevitable evil, which should not surpass the limits of strict necessity. . . . Reason and humanity, as the self-interest of nations, has consecrated this fundamental rule: 'Do not cause more harm to your enemy during war than the necessity of bringing him back to reason requires'. The ancient maxim of war on the contrary wished that one did all the harm possible that one could to the enemy and that one judged desirable" (my translations). August Wilhelm Heffter, *Le Droit international de l'Europe*, trans. Jules Bergson, 3d French rev. ed. (Berlin: Schroeder Librairie, 1973), 227. Heffter held that one need not observe the laws of war in fighting savages who do not observe any "human" law, ibid.

Robert Phillimore goes beyond "civilized" to "Christian." He says, "It would be disgraceful to Christian Governments if they assented to the doctrine that in War the furies are to be let loose, and each party is to do that which seems good in his own eyes." Sir Robert Joseph Phillimore, *Commentaries upon International Law*, 4 vols., 3d ed. (London: Butterworth, 1879–86), 3:79.

10. Best, *Humanity in Warfare*, 141–43, 148–57.

11. Ibid., 160–66.

12. See generally Alfred Vanderpol, *La Doctrine scolastique du droit de guerre* (Paris: Pedone, 1919); John Eppstein, *The Catholic Tradition of the Law of Nations* (Washington, D.C.: Carnegie Endowment for International Peace and The Catholic Association for International Peace, 1935), chaps. 4 and 5.

13. Johnson, *Ideology, Reason, and the Limitation of War*, 27–30.

14. Ibid., chap. 1.

15. St. Thomas relies on quotations from St. Augustine; see note 17. See also Johnson, *Ideology, Reason, and the Limitation of War*, 40.

16. Paul Ramsey, *War and the Christian Conscience: How Shall Modern War Be Conducted Justly?* (Durham, N.C.: Duke University Press, 1961); idem, *The Just War: Force and Political Responsibility* (New York: Charles Scribner's Sons, 1968). See Johnson's critique in *Just War Tradition and the Restraint of War*, 347–57. For different views challenging Ramsey's interpretation of St. Augustine, see Charles E. Curran, *Politics, Medicine, and Christian Ethics: A Dialogue with Paul Ramsey* (Philadelphia, Pa.: Fortress Press, 1973); Richard Shelly Hartigan, "St. Augustine on War and Killings: The Problem of the Innocent," *Journal of the History of Ideas* 27 (1966): 195–204; William V. O'Brien, "Morality and War: The Contributions of Paul Ramsey," in *Love and Society: Essays in the Ethics of Paul Ramsey*, ed. James Johnson and David Smith (Missoula, Mont.: Scholars Press, 1974), 163–84.

17. St. Thomas's third *jus ad bellum* condition, following competent authority and just cause, is right intention:

Thirdly, there is required a right intention on the part of the belligerents: either of achieving some good object or of avoiding some evil. So St. Augustine says in the book *De Verbis Domini*: "For the true followers of God even wars are peaceful, not being made for greed or out of cruelty, but from desire of peace, to restrain the evil and assist the good." So it can happen that even when war is declared by legitimate authority and there is just cause, it is nevertheless made unjust through evil intention. St. Augustine says in *Contra Faustum* (*LXXIV*): "The desire to hurt, the cruelty of vendetta, the stern and implacable spirit, arrogance in victory, the thirst for power, and all that is similar, all these are justly condemned in war."

St. Thomas Aquinas, *Summa Theologica, secunda secundae*, no. 15, Question 40, art. 1, in *Aquinas: Selected Political Writings*, ed. A. P. D'Entrèves, trans. J. G. Dawson (Oxford: Blackwell, 1948), 159–61. See Vanderpol, *Doctrine scolastique du droit de guerre*, 85–88; Johnson, *Ideology, Reason, and the Limitation of War*, 40–43.

18. Johnson, *Ideology, Reason, and the Limitation of War*, chap. 1.

19. For example, Grotius cites the authority of Victoria extensively on issues of direct intentional killing, exemption of religious from attack, treatment of prisoners, hostages, destruction of property, and captured property. Hugo Grotius, *De Jure Belli et Pacis Libri Tres*, trans. by Francis W. Kelsey (Oxford: Clarendon Press, 1925), bk. 1 chaps. 12–14, pp. 722–69.

20. U.S. Department of the Air Force, *International Law: The Conduct of Armed Conflict and Air Operations, 19 November 1976*, Air Force Pamphlet AFP 110-31 (Washington, D.C.: Headquarters of the Air Force, 1976).

21. U.S. Department of the Army, *The Law of Land Warfare, July 1956*, FM 27–10 (Washington, D.C.: Department of the Army, 1956).

22. U.S. Air Force, *International Law*, chapter 1, 5–6.

23. Ibid., chapter 1, 6.

24. Ibid.

25. See Suarez's response to the questions, "Quelle est la manière convenable de faire la guerre?" Francisco Suarez, *De Bello* 7, reproduced in translation in Vanderpol, *La Doctrine scolastique du droit de guerre*, 397–412. See Vanderpol's criticism of this change, ibid., 253–54.

26. My translation from Suarez, *De Bello* 7, quoted in Vanderpol, *La Doctrine scolastique du droit de guerre*, 410.

27. Hague Convention IV Respecting the Laws and Customs of War on Land, 18 October 1907, 35 Stat. 2277; Treaty Series no. 539; Malloy Treaties, vol 2: 2269.

28. My translation from Vanderpol, *La Doctrine scolastique du droit de guerre*, 335, Victoria's *De Jure Belli, Fourth Principal Question*.

29. My translation from Vanderpol, *La Doctrine scolastique du droit de guerre*, 399–400, Suarez's *De Bello* 7.

30. My translation from "In war, is it permitted to lay ambushes?" St. Thomas Aquinas, *Summa Theologica, secunda secundae*, q. 40, art. 3, quoted in Vanderpol, *La Doctrine scolastique du droit de guerre*, 317–18.

31. Johnson, *Ideology, Reason, and the Limitation of War*, 196.

32. Ibid.

33. My translation from Suarez, *De Bello* 7, question 2, quoted in Vanderpol, *La Doctrine scolastique du droit de guerre*, 402–3, original emphasis; see Johnson, *Ideology, Reason, and the Limitation of War*, 197.

34. Hague Convention IV (1907), cited in note 27.

35. Johnson, *Ideology, Reason, and the Limitation of War*, 197.

36. William V. O'Brien, *Nuclear War, Deterrence, and Morality* (Westminster, Md.: Newman, 1967), 30–31.

37. See Stephen E. Lammers, "Approaches to Limits on War in Western Just War Tradition," and Robert L. Phillips, "Combatancy, Noncombatancy, and Noncombatant Immunity in Just War Theory," in *Cross, Crescent, and Sword: The Justification and Limitation of War in Western and Islamic Tradition*, ed. James Turner Johnson and John Kelsay (Westport, Conn.: Greenwood Press, 1990).

38. G.I.A.D. Draper, "The Interaction of Christianity and Chivalry in the Historical Development of the Law of the War," *International Review of the Red Cross* 5 (1965): 18–19.

39. Grotius, *De Jure Belli ac Pacis*, bk. 3, chap. 4, nos. 15–17, pp. 651–53. Grotius cites no classic war writers. The use of poison and poisoned weapons is prohibited by Article 23(*a*) of 1907 Hague Convention IV and is considered to be declaratory of long-standing customary international law.

40. Hague Convention IV (1907), cited in note 27.

41. My translation from Victoria, *De Jure Belli*, pt. 3, quoted in Vanderpol, *La Doctrine scolastique du droit de querre*, 349. See Johnson, *Ideology, Reason, and the Limitation of War*, 200–201.

42. Hague Convention IV (1907), cited in note 27.

43. My translation from Victoria, *De Jure Belli*, pt. 3, 7th question, quoted in Vanderpol, *La Doctrine scolastique du droit de guerre*, 355–56.

44. See Hague Convention IV (1907), cited in note 27, Articles 4–20; 23(*c*) and (*d*); Geneva Convention Relative to the Treatment of Prisoners of War (1949), 6UST 3516, T.I.A.S. 3365; 75 UNTS 287.

45. My translation from Victoria, *De Jure Belli*, pt. 3, 6th question, quoted in Vanderpol, *La Doctrine scolastique du droit de guerre*, 353–54. Emphasis added.

46. See Best, *Humanity in Warfare*, 141–43, 157–66.

47. See Victoria as cited in note 41 and quotation in accompanying text.

48. My translation of Victoria, *De Jure Belli*, pt. 3, 7th question, quoted in Vanderpol, *La Doctrine scolastique du droit de guerre*, 354–56.

49. My translation of Victoria, *De Jure Belli*, pt. 3, 4th question, quoted in Vanderpol, *La Doctrine scolastique du droit de guerre*, 351.

50. See Suarez's statement quoted in the section on "Combatant and Non-combatant Status."

51. See St. Thomas Aquinas's discussion cited in note 30.

52. See U.S. Army, *Law of Land Warfare*, chap. 8, pp. 176–83.

53. See note 37.

54. See the several versions of Father Murray's principal contribution: "Theology and Modern War," *Theological Studies* 20 (1959): 40–61; *Morality and Modern War* (New York: Church Peace Union, 1959); *We Hold These Truths* (New York: Sheed and Ward, 1960), 249–73.

55. Paul Ramsey, "How Shall Counterinsurgency Warfare Be Conducted Justly?" in *Just War*, 430–31; emphasis in original.

56. Ibid., 432–40.

57. Ibid., 440–46.

58. Paul Ramsey, "The Just Revolution," *Worldview* 16, no. 10 (October 1973): 37; emphasis in original.

59. Ramsey; "Incapacitating Gases," in *The Just War*, 477.

60. Ibid., 477–78.

61. Johnson, *Just War Tradition and the Restraint of War*, 86–94.

62. Ibid., 219–24.

63. Ibid., chaps. 7 and 9.

64. Ibid., 11, 23, 41–44, 82–84.

65. Ibid., 61–69.

66. Ibid., 87.

67. Ibid., 219–20.

68. Ibid., 220–24.

69. See ibid., chap. 9.

70. Ibid., 43–44; see also 82–84.

71. Ibid., 61, 147.

72. E.g., ibid., chap. 3.

73. Michael Walzer, *Just and Unjust Wars* (New York: Basic Books, 1977), xvi.

74. Ibid., xii–xiii.

75. Ibid., xiii.

76. See my discussion in the summary of my own work, later in this chapter (immediately following note number 97).

77. See the section on "Modern Just War Doctrine and the Law of War," especially the subsection on Ramsey.

78. Walzer, *Just and Unjust Wars*, xvi.

79. Ibid., 144.

80. Ibid., 145–59.

81. Walzer quotes M. Greenspan, *The Modern Law of Land Warfare* (Berkeley: University of California Press, 1959), 313–14.

82. See the section on "Basic Principles of the Law of War."

83. William V. O'Brien, "The Meaning of 'Military Necessity' in International Law," *World Polity* 1 (1957): 109–76.

84. See the section on "Basic Principles of the Law of War."

85. Walzer, *Just and Unjust Wars*, 16, 34, 37, 45.

86. Ibid., 182–96.

87. Ibid., 184–85.

88. Ibid., 195–96.

89. Ibid., chap. 10.

90. Ibid., 174–75.

91. Geneva Convention Relative to the Protection of Civilian Persons in Time of War (1949), 6UST 3516; T.I.A.S. 3365; 75 UNTS 287.

92. See Walzer, *Just and Unjust Wars*, chap. 16, "Supreme Emergency," and chap. 17, "Nuclear Deterrence."

93. Ibid., 215.

94. See the section on "Sanctions" and note 52.

95. Walzer, *Just and Unjust Wars*, 215.

96. Ibid., chap. 19.

97. William V. O'Brien, *The Conduct of Just and Limited War* (New York: Praeger, 1981).

98. See Johnson, *Just War Tradition and the Restraint of War*, chap. 7.

99. O'Brien, *Conduct of Just and Limited War*, chap. 13, "Modes and Channels for the Limitation of War."

100. Ibid., 66. This is my definition of military necessity based on "Meaning of 'Military Necessity' in International Law" and developed further in "Legitimate Military Necessity in Nuclear War," *World Polity* 2 (1960): 35–120.

101. O'Brien, *Conduct of Just and Limited War*, 66.

102. See the section on "Combatant and Noncombatant Status."

103. O'Brien, *Conduct of Just and Limited War*, 184–89.

104. Ibid.

105. Ibid., 110–14.

106. Ibid., 83.

107. Ibid., 119–26.

108. Walzer, *Just and Unjust Wars*, 179–82.

109. O'Brien, *Conduct of Just and Limited War*, 98–104.

110. Ibid., 59.

111. Geneva Convention on Prohibitions of Restrictions on the Use of Certain Conventional Weapons Which May Be Deemed to Be Excessively Injurious or to Have Indiscriminate Effects (October 10, 1980). *International Legal Materials* 19(1980):1523–36. (Treaty not yet ratified by U.S.)

112. O'Brien, *Conduct of Just and Limited War*, 104–5.

113. Ibid., 59–60, 105–10.

114. Gerald F. Ford, "Renunciation of Certain Uses in War of Chemical Herbicides and Riot Control Agents," *Federal Register* 40 (April 10, 1975): 16187. See U.S. Air Force, *International Law*, 6–10.

115. O'Brien, *Conduct of Just and Limited War*, 197–98.

116. Ibid., 198.

117. Ibid., 67–70.

118. See Guenter Lewy, *America in Vietnam* (New York: Oxford University Press, 1978), chap. 10.

119. Murray, *We Hold These Truths*, 256–60.

120. Ibid., 261.

121. Pope Pius XII, "The Threat of ABC Warfare," Address to the Peoples Assembled in St. Peter's Square, April 18, 1954, quoted in translation in *Pattern for Peace*, ed. Harry W. Flannery (Westminster, Md.: Newman Press, 1962), 234–35.

122. National Conference of Catholic Bishops, *The Challenge of Peace: God's Promise and Our Response: A Pastoral Letter on War and Peace* (Washington, D.C.: United States Catholic Conference, 1983).

123. William M. Abbott, ed., *The Documents of Vatican II* (New York: Guild Press/America Press/Association Press, 1966), no. 79, p. 292.

8

War and Peace in the Islamic Tradition and International Law

Ann Elizabeth Mayer

INTRODUCTION

Historical Background

The Islamic tradition on questions of war and peace bears a different historical relationship to international law than does the Western one, a factor that may account for the dissimilar orientations of persons writing on war and peace in these two traditions. In this regard it should be recalled that the West today deals with international law as a familiar and integral component of Western civilization that has evolved pari passu with Western culture and religion over centuries. In contrast, the Islamic doctrines on war and peace have been part of a juristic culture that has remained closer to its premodern roots.

Although Islam is a younger religion than Christianity, its tradition on war and peace coalesced earlier than the Christian one did. The sources of the tradition were rules in the Qur'an, which dates from the seventh century C.E., and the example of the Prophet Muhammad (d. 632 C.E.) in matters involving warfare and the conduct of statecraft. The Islamic law on war and peace was elaborated by jurists during the centuries after the Prophet's death. Thus as early as the eight century C.E. one has the important treatise by the Sunni jurist Muhammad al-Shaybani (d. 805 C.E.), *Al-Siyar al-kabir*. On the Twelver Shi'i side, the law on war was largely established at the time of the influential treatise *Al-Nihaya* by Abu Ja'far al-Tusi (d. 1067 C.E.).[1]

The Islamic jurists did not treat the conduct of actual states as a source of law except in the rare cases of governments that were headed by exemplary rulers, like the rightly guided caliphs of the Sunnis and the *imams* of different Shi'i groups. Instead of examining the actual conduct of governments, succeeding generations of Islamic jurists tended to perpetuate the ideas that had been set forth by their predecessors in the first centuries of Islam without bothering to take into account altered political circumstances. In consequence, the Islamic tradition on war and peace issues became seriously estranged from the rules embodied in the actual conduct of states. For example, jurists continued to speak of a world divided into a *dar al-islam* and a *dar al-harb* long after these categories had become anachronistic.

Premodern Islamic law contemplated that the Muslim community would conduct ongoing *jihad* against the infidels to bring them all within the Islamic fold. Thus only temporary truces, not permanent peace treaties, were permissible with the so-called "abode of war." In contrast, governments of Muslim states centuries ago had to begin to adjust their ambitions and practice to the realities of their declining prowess and to enter into permanent peace treaties with European governments. Following the rules on war and peace of Islamic international law, which presupposed a continued pattern of Islamic military expansion at the expense of non-Muslim countries, proved impossible in a situation in which Muslims routinely had to deal with their foes from a position of vulnerability and weakness. The practical abandonment by governments of much of the premodern tradition became particularly striking from the seventeenth century C.E. onward, as the relative military and economic strength of Muslim countries began to decline sharply vis-à-vis European might.

The 1606 Treaty of Zsitvatorok contracted between the holy Roman emperor and the Ottoman sultan, long the most formidable Muslim ruler, may be seen as one turning point. The Ottoman sultan did not allow religious scruples to stand in the way of acceding to a permanent peace with the Christian emperor, a peace that was contracted by the two rulers on a footing of full equality. Later, by signing the 1856 Paris Peace Treaty, the sultan joined the Concert of Europe, thereby effectively submitting to the European scheme of international relations.

The Muslim world was largely subjugated to Europe during the age of imperialism. After freeing themselves of European domination, Muslim countries did not revert to using the premodern rules on war and peace. Instead, governments in the Muslim world recognized the authority of public international law. This is manifested, among other things, in the fact that all have chosen to join the United Nations. The United Nations Charter calls in Article 1 for the settlement of international disputes in conformity with justice and international law. The UN stress on international law is reinforced by the preamble to the Charter of the Organization of the Islamic Conference, the international organization that all Muslim countries have chosen to join, which reaffirms their commitment to the UN Charter, "the purposes and principles of which provide the basis for fruitful cooperation amongst all people." Within the framework of the Islamic Conference, it would have been possible for Muslim countries to choose to regulate their relations by a special law like Islamic law, just as, for example, European Community countries have set up a special law to regulate their relations. That Muslim countries have elected to follow international law and the UN Charter in their mutual relations indicates that the choice was not forced on them by a need to accommodate non-Muslim countries but represented their actual preference. Indeed, Muslim countries do not just utilize public international law as the law governing the relations between states; with the assistance of distinguished Muslim jurists, they have also contributed to its development.

The Contemporary Status of the Islamic Tradition on War and Peace

Although state practice has relegated much premodern doctrine on war and peace to a condition of desuetude, the Islamic tradition in this area is not so much dead as undergoing a process of adjustment. The hold of certain aspects of the premodern juristic tradition on war and peace may now be weakening, but its concepts have by no means ceased to influence Muslims' perspectives. Much work is being done to revise and update the tradition and to narrow the gulf between Islamic theory and contemporary state practice. In recent decades Muslims have produced a sizeable literature on war and peace that is designed to offer new doctrines that are more in accord with political realities and more congruent with the standards of international law than certain of the rules of the premodern *shari'a*. So far, none of the many attempts to reformulate the Islamic law of war and peace seems to have won general recognition by Muslims as the definitive statement of where Islamic doctrine now stands.

It should be noted that the Islamic tradition today seems most alive in the area of the *jus ad bellum*. *Jus in bello* issues do not seem to be attracting comparable attention among Muslims concerned with the application of their tradition to contemporary problems.[2] The deemphasis on *jus in bello* in the contemporary literature by Muslims contrasts with the orientation of the premodern jurists, who were very interested in elaborating rules for the treatment of the non-Muslims who were vanquished or captured in the *jihad*.[3] These rules were formulated in an era of continued Islamic conquests at the expense of non-Muslims. From the jurists' perspective, non-Muslims had no right to resist Islamic military expansion, and the rules for treating the conquered peoples reflect the jurists' premise that in refusing to submit to Islam, they were doing a wrong that justified harsh treatment.[4] Some of the premodern juristic rules affecting the *jus in bello* would, if applied, violate international rules for the treatment of combatants and noncombatants under various Geneva conventions and protocols and UN General Assembly resolutions.[5]

In practice, the premodern *shari'a* rules pertaining to the conduct of war are in abeyance. Muslims today seem to concur that modern norms of "humane treatment" should be accorded to both combatants and noncombatants. In the absence of updated versions of the premodern *shari'a* rules regulating the conduct of war, the international legal standards have become the operative norms.

It is in the area of the *jus ad bellum* that references are still made to the *shari'a*, but contemporary Muslims' opinions differ on so many points that one can no longer ascertain "a single, recognizable cultural consensus on the justification and limitation of violence," that is to say, a "tradition" of thinking about resort to war.[6] Despite the diversity in opinion, one can see that a convergence of ideas and political circumstances is encouraging certain modifications in the Islamic tradition that reflect the outlooks and experiences of contemporary Muslim societies. These modifications comprise significant trends that will now be considered.

One trend is to establish a justification for Muslim adherence to public international law. This entails providing theoretical rationales for using international law and demonstrations of the essential compatibility of international law and the *shari'a*. Another trend is that of abandoning the *shari'a* scheme of division of the world into a *dar al-islam* and a *dar al-harb* and recognizing the legitimacy of the modern nation-state. Most important, features of the traditional *jihad* are being reconsidered in the light of recent developments in international law and new concepts of just war. This involves defining where Islam stands vis-à-vis national liberation struggles, reflecting the context in which the Islamic tradition is presently evolving and to which it has become increasingly responsive.

Muslim Perspectives on the Relationship of Islamic Law and Public International Law

Since the end of World War II and the founding of the United Nations, public international law has become a universal law formulated with the participation of the countries of the world. Public international law has been largely purged of features that used to reflect its Christian/European origins. Notwithstanding the internationalization and religious neutrality of international law today, special obstacles remain in the way of fully integrating international law into the Islamic tradition.

Accepting the authority of international law means superseding Islamic international law, which has its own specific rules on questions of war and peace, but doing this offends the theory of the supremacy of Islamic law. The theory of Islamic law does not admit that any laws of human origin may override Islamic rules, which are considered to be divinely mandated. Furthermore, the origins of international law in Europe mean that for at least some Muslims, acknowledging its authority is perceived as entailing a victory for Western culture at the expense of Islamic culture. Regardless of whether public international law should be associated with Christianity, as opposed to Western culture generally, Muslims may associate international law with the Christian religion, which can exacerbate concerns about the appropriateness of its use.

The large volume of writing that has recently been produced by Islamic scholars and Muslim law professors on the relationship of Islamic law and international law indicates that the difficulties created by the reception of international law are of considerable interest.[7] Unfortunately, the existing literature does not always treat problematic issues in an objective and coherent fashion or adequately analyze methodological questions.[8]

Among Muslims who do attempt to offer rationales for following international law, the most common approach is to maintain that international law either definitely or presumptively derives from Islamic law.[9] If international law derives from Islamic law, employing it should violate no Islamic religious precept. However, the weight of evidence from history and prevailing scholarly opinion supports the conclusion that international law derives from European thought, although it remains possible that evidence proving Islamic influences may yet be uncovered. This chapter does not propose to deal with this question, which will be resolved, if at all, only by extensive legal historical research in medieval sources. Regardless of the strength of its scholarly underpinnings, the theory that international law derives from Islam can function like a benign fiction that facilitates the reception of international law in the Muslim world. The consequences for scholarship may be less positive. Having accepted this fiction, Muslims may be disinclined to examine critically points of difference and the reasons why the Western and Islamic traditions differ.

Not all Muslims are prepared to reach an accommodation with public international law. One finds Muslims who continue to adhere to the shari'a in its premodern juristic formulations and refuse to acknowledge the legitimacy of any non-Islamic legal system. These include members of some of the radical, fundamentalist groups in the Muslim world, aspects of whose views will be treated subsequently.

In the absence of any settled theory authorizing Muslims to resort to international law, the reliance by the educated classes and governmental elites on international law seems to imply that the two are presumed to coexist as complementary systems. However, there is evidence of some concern for the need to resolve the conflicts that might result from the duty to abide by the *shari'a* and the obligations that are imposed under international law. The potential tensions between these two legal systems have been deemed sufficiently serious by the Organization of the Islamic Conference to warrant its expressing an interest in setting up an international court that would reconcile *shari'a* and public international law.[10] The existence of this project amounts to an acknowledgment that governments of Muslim countries recognize that the two traditions are distinct, that their relationship is problematic, and that the possibility of conflicts is real enough to justify such formal institutional mediation.

The problems of reconciling the two traditions do not come up in those areas where the Islamic tradition is underdeveloped or where it has gaps. It should be stressed that the premodern *shari'a* rules cover far less ground than do their international counterparts. Since the *shari'a* rules on war and peace were formulated at such an early stage of Islamic history, when warfare and statecraft did not involve the same problems that we face in the twentieth century c.e., the failure to address all the topics that are treated in modern international law is hardly surprising. Islamic doctrines could potentially be expanded to cover these areas, but at the moment they provide scant guidance for a person seeking to understand precisely where the Islamic tradition stands on subjects such as economic aggression, armed reprisals, state-sponsored terrorism, belligerent occupation, collective self-defense, collective punishment, multilateral peacekeeping forces, disarmament schemes, war-crimes tribunals, and the use of modern weaponry like nuclear and chemical weapons. Premodern Islamic doctrine also does not contemplate a role for an international organization like the United Nations or even an organization of Muslim countries like the Organization of the Islamic Conference.

In other areas specific Islamic rules or general principles taken from the Islamic tradition prove to be ones that readily harmonize with and accommodate modern international norms. One example is the principle *pacta sunt servanda*, a fundamental tenet of Islamic as well as of international law.

ISLAMIC LAW REGARDING INTERNATIONAL TREATIES

International agreements are a central feature of public international law regarding war and peace. It is therefore relevant to consider how Islamic law might affect international agreements.

Where Muslims are concerned, their religious law gives them every incentive to honor contracts that they have entered into. Generally speaking, in Islamic law, abiding by a valid contract is deemed to be both a religious and a legal obligation.[11] The fact that one party is a non-Muslim should not diminish the responsibility of the Muslim party to live up to valid contractual commitments.

The question remains: are modern international agreements valid under Islamic law? Premodern Islamic law did not deal specifically with the kinds of international peace treaties that the modern international system relies on. It did allow Muslim rulers to make certain temporary truces or agreements establishing tributary relations with non-Muslims. In consequence, there may be some uncertainty about the binding force of some treaties, such as ones that would permanently fetter Muslims' ability to conduct a *jihad*.[12]

Ayatollah Khomeini had said that he opposed treaties that contradict Islamic law.[13] This does suggest that he believed that at least some international treaties may violate Islamic law. One also finds Sheikh Mahmud Shaltut, a former rector of al-Azhar, asserting that when the harm to Muslims caused by a treaty exceeds the advantages it offers Muslims, Muslims are free to denounce it.[14] One sees occasional evidence of a belief that Muslims are not bound by treaties with non-Muslims. Such an attitude was evinced by Sadat's assassins, whose ideas will be treated in a later section.

Therefore, while Islamic law on contracts is basically in harmony with the international principle *pacta sunt servanda*, a principle that, it has been suggested, could be one that international law took from the Islamic tradition,[15] challenges to treaties between Muslim and non-Muslim countries could, at least hypothetically, result from the application of Islamic law.

One of the most interesting tests of how a state officially professing adherence to Islamic law has treated its obligations under international law lies in the attempts by the Islamic Republic of Iran to justify its conduct in the seizure of the American embassy in Tehran in 1979 that led to American diplomats being held hostage. Although not a hot-war situation, the hostage crisis was certainly a major international conflict, one that, if not settled, could have led to military actions beyond the scope of the unsuccessful American rescue mission of April 1980. It is relevant as an illustration of what law a contemporary government of a Muslim country follows or treats as the binding norm when hostilities seem imminent.

Iran refused to appear at the International Court of Justice (ICJ) to defend its actions, which were in flagrant violation of the Vienna Convention on Diplomatic Immunity. Instead, two communications sent by the Iranian foreign minister were Iran's only direct communications to the ICJ about Iran's position.[16] At a time when Islamic fervor in Iran was intense and a policy of applying Islamic law was being vigorously pursued by the Khomeini regime, Iran's foreign minister did not invoke *shari'a* criteria but couched Iran's defense in terms of international law. It is especially noteworthy that no argument was offered to the ICJ by the foreign minister to the effect that Iran's following Islamic law excused it from abiding by its obligations under international law or allowed it to violate a treaty with non-Muslims. Indeed, the foreign minister condemned the United States for breaching its obligations under international law in its pattern of interfering in Iranian politics, exploitation of Iran, and crimes against the Iranian people. Iran's defense did not challenge the applicability of international law but instead pled that there were special facts that bore on the case, such as the complicated prior history of American interference in Iranian internal affairs and the revolutionary situation in the country, that justified its refusal to submit this particular case to a ruling by the ICJ.[17] By the nature of its arguments, Iran effectively indicated that it regarded the international law on treaties regarding embassies and diplomats as legitimate.

Observers of the Islamic resurgence have occasionally voiced apprehensions that the revival of Islamic law could lead to a situation where Muslim countries would be bound by laws that would block the possibilities of cooperation with non-Muslim countries.[18] The Iranian case suggests that the likelihood of a Muslim government using Islam as a justification for breaking with the system of international law governing the relations among states is small.

CONTEMPORARY MUSLIM PERSPECTIVES ON JIHAD

Jihad—A War of Aggression or Defense?

The rules of *jihad* elaborated by the early jurists regarding what constituted justifications for fighting are facets of Islamic law that directly conflict with the modern international norms regarding war and peace. Briefly, the jurists generally supported the view that wars to conquer the *dar al-harb* were a religious obligation and that the *jihad* should be conducted by the Muslim community against the *dar al-harb* until all unbelievers submitted to Islamic rule.

Views sanctioning recourse to military aggression are obviously at odds with international law regarding war. In 1945 the UN Charter banned not only war but also the use of force short of war and even the threat of force. Recourse to armed aggression is prohibited under Article 2(4) of the UN Charter and elsewhere, including several UN General Assembly resolutions. There is a clear international consensus prohibiting acts of military aggression. Recourse to military force to defend a state that is the victim of aggression, meaning that force is utilized only in self-defense, is permissible. This principle is established in Article 51 of the UN Charter and elsewhere.

Muslims can maintain that Islamic law conforms to international law if they redefine the *jihad* as a war fought exclusively for defensive reasons. Reinterpretations of *jihad* that deny that it could sanction military aggression and assertions that Islam is meant to be spread exclusively by peaceful means are both common today. Contemporary Muslims regularly take the position that legitimate *jihad* is undertaken exclusively for the defense of the Muslim community.[19] For those Muslims who do reinterpret the *jihad* as an entirely defensive war, there is justification for saying that Islam calls for peace and condemns war. The assumption is made that *jihad* is the only form of armed conflict that Islam approves, and if *jihad* is only for purposes of defense, aggression or the recourse to force can be said to be prohibited in Islam.

Hasan Moinuddin, in the course of a thoughtful study that devotes considerable attention to reconciling Islamic and international law, offers the opinion that *jihad* is permitted against those who fight Muslims, but that Muslims are not permitted to begin hostilities or to commit aggression. He characterizes *jihad* as "the *bellum justum* of Islam because it is to be waged for a just cause as a consequence of some wrong or injury inflicted upon the Muslims; it includes the inherent right of self-defense; and it must be conducted in accordance with upright intentions and not for material gains or the sake of glory and power."[20]

Excerpts from an article on international law in the light of Islamic doctrine by Sobhi Mahmassani indicate how far modern interpretations of the rules of war in Islamic law have moved in the direction of harmonization with principles of public international law. Mahmassani describes Islamic doctrine on war as follows:

Islamic law ... is essentially a law of peace, built on human equality, religious tolerance and universal brotherhood....

War, in theory, is just and permissible only as a defensive measure, on grounds of extreme necessity, namely to protect the freedom of religion, to repel aggression, to prevent injustice and to protect social order....

This defensive war, when permissible, is moreover subjected by Islamic jurisprudence to strict regulations and rules. In their humane character they were unparalleled in their time and are comparable in content only to modern regulations recognized to-day [*sic*] by international conferences and treaties.

Thus, a declaration of war has to be preceded by notification sent to the enemy. Detailed provisions are laid down for the use of humane methods of warfare and fair treatment of enemy persons and property. Acts of cruelty and unnecessary destruction and suffering are expressly proscribed. Provision is also made for the termination of war and the settlement of its consequences.[21]

While taking positions that are generally close to international law, Mahmassani's comments on justifications for recourse to war also show the influence of the premodern *shari'a* tradition. His elaboration of what constitutes "extreme necessity" is not identical with what one would find in a textbook on international law and leaves the door open for interpretations that would conflict with the rules of international law. International law conceives of self-defense as involving only a response to military aggression. In international law an attack can be made in anticipatory self-defense only where the need to attack is instant, is overwhelming, and leaves no choice of means and no moment for deliberation.[22] Depending on the interpretations of Mahmassani's words, rubrics like the need to "protect freedom of religion," "prevent injustice," and "preserve social order" might be used to justify a recourse to force that would be impermissible in international law. As one sees in Mahmassani and in the comments of other Muslims on defensive war that follow, the justifications for launching an Islamic "defensive" war may include justifications for war that are not recognized in public international law.

Sheikh Shaltut of al-Azhar took the position in a pamphlet published in 1948 that verses of the Qur'an had aimed at securing peace and exterminating rebellion and aggression long before the League of Nations had done so, suggesting that the Islamic and international concepts of illegal aggression would be similar. To prove his thesis, he offered explanations for those Qur'anic verses that might seem to condone aggression but in his view did not. He denied that Islam had been spread by force. In Islam fighting is justified, he maintained, only to repel aggression, to protect the Islamic mission, and to defend religious freedom.[23]

The elaboration of this theme indicates that Shaltut's ideas about legitimate recourse to war sometimes diverge from the concepts familiar in international law. To construct his theory of fighting in Islam, he reviewed the early conquests of Islam, justifying the wars waged by the first two caliphs on the grounds that they had to "repel evil, to give the people opportunities to hear the Message [of Islam] and to give security to Moslems with regard to their religion and their countries."[24] He justified the Muslim conquests of Byzantine and Persian territory on the grounds of the hostility shown by the Byzantines and Persians to communications calling on them to convert to Islam.[25] Shaltut asserted in this connection:

Moslems only attacked people when they showed a spirit of hostility, opposition and resistance against the mission and a contempt for it. When such a hostile spirit became manifest to them and they were convinced of its danger to themselves and to the mission, they hastened to put it out of the way before its evil would grow beyond control. They did not wait for the enemy to attack them in their own country.[26]

Here, religious reasons, resistance to converting to Islam and contempt for Islamic missionaries, apparently justify recourse to military force—at least where the states attacked are perceived to be a danger to Muslims or the spread of Islam. By the standards of international law, such reasons make for a concept of self-defense that is too broad.

Other examples of religious reasons for which contemporary Muslims believe that "defensive" *jihad* can be launched include repelling oppression and persecution of Muslims outside the *dar al-islam*,[27] ridding a society of evil polytheist beliefs, and destroying obstacles in the way of propagating Islam.[28] None of these religiously grounded reasons for war would justify recourse to armed force under international law or fall within the scope of permissible self-defense. Thus, while Muslims are clearly moving to redefine *jihad* as a defensive war, assertions that Islam allows wars only in self-defense must be subjected to scrutiny to ascertain whether the Islamic concepts of self-defense being used do in fact correspond to the concepts of international law.

The Influence of Islam's Third World Context

Distinctive Third World perspectives have evolved on certain contested points of international law.[29] These are affecting the way Muslims understand their own tradition and do much to explain why certain topics in the area of war and peace come consistently to the fore.

Islam is today overwhelmingly a religion of the Third World. In many countries where Muslims predominate, subjugation by Western imperialism—or Eastern imperialism, in the cases of central Asia and Afghanistan—is bitterly resented. Due to the relative technological and military weakness of the Muslim world vis-à-vis the superpowers, there is apprehension about subordination to Western economic power and, to a lesser extent, fear of domination by the Soviet Union. In this situation there is a natural sympathy for struggles against imperialism and alien domination. In particular, there is strong Muslim support for the cause of Palestinian liberation. Analysis of current expositions of the doctrine of *jihad* shows that *jihad* is frequently redefined to legitimate the use of force on behalf of goals that reflect the influence of the general Third World backing for national liberation struggles.

Contemporary discussions of *jihad* now often assert that wars are justified in Islamic law when they are conducted to end exploitation and oppression by the superpowers or to achieve liberation from the forces of imperialism. As the French scholar Jean-Paul Charnay has noted, contemporary discussions of *jihad* reflect the deconfessionalization of political struggles in the Middle East, which are pursued on behalf of causes like nationalism or internationalist revolution.[30] Thus Islamic principles of war, at least in some interpretations, may be becoming less distinctively Islamic and more like ideas shared by Third World opinion generally.

Ayatollah Khomeini's Ideas on War

The ideas of Ayatollah Khomeini, a highly influential figure in the Iranian and Shi'i milieus, merit special attention. Ayatollah Khomeini and his allies in the clergy had great influence on the drafting of the 1979 Iranian Constitution. It includes in its preamble a passage that seems to be a reiteration of traditional notions of *jihad*. The passage states that the Iranian army "will be responsible not only for safeguarding the borders, but also for accomplishing an ideological mission, that is, the Jihad for the sake of God, as well as for struggling to open the way for the sovereignty of the Word of God throughout the world." One is prompted to inquire what this constitutional provision for *jihad* means, especially since in the Iran-Iraq War both Iran and Iraq rhetorically appealed to *jihad* to justify fighting the other side.[31]

Ayatollah Khomeini characterized a variety of struggles as constituting *jihad*. One might expect that as a jurist with a traditional education, he would be inclined to adhere to the rules on *jihad* set forth in the treatises of the premodern Shi'i jurists, but the views he articulated on justifications for war were tied as much to Iran's current political environment as they were to traditional views. In particular, he took into account the military power of the modern superpowers and linked Islamic concepts to the more general Third World struggle to throw off the yoke of exploitation and domination by the great powers, particularly those in the West. Poised between the premodern Islamic tradition and the ideas that naturally circulate in a revolutionary Third World environment, Khomeini made a variety of statements about justifications for war.

Thus Khomeini divided the world into oppressed and oppressors and called for wars by the oppressed against domination by the superpowers and the oppressors of the downtrodden.[32] In this regard Israel figured prominently among the ranks of oppressors, because Khomeini saw it as an outgrowth of the collusion of Eastern and Western imperialism to suppress and exploit the Muslim peoples.[33] Such views closely approximate statements of Third World positions on justifications for recourse to armed struggle.[34]

At other times Khomeini employed distinctively Islamic categories. He condemned *taghuti* war, using a term taken from the word *taghut*, which in the Qur'an denotes a demon or source of wickedness.[35] He supported *tawhidi* wars, divinely sanctioned wars that are led by (Muslim) prophets, *imams*, and believers to convert rebellious people and reform them.[36] *Tawhidi* wars are obviously like the premodern *jihad*, being wars that are fought on behalf of the Islamic cause and justified by belief in the need to spread Islamic rule. According to Khomeini, *jihad* "means expansion and the taking over of other countries"; Muslims are bound "to fight and to spread Islamic laws throughout the world."[37] Khomeini expressly distinguished *jihad* from *defa*ʿ ("defense" in Persian). The latter, he said, is fought to defend one's independence and does not require religious leadership.[38]

In other statements Khomeini abjured any intent to resort to force. He professed that security and peace were his policies and disavowed any intent to use armed force to achieve his objectives, which were to be realized by spiritual means.[39] His disavowal of any intent to resort to wars of aggression could be seen as being prompted by a wish to avoid a clash with the current norms of international law prohibiting the use of force.

Taken together, Khomeini's positions do not correspond precisely to the classical theory of *jihad*, the condemnation of war in public international law, or Third World support for struggles to throw off the yoke of superpower domination. Instead, one sees reflections of all three. For example, these are excerpts from a long speech that he made on July 20, 1988, in connection with the Iranian acceptance of the cease-fire with Iraq:

We have repeatedly shown in our foreign and international policy that we have been and are intent on expanding the influence of Islam in the world and lessening the domination of the world devourers. Now, if the servants of the United States cite this policy as being expansionist and motivated to establish a great empire, we will not fear it but welcome it.

We are intent on tearing out the roots of corrupting Zionism, Capitalism, and Communism in the world. We have decided to rely on God Almighty to destroy the regimes which are based on these three pillars, in order to spread the regime of the Islam of the messenger of God. . . .

O Muslims of all the world . . . think of attacking the enemies of Islam, because glory in life can be achieved through struggle. . . . it is necessary to break the sovereignty of global infidelity, particularly of the United States. . . .

We must smash the hands and the teeth of the superpowers, particularly the United States. And we must choose one of two alternatives—either martyrdom or victory, which we both regard as victory. . . .

Our war is one of ideology and does not recognize borders or geography. We must ensure the vast mobilization of the soldiers of Islam around the world in our ideological war. God willing, the great Iranian nation, through its material and moral support for the revolution, will compensate for the hardships of the war with the sweetness of the defeat of God's enemies in the world. What is sweeter than the fact that the great Iranian nation has struck the United States on the head like lightning? . . .

We say that as long as there is infidelity and poletheism [*sic*], there is struggle, and as long as there is struggle, we will be there.

We are not fighting anyone over towns or territory. We are determined to raise the glorious banner of "There is no God but God" on the heights of magnanimity and generosity. Therefore, O my army, IRGC [revolutionary guards], and mobilization corps children! O you popular forces, never talk of the loss of a position with sadness or talk about the capture of another with pride and happiness as these are insignificant compared with your goal.[40]

This speech, which is representative of the transitional stage in which Islamic doctrines relating to war currently find themselves, combines elements of Islamic and Third World concepts of struggle. In the excerpts Khomeini seems to endorse wars of expansion to form "a great empire," which would be in conflict with international law. The objective of the fighting, insofar as it is rooting out Zionist, capitalist, and Communist ideologies, is different from the goals of the *jihad* as these were defined by the premodern jurists and more like the political goals espoused by Third World advocates of liberation struggles. But to the extent that the justification for Khomeini's war involves spreading Islam and eradicating infidelity and polytheism, it looks much more like premodern *jihad*. It is noteworthy that these bellicose remarks were not addressed to the international community but to an internal audience, which could be expected to be stirred by the imagery of conquests to come. Khomeini's government was working even as he spoke under the auspices of the United Nations to arrange the conditions for a cessation of hostilities with Iraq, a fact that indicates that his strong rhetoric did not mean that Iran could not cooperate with established international organizations or work within the framework of international law.

The Invocation of Jihad to Justify Offensive Wars

The foregoing review of Ayatollah Khomeini's views suggests the ambivalence contemporary Muslims feel as to whether offensive wars justified by religious criteria are still permissible. Khomeini's views on this issue may be contrasted with the views of unreconstructed advocates of the *jihad* in the traditional sense of a war against the infidels. There are contemporary Islamic movements that profess a commitment to fight the *jihad* and that denounce Muslims who fail to recognize that fighting the *jihad* is a religious duty.[41] However, even in the case of these movements, there are important divergences from the *jihad* envisaged by the premodern jurists. In particular, the contemporary advocates of *jihad* often see it as a vehicle for advancing the Palestinian national cause. For reasons that will be discussed, *jihad* principles seem to many Muslims to have a particular application to the conflict between the Arab countries and Israel.

An example of this was offered in 1981 in Egypt. Because Zionism is viewed as a force hostile to Islam and Israel is seen as the natural target of *jihad*, President Sadat of Egypt outraged Muslim opinion by entering into a peace treaty with Israel, even though he took the precaution of first obtaining from al-Azhar a ruling that the treaty did not violate the *shari'a*. It is significant that Sadat concluded that Islamic sensibilities dictated that he obtain a prior religious authorization for peace. This suggests the way that the persistence of traditional notions of *jihad* can affect the approach of contemporary Muslims to questions of war and peace.

Sadat's precautionary measure was in vain, since his entering into a treaty with Israel was later cited by his assassins as one of the justifications for their action. In a pamphlet entitled *Al-Farida al-gha'iba* (the neglected duty [to fight the infidel]), the group behind the assassination decried attempts to interpret the *jihad* as a defensive war, asserting that Islam had been spread by the sword and that Muslims were duty bound to take the military initiative against unbelievers.[42] Furthermore, while not discussing international law per se, the pamphlet took positions that were incompatible with adherence to international law and to international treaties, stating that Muslims were free to abrogate treaties with non-Muslims[43] and condemning the following of laws that were not Islamic.[44]

Was this actually a call to *jihad* in the traditional sense of launching a war against the *dar al-harb*? The situation was in fact more complicated. The pamphlet stated that the *jihad* could not be pursued by contemporary nation-states. According to the pamphlet, an Islamic state and an Islamic order would first have to be established, which would require the extermination of the current "infidel leaders" of Muslim countries.[45] That is, the pamphlet was in the first instance concerned with instigating internal Islamic revolutions to set up an Islamic government and only secondarily with launching a holy war against foreign infidels. The group's professed commitment to wage *jihad* against Israel seems to have been designed to mobilize domestic support for its cause, the goal of which was to seize power in Egypt as a first step toward reuniting the Islamic *umma* or community.

ISLAMIC LAW AND NATIONAL LIBERATION STRUGGLES

Confronting the Problems of Legal Personality of Peoples Seeking Self-Determination

In the premodern period Islamic jurisprudence contemplated that there would be a legitimate Islamic polity to conduct the *jihad*, such as the *umma* that the Egyptian Sunni group just mentioned aspired to reestablish, or, for Shi'is, a community led by a divinely inspired Imam. By contrast, many contemporary Muslims seem to discount the importance of the requirement that the entity conducting *jihad* conform to the traditional models of the legitimate Islamic *umma* or *imamate*. If *jihad* may only be conducted by a unified Islamic community, it becomes irrelevant in today's system, in which the nation-state is the only viable political entity. For *jihad* principles to be applicable in the context of problems meaningful to contemporary Muslims, it is essential to rethink what political entities have the capacity to wage *jihad*.

To sort out Islamic doctrines on war and peace, Muslims have had to face the problem of deciding what entities should be accorded legal personality. As will be shown, the newly emerging Islamic doctrines in this area have not attained a definitive formulation or a universal acceptance. Defining the requisites for legal personality happens also to be an issue of acute interest to the world community, but one that has not thus far been resolved in international law. That is, international law itself is presently in disarray on this subject.

In general, only states have enjoyed personality under public international law. The influential 1933 Montevideo Convention expounded the criteria for statehood in an era before modern ideas of self-determination and human rights developed. Pressures for revising the criteria for recognizing legal personality have come from many political groups that lack the characteristics of states but have sought to have their personality recognized by the international community. International law is presently struggling to settle the degree to which the rights accorded states under international law may be claimed by national liberation movements, which inevitably constitute a challenge to the territorial sovereignty of existing, recognized states.[46]

In sources that state principles of public international law like the 1966 International Covenants on Human Rights and the 1970 Declaration of Friendly Relations between States, it is established that "all peoples" have a right to self-determination. States that deny "peoples" this right would therefore seem to be in violation of international law. But there are many disagreements regarding what the term "peoples" entails and how "peoples" denied this right may seek redress.

According to Third World countries and the socialist bloc, "peoples" engaged in national liberation struggles enjoy legal personality and are covered by international law. In contrast, the Western powers tend to support the view that international law only addresses conflicts between states.[47]

Debates in international forums on this subject have been inconclusive, and the juridical status of "peoples" fighting for their right to self-determination remains uncertain. As yet, they have not been given a status on a par with the other subjects of international law, but they nonetheless have achieved a kind of locus standi in the international system.[48]

Frustrated in their demands for self-determination, many national liberation movements have turned to armed force. Unsatisfied demands for self-determination are a serious threat to peace and have resulted in rebellion, armed conflict, civil wars, and protracted guerrilla warfare. Western countries have condemned such recourse to force, giving priority to preserving the peace and the status quo over remedying injustices caused when peoples are subjugated by states that deny them their right to self-determination. In this the West currently disagrees with the Soviet and Third World blocs, which have generally accepted the legitimacy of the use of armed force on behalf of national liberation movements, according higher priority to realizing the goal of justice for subjugated peoples than to maintaining the peace.[49]

The Third World, supported by the socialist bloc, has since the 1970s taken the position that the use of force by national liberation movements is a form of self-defense and is therefore not affected by the ban on war.[50] Arguments have been made by spokespersons for the Third World that "peoples" may fight "with all necessary means" or "by all means at their disposal" for liberation. National liberation struggles are thus seen as new forms of just war, legitimate uses of armed force that are justified because they are fought for an approved objective.[51]

In the Middle East the disputed status of peoples seeking independence is not a theoretical question but a major political preoccupation. It lies at the base of the most explosive regional conflict, that between Israel and the Palestinians. The status of the Palestine Liberation Organization (PLO) has been a particularly contentious issue. Prior to the declaration of a Palestinian state in November of 1988, the PLO had been recognized as the legitimate representative of the Palestinian people by 117 countries and had missions in 60. The PLO was a member or observer in many international organizations and conferences, and the personality of the PLO as a quasi-governmental entity was widely recognized by the international community.[52] As might have been predicted, Israel and the United States opposed any such recognition. The recent declaration of a Palestinian state promises to create many new controversies that will test international legal doctrines in this area. Similar issues, where Muslims are either on one or both sides of national liberation struggles, have arisen in such diverse areas as the Western Sahara, Eritrea, the Philippines, Bangladesh, the Sudan, Algeria, Kurdistan, and Baluchistan.

Islamic Law and Legal Personality

Muslims are naturally interested in how Islamic principles apply to people's demands for self-determination and the use of armed force to achieve national liberation. On this topic they will find no explicit guidance in the premodern juristic treatises, but they can consult a growing body of literature by contemporary Muslims. A variety of positions has been articulated in works seeking to accommodate the legal personality of national liberation movements within an Islamic framework, but these necessitate doctrinal adjustments in the relevant Islamic legal theories.

An initial problem is that the nation-state, the goal of every national liberation struggle, has never been definitively reconciled with Islamic theory, which in its traditional formulation recognized only the *umma*, or community of believers. There have been Muslims who, despite the entrenched character of the system of nation-states in the modern world, still adhered to the traditional opinion that any political subdivisions of the Islamic *umma* were inimical to Islam.[53] Others have accepted these divisions[54] or tolerated them on the assumption that they are a temporary phenomenon.[55]

The idea that Islam recognizes the legal personality of "peoples" struggling to establish their own nation-states at the expense of existing states is too recent to be treated as a settled component of the Islamic tradition, but it seems to be gaining in popularity. Some representative positions will be surveyed in what follows, and Islamic perspectives on the Palestinian conflict, which will be treated separately, should also be considered in this connection.

The prominent Egyptian intellectual Hassan Hanafi has articulated a position that seems to be growing in popularity. Hanafi maintains that Islam naturally espouses a theology of national liberation.[56] He asserts that Islam supports the idea that every people deserves its own nation-state.[57] It is probably significant that Hanafi is not an Islamic cleric but a professor who trained at the Sorbonne, where he worked on Islamic law and Islamic intellectual history, and that in his work he has attempted to reconcile his sympathies for leftist causes with adherence to Islamic doctrine.

A detailed argument on behalf of the proposition that Islamic law accords legal personality to national liberation movements was set forth in a treatise published in Egypt in 1970–71 on legal personality in Islamic and international law. Here the claim is made that the limitation of legal personality to states was a way to authorize Western domination of other communities under "European International Law."[58] In contrast, the author asserts that Islamic law grants nations and communities legal personality even where they have been subjugated to foreign powers, as long as the community has sociocultural unity, unity of political leadership, and a unity of legal system.[59] According to the author, Islamic law buttresses the international status of the Palestinian people, which, he says, has been denied recognition under the "European" theory of legal personality.[60]

The 1972 Charter of the Organization of the Islamic Conference is based on the system of nation-states and also recognizes the right of "all peoples" to self-determination, with a special endorsement of the struggle of "Moslem peoples" for "dignity, independence, and national rights" in Article II(A)6.[61] To the extent that one accepts the "Islamic" character of the charter, which in its preface officially aims at preserving "Islamic spiritual, ethical, social and economic values," one may take this endorsement as additional evidence that there is an Islamic warrant for granting "peoples" personality in the international system. However, only one national liberation struggle is specifically endorsed in the charter, which pledges efforts for "the struggle of the people of Palestine, and [to] help them to regain their rights and liberate their land" in Article II(A)5. In contrast, Article II(B)3 enunciates the principle of "the sovereignty, independence and territorial integrity of each member State," which rules out any support for liberation struggles against governments that belong to the organization.[62]

Turning from the theory in this area to government practice, one sees that the response of the contemporary governments of Muslim countries to national liberation movements on their own territories has not been more accommodating than the response of non-Muslim countries whose sovereignty has been challenged by such movements. Islamic theories of legal personality do not seem to play a determinative role in resolving such disputes.

The 1975 Western Sahara Case

There has been a recent instance where highly developed, formal legal arguments on a people's right to self-determination were presented in the context of a war of national liberation fought in the Muslim world. In the 1975 ICJ case on the Western Sahara, Islamic doctrines on the legal personality of national liberation movements, if any existed and were accepted as authority, should have been central. The main parties presenting arguments in the case, Algeria, Mauretania, and Morocco, were all Muslim, as were the Sahrawis, whose status was in question. The reports of the pleadings, which fill five volumes, show that Islamic law was referred to, albeit only occasionally and only to establish the historical background of the dispute. In contrast, international law was referred to by all parties as the controlling standard on issues of self-determination and legal personality.

The case arose in the following context. When in 1974 Spain decided to abandon its colony Rio de Oro, the inhabitants of the territory claimed that they were entitled to independence and formed the Polisario movement. This was supported by Algeria, but neighboring Morocco and Mauretania insisted that the Spanish colony had merely occupied a territory that each claimed belonged to it. When Morocco moved to occupy and annex most of the territory, Polisario rebels launched a war of national liberation in which they were backed by Algeria and called for international recognition of an independent state, the Saharan Arab Democratic Republic. The Polisario movement was recognized by 70 countries, with Muslim countries being sharply divided on whether the Sahrawi people were entitled to self-determination, a decision that suggests that common adherence to Islam had no bearing on the nations' positions.

At the outset of the conflict in 1975 the ICJ was asked for an advisory opinion.[63] Among the issues that the ICJ had to address was whether the people of the Western Sahara deserved recognition and self-determination even though there had not been a formal, Western Saharan state in the past and even though Mauretania asserted that the Western Saharans were just one part of the Shinguitti "people" living both in the Western Sahara and in Mauretania.

Islamic law was discussed in connection with whether the territory had, as Morocco said, owed allegiance to the Moroccan sultan prior to the Spanish colonization. Islamic law was referred to by Algeria, which claimed that the territory belonged to the *dar al-islam*, taking the position that Islamic law did not recognize nation-states on the European model.[64] However, Algeria noted that its reference to the *dar al-islam* concept was merely incidental, that it should not figure as a determinative part of its argument and even less as a determinative element in the broader debate.[65] Even so, Morocco strongly objected to this argument, asserting that Algeria was trying to use the concept of *dar al-islam* to show that ties to a state have no meaning in an Islamic system in order to controvert Moroccan claims that the disputed territory had had ties to the Moroccan state before Spain conquered it.[66] Morocco denied that the notion of the *dar al-islam* meant a negation of the state or state sovereignty. Morocco emphasized that in the Muslim world the system of separate states had coexisted with the concept of the *dar al-islam*. According to Morocco, the historical existence of states within the *dar al-islam* could be proved by the facts that Muslim states had historically exercised sovereignty over specific territory and had maintained diplomatic relations with other Muslim states.[67]

Challenging the Moroccans, the Mauretanian representatives asserted the traditional position, advising the ICJ that nation-states could have no legitimacy in Islam and that any recognition of statehood inside the boundaries of the *dar al-islam* was of a de facto, not a de jure, character. Muslims did not feel at home in the European-style nation-state, Mauretania asserted, because it was too rigid and oppressive for them. In this connection Mauretania concluded that the existence of an autonomous people on the Saharan territory that was not tied to the surrounding states was not in violation of the *shari'a* since the *shari'a* did not require obedience or submission to de facto powers.[68] Mauretania also argued that the Sahrawis and Mauretanians were parts of one Shinguitti "people" or "nation" that shared a common language, way of life, religion, and system of laws.[69] On that basis the people deserved to be united.

Neither Algeria nor Mauretania claimed that there existed an Islamic theory of legal personality that could be used to support their positions. Both used Islamic law only in a negative way to try to undermine the Moroccan claims that former sultans had ruled over the Western Saharan territory.

The arguments in this case reveal how divided Muslims currently are on how Islamic law applies to the nation-state and legal personality. They also show the very marginal role Islamic law plays in supplying the principles that are actually referred to in resolving armed conflicts, even where all parties are Muslim. All parties in the case shared the conviction that the right of self-determination for the Sahrawis and other issues had to be governed by international law, which was what the ICJ used to resolve the dispute.

The ICJ rejected both Morocco's and Mauretania's claims to the territory, saying that the people of the territory should have the right to self-determination. Because the parties could not agree to the conditions for the exercise of that right, the war continued for over a decade. In 1990 it seemed that the ICJ proposal for allowing the Sahrawi people to settle their future by a vote might be implemented, in part due to the Algerian disinclination to offer further backing for the Polisario movement.

Islamic Doctrines on War and National Liberation in Relation to the Palestinian Issue

It seems impossible to exaggerate the impact that the Arab-Israeli conflict and especially the 1967 Israeli conquest of Old Jerusalem with its Islamic holy places has had on Muslims' perceptions of the relevance of *jihad* principles to their present situation. In the absence of this particular conflict, Muslims' ideas regarding the legality of war might have moved closer to the secular model of public international law.

When one considers the many wars that have raged in the Middle East since World War II, one realizes that the conflict with Israel resembles the model of a *jihad* conducted by the *dar al-islam* against the *dar al-harb* more than most. For example, the *jihad* model seems to have scant applicability to instances of warfare involving Iran and Iraq, Libya and Chad, Pakistan and Bangladesh, Egypt in the Yemen, and Morocco in the Western Sahara, or among competing sides in Lebanon, Oman, Baluchistan, and Kurdistan. Even where one side is or was non-Muslim, as in the independence wars in Algeria and Eritrea, the Egyptian fight against the invasion of 1956, Pakistan's wars with India, the Turkish invasion of northern Cyprus, and the Sudanese civil war, many factors, such as the secular nature of both the political leadership and the military objectives, diverge from the *jihad* model. Perhaps a closer analogy to the *jihad* lies in the fight of the *mujahidin* in the Afghan civil war, but that is a civil war in which Muslim Afghans lead, at least formally, both camps and the *mujahidin* factions are themselves bitterly divided about what they are fighting for and who should lead them.

The religious dimensions of the Arab-Israeli conflict are much more pronounced. Israel is seen as constituting a Jewish and Christian (the latter because of European and American military and political support) incursion onto territory that has traditionally formed the core of the *dar al-islam*. Control of the city of Jerusalem is fraught with religious significance for Muslims. The fact that Israel is a self-proclaimed Jewish state accentuates the religious nature of the conflict. All this suggests that the categories of *dar al-islam* and *dar al-harb* remain relevant. Furthermore, on the issue of Palestine, the religious and political sentiments of Muslims around the world are united in support for Palestinians' right of self-determination. It is not surprising that in discussing the Palestinian cause, Muslims frequently appeal to *jihad*. In Muslims' vocabulary *jihad* is associated with a war of unchallengeable legitimacy, a righteous struggle on behalf of just cause.

Jihad has been appealed to in the conflict with Israel in a variety of contexts. For example, even before the State of Israel was founded in 1948, Zionist settlement in Palestine was viewed as a threat to Islam, and there were many calls for *jihad* against the Jewish settlers.[70] Since 1967 *jihad* has routinely been called for to liberate Jerusalem from Israeli control. While the PLO is a movement that is secular both in terms of its membership and its goals, in 1978 in Mecca Yasir 'Arafat declared a holy war to liberate Palestine and recover Jerusalem.[71] The Third Islamic Conference, held at Ta'if in Saudi Arabia in 1981, called for a *jihad* to liberate Jerusalem and the Occupied Territories by all military, political, and economic means.[72] How far the doctrines of *jihad* have merged with Muslims' support for the Palestinian cause is perhaps most perfectly symbolized by the name adopted by the contemporary Lebanese organization Islamic Jihad for the Liberation of Palestine. It may be significant that in an era when the *jihad* concept has been widely deconfessionalized, the group thought it necessary to add the seemingly redundant adjective "Islamic"; the name suggests an awareness that *jihad* may now have a predominantly secular political connotation in addition to its original religious sense.

Nels Johnson seems to have accurately assessed the ambiguous symbolism involved in current patterns of usage of *jihad*. He says that the defeat of the Palestinians and the limitations on effective political action that resulted from Israeli domination led to Islam becoming a vehicle for a redemptive process. As he notes, when Muslims were faced "with a foreign enemy of two different religions [British Christians and Zionist Jews] who sought domination over the second holiest land of the Faith, Islam provided the cultural categories, in the conceptual field of jihad, to encompass and organize resistance."[73] According to Johnson, in Palestinian political culture Islamic concepts have expanded beyond their traditional religious definitions, so that "Islamic ideation exists as highly ambiguous symbolic formulations which are susceptible to wide application and interpretation by individuals and groups in modes which can be both secular and religious in connotation."[74]

When Muslims speak of a *jihad* to liberate Palestine, they do not mean the *jihad* as defined in the premodern treatises, which would not fit the circumstances of the Palestinian people. Many Palestinians and members of the PLO are Christian, and the PLO follows a nonsectarian policy. The PLO has no aspirations to convert non-Muslims to Islam or to impose *dhimmi* status on Jews and Christians in Palestine. The deconfessionalization of the *jihad* concept as it relates to the Palestinian cause is demonstrated by a call for *jihad* made by the rector of al-Azhar in 1973, asserting that *jihad* against Israel was an obligation incumbent on Egyptians, regardless of whether they were Christian or Muslim.[75] The call for Christian participation in the *jihad* is tantamount to acknowledging that *jihad*, when conducted on behalf of the Palestinians, has been drastically transformed.[76]

ISLAM AND TERRORIST VIOLENCE

Terrorism may be viewed as a form of warfare. Given the assumptions that are frequently made in the West regarding links between Islam and terrorism, how the Islamic tradition deals with terrorism must be considered here. But what is "terrorism"?

To date, the international community has been unable to reach a universally accepted definition of "terrorism." For convenience, I shall make use of the following as a working definition of terrorism: violent acts or the threat of violence against third parties, often innocent civilians, to achieve political concessions or changes in policies by states or persons in authority.[77] In the same vein, in my working definition international terrorism will be "isolated assassination and 'hostility' missions or the intermittent use or threat of force against person(s) to obtain certain political objectives of international relevance from a third party."[78]

Recourse to acts that fall within these definitions of terrorism has been deemed expedient by groups around the world fighting foreign occupation or conducting liberation struggles. In such contexts terrorism may be supported and rationalized as a variant of guerrilla warfare, the tactics that the weak necessarily are forced to resort to in a contest with the strong, the strong having at their disposal military might that dooms the weak to certain defeat if they carry on their struggle via conventional warfare.

Historically, sympathy for perpetrators of terrorist acts confronting a more powerful foe while engaged in a struggle on behalf of peoples denied rights and freedoms is not strange. Such attitudes inevitably affect judgments about which acts may be characterized as "terrorism." People's political sympathies tend to correlate with whether or not they use the highly pejorative term "terrorism" to characterize certain uses of violence to achieve political goals. It is hardly original to observe that in consequence, one person's "terrorist" will be another's "freedom fighter." Thus it would be rare to find any group or government, Muslim or non-Muslim, that is involved in acts that would fit in the above definitions of terrorism that would be prepared publicly to acknowledge that they support or engage in "terrorism." In consequence, when "terrorism" is used here, it must be recognized that the term is applied in a purely formal sense. The persons and groups characterized as engaged in terrorism would, no doubt, reject the label.

Despite the inability of the international community to agree concerning what falls within the category of "terrorism," there is agreement that acts of international terrorism contravene international law. Thus there are international conventions designed to promote international cooperation in preventing and punishing terrorism. State sponsorship or facilitation of international terrorism is a violation of international law.

Mainstream Islam does not condone terrorism, whether intrastate or international. The connections between Islamic institutions and doctrines and any distinctively Islamic form of terrorism are very weak. Of course, there are Muslims who sponsor or perpetrate terroristic acts either in a governmental or a private capacity. There are even examples from history, such as the notorious medieval Order of the Assassins, that show that certain Islamic beliefs have correlated with a commitment to use terrorism.[79] While Muslims who engage in acts of what others would characterize as terrorism may have subjective convictions that their acts are undertaken pursuant to the dictates of their religion, these beliefs have very tenuous foundations in Islamic law or theology.

Acts that could fall within the definition of international terrorism have been carried out in the last decades by Muslims and often in ways that associate terroristic acts with the Islamic religion. For example, the Islamic Jihad organization in Lebanon has boasted of bombing the American marines and embassy and holding American hostages in Beirut.

That Islam has been mined by the Islamic Jihad for useful conceptual categories and positive symbolic associations does not, however, mean that the members of the organization resorted to terrorist tactics because they were Muslims or pursuant to the mandates of Islamic doctrine. Islamic nomenclature should not obscure the fact that Muslim terrorists use the same tactics and pursue basically the same kinds of political results as do non-Muslim organizations involved in terrorism, such as the Irish Republican Army, the Jewish Defense League, Puerto Rican nationalists, Basque separatists, the Sendero Luminoso of Peru, Sikh separatists, Tamils in Sri Lanka, the Italian Red Brigades, the Baader-Meinhof group, Germans in the South Tyrol, Croatians in Yugoslavia, Corsicans opposed to French rule, the Japanese Red Army, and other groups involved in terrorist activities, not excepting Zionist militants in Palestine. Any balanced survey of the record of international terrorism would establish that there is no uniquely Islamic proclivity to condone or indulge in acts of international terrorism.

Nonetheless, Islam has become closely associated with terrorism in the minds of people in the West, where the media have propagated the notion that there exists a natural connection between terrorism and a supposed, peculiar Islamic fanaticism and militance. An example of a work promoting the view that Islam acts as an independent factor in some sense causing terrorism is *Sacred Rage: The Wrath of Militant Islam* by Robin Wright, who enjoys considerable cachet as a media "expert" on Islam. The subtitle is emblematic of Wright's approach, which imagines a reified, militant "Islam" as the cause of terrorist horrors and outrages. In pursuing her characterizations of Islam, Wright at one point quotes Shaykh Muhammad Husayn Fadlallah, a patron of Shi'is in the Hizbullah, or party of Allah, faction in Lebanon, but she seems to miss the significance of his comments. While not disavowing the influence of religious factors in the violence in Lebanon, Shaykh Fadlallah condemned the tendency to evaluate what Shi'is did outside the context of Lebanon's peculiar conditions and without looking at what went on in other Lebanese communities. He expressed unhappiness that the Western media and others were associating Islam with terrorism. He insisted that the Hizbullah was a party like other parties in Lebanon that had resorted to the use of arms. He admitted that the Hizbullah might have violated laws and made mistakes, but he defended Hizbullah tactics as a way of confronting America, France, and Israel.[80]

That is, while the Western observer, Wright, was inclined to sacralize the origins of terrorist violence in Lebanon and view it as a manifestation of "sacred rage," an exotic, Islamic phenomenon, the Shi'i cleric, Sheikh Fadlallah, was pointing out that the roots of terrorism lay in Lebanese political conditions and that religious categories were not helpful in identifying the real sources of the violence. Wright's thesis, that there are peculiar affinities between Islam and terrorism, distracts attention from the real factors that have shaped the agony of Lebanon. If anything else were needed to disabuse people of the notion that Islamic principles of *jihad* somehow account for violence in Lebanon, the bloody conflict between the Shi'i Amal and Shi'i Hizbullah forces in Lebanon should serve. Despite being adherents of the same Islamic sect, Twelver Shi'ism, members of Amal and Hizbullah in 1988 engaged in some of the most lethal warfare Lebanon has seen. As the conflict intensified in 1989, it should have been obvious that constructs like Muslims' duty to fight the *jihad* against unbelievers or a fanatic Shi'i hatred of the West could not account for warfare where Shi'is were equally perpetrators and victims. Similarly, the bitter warfare between Lebanese Christian factions in late 1989 and early 1990 undermines assumptions that adherence to Islam is an explanatory category in the analysis of Lebanese violence.

CONCLUSION

As this brief survey attempts to show, the relationship between the Islamic tradition on war and peace and international law is presently an ambivalent one. While the modern Christian tradition on war and peace may be said to have been subsumed in the Western tradition, so that it would be hard to find elements in the Christian tradition that one could distinguish from principles of international law, it is still possible to make differentiations between Islamic doctrines and their counterparts in international law. While Muslim countries follow international law in matters of war and peace, the evidence shows that Muslims remain convinced that their own religious tradition is relevant for the disposition of such matters. The *shari'a* doctrines found in the treatises of premodern jurists have long been consigned to desuetude by governments bent on modernization, but those doctrines are now being reconsidered and updated in the light of the contemporary experiences of Muslim societies. As Muslims work to define Islamic positions on issues of war and peace facing the world community like the rules affecting national liberation struggles, the Islamic and international legal traditions, long separated by different perspectives, are now starting to converge in areas of common concern.

NOTES

1. On al-Shaybani, see John Kelsay, "Religion, Morality, and the Governance of War: The Case of Classical Islam," in *Journal of Religious Ethics* 18, no. 2 (Fall 1990): 123–39. On al-Tusi, see Etan Kohlberg, "The Development of the Imami Shi'i Doctrine of *jihad*," *Zeitschrift der Deutschen Morgenlaendischen Gesellschaft* 126 (1976): 80. Kohlberg remarks on the general similarity of Sunni and Shi'i doc-

trines on *jihad*, ibid., 64, 68. An important distinction, the requirement in traditional Shi'i jurisprudence that the *jihad* be led by a divinely inspired Imam, is noted in Abdulaziz Sachedina, "The Development of *Jihad* in Islamic Revelation and History," *Cross, Crescent, and Sword: The Justification and Limitation of War in Western and Islamic Tradition,* ed. James Turner Johnson and John Kelsay (Westport, Conn.: Greenwood Press, 1990).

2. Compare William V. O'Brien, "The International Law of War as Related to the Western Just War Tradition," in this volume.

3. These rules are discussed by John Kelsay, "Religion, Morality, and the Governance of War," and also in Majid Khadduri, "International Law," in *Law in the Middle East,* vol. 1, eds. Majid Khadduri and Herbert Liebesny (Washington, D.C.: Middle East Institute, 1955), 355–56; cf. also Muhammad Hamidullah, *The Muslim Conduct of State* (Lahore: Muhammad Ashraf, 1968), 212–65.

4. Sobhi Mahmassani, an internationally renowned Lebanese scholar of Islamic and international law who has generally taken the position that Islamic and international principles are congruent, has acknowledged that in this area the premodern *shari'a* rules would be at odds with the international standards. Sobhi Mahmassani, "International Law in Light of Islamic Doctrine," *Academie de droit international, Recueil des cours* 117 (1966): 307–8.

5. These rules prohibit, among other things, killing or mistreatment of prisoners of war and the murder or collective punishment of enemy civilians, taking them hostage, and meting out to them humiliating or degrading treatment, such as indecent assault or enforced prostitution. Slavery is also prohibited. These are discussed in Ingrid DeLupis, *The Law of War* (Cambridge: Cambridge University Press, 1987), 130–37, 271–93.

6. The phrase is borrowed from James Turner Johnson, "Historical Roots and Sources of the Just War Tradition in Western Culture," in this volume.

7. It is instructive to contemplate the comparative paucity of recent works by Christians on the relationship of Christianity and international law, a phenomenon that suggests that the fundamental questions about that relationship may already have been satisfactorily resolved in the minds of most Christians.

8. In contrast to the authors of the premodern juristic treatises, who worked within an intact, self-contained cultural tradition, contemporary Muslims writing on war and peace are coping with a fractured tradition and one that is also permeated by Western influences. Unlike Western writers on international law, who appear uninterested in the Islamic tradition and how it may differ from the *siyar*, Muslims who write on international law do so with an awareness that public international law, a product of Western culture, is universally entrenched as the normative standard and will be used to judge Islamic legal doctrines, which will be deemed defective if they violate the international norms. Muslims may adopt a defensive stance when comparing Islamic rules on war and peace with their international counterparts, so that apologetic preoccupations rather than scholarly ones ultimately inform their work. Concerns about the adequacy of the literature produced in these circumstances are shared by Rudolph Peters. See his *Islam and Colonialism: The Doctrine of Jihad in Modern History* (The Hague: Mouton, 1979), 138.

9. See, for example, a work by a professor of comparative jurisprudence at the women's section of al-Azhar University, Khadija Ahmad Abu Atlah, *Al-*

Islam wa al-ʿalaqat al-dawliya fi al-silm wa al-harb (Cairo: Dar al-maʿarif, 1983), 194; a book by a professor of international law at the University of Alexandria educated at the Universities of Cairo and London, Mohammed al-Ghunaimi, *The Muslim Conception of International Law and the Western Approach* (The Hague: Nijhoff, 1968), 82–84; a book that has been widely cited since its original publication in 1941, authored by a Muslim from Hyderabad whose studies included work at the University of Bonn and the Sorbonne, M. Hamidullah, *Muslim Conduct of State*, 65–69; a Ph.D. dissertation that deals in unusual depth with the relationship of international law and Islamic law, Muhammad Kamil Yaqut, *Al-Shakhsiya al-dawliya fi al-qanun al-dawli al-ʿamm wa al-shariʿa al-islamiya* (Cairo: ʿAlam al-kutub, 1970–71), 14 [English section]; and a professor of Islamic jurisprudence who has written important studies on jurisprudence and Hanbali doctrine and teaches at the University of Damascus, Wahba al-Zuhaili, *Al-ʿAlaqat al-dawliya fi al-Islam muqarana bi al-qanun al-dawli al-hadith* (Beirut: Muʾassasat al-risala, 1981), 19–20. A rare Western scholar supporting the proposition that Islamic influence likely accounts for the development of international law in Europe is Marcel Boisard, "On the Probable Influences of Islam on Western Public and International Law," *International Journal of Middle Eastern Studies* 11 (1980): 429–50. A similar approach, citing Boisard, can be seen in a recent Ph.D. dissertation for the University of Bochum: Hasan Moinuddin, *The Charter of the Islamic Conference and Legal Framework of Economic Co-operation among Its Member States* (Oxford: Clarendon Press, 1987), 43–45.

10. Jean-Paul Charnay, *L'Islam et la guerre: De la guerre juste à la révolution sainte* (Paris: Fayard, 1986), 114.

11. Moinuddin, *Charter of the Islamic Conference*, 48.

12. Al-Ghunaimi, *Muslim Conception*, 184–85.

13. Farhang Rajaee, *Islamic Values and World View: Khomeyni on Man, the State, and International Politics* (Lanham, Md.: University Press of America, 1983), 81.

14. Rudolph Peters, *Jihad in Medieval and Modern Islam* (Leiden: Brill, 1977), 70.

15. Moinuddin, *Charter of the Islamic Conference*, 211.

16. One copy is reproduced in United States Diplomatic and Consular Staff in Tehran, I.C.J. Reports 1980, 8–9.

17. An extensive record of statements by Iranian government officials was included by the United States in its pleadings before the ICJ, which elaborated on the points raised by the foreign minister. The pleadings are in United States Diplomatic and Consular Staff in Tehran, I.C.J. Pleadings, 1982.

18. For example, this troubles al-Ghunaimi; see *Muslim Conception*, 222–23. Moinuddin has noted Western concerns about this as well. Moinuddin, *Charter of the Islamic Conference*, 3.

19. See, for example, Moinuddin, *Charter of the Islamic Conference*, 21–28; Peters, *Islam and Colonialism*, 110–11; Yaqut, *Al-Shakhsiya*, 372–73, 388; Mehdi Abedi and Gary Legenhausen, eds., *Jihad and Shahadat: Struggle and Martyrdom in Islam* (Houston: Institute for Research and Islamic Studies, 1986), 13, 103. The last work treats recent Twelver Shiʿi views. Al-Ghunaimi, *Muslim Conception*, 136, 163, treats the traditional view, that *jihad* was a war of aggression, as the product of juristic misuse of the term and confusion with the word *qital*. For a different

type of argument in favor of the notion of *jihad* as a defensive war, see Abdulaziz Sachedina, "Development of *Jihad*."

20. Moinuddin, *Charter of the Islamic Conference*, 28.

21. Mahmassani, "International Law," 320–21.

22. See, for example, Rosalyn Higgins, "The Attitude of Western States towards Legal Aspects of the Use of Force," in *The Current Legal Regulation of the Use of Force*, ed. A. Cassese (Dordrecht: Martinus Nijhoff, 1986), 442.

23. Peters, *Jihad in Mediaeval and Modern Islam*, 37–55.

24. Ibid., 75.

25. Ibid., 75–78.

26. Ibid., 78.

27. Peters, *Islam and Colonialism*, 123.

28. Abedi and Legenhausen, *Jihad and Shahadat*, 110–11. The comments referred to were made in the course of a lecture by Ayatollah Mutahhari on "Defense—the Essence of Jihad." Fighting countries that present obstacles to the propagation of Islam is in his view not only defensive but is in the cause of right and freedom of humanity. Ibid., 109–13.

29. See, for example, Frederick Snyder and Surakiart Sathirathai, eds., *Third World Attitudes toward International Law* (Dordrecht: Martinus Nijhoff, 1987).

30. This is the general theme of Charnay's book, *L'Islam et la guerre* and is discussed specifically there, 48–55.

31. In contrast, in serious attempts to establish the rationales and legal defenses for their military actions, both resorted to arguments based on public international law and each accused the other of violating public international law. Examples of positions taken by the Iranian and Iraqi representatives were presented at a Princeton conference on the war. See Ali Dessouki, ed., *The Iraq Iran War: Issues of Conflict and Prospects for Settlement* ([Princeton]: Center of International Studies, Woodrow Wilson School of Public and International Affairs, Princeton University, 1981). Government spokespersons in the course of wars have a tendency to appeal to religious symbolism, and Muslim political leaders are no exception in this regard. One sees that *jihad* is regularly used by Muslim politicians, though they often apply it to circumstances where it does not fit. It becomes, therefore, essential to distinguish between operational legal norms and politically inspired rhetoric.

32. Rajaee, *Islamic Values*, 79–81.

33. Ibid., 87.

34. See, for example, the General Assembly Resolution 2649(XXV) (1970) affirming "the legitimacy of the struggle of peoples under colonial and alien domination" and "the legality of the people's struggle for self-determination and liberation from colonial and foreign domination and alien subjugation," with special mention of the Palestinian people, among some others. As will be discussed, this struggle may involve warfare.

35. A discussion of the connotation of the term *taghut* in the contemporary Iranian scene is offered by Khomeini's erstwhile ally and later nemesis, Ayatollah Taleghani. See Abedi and Legenhausen, *Jihad and Shahadat*, 51–53.

36. Rajaee, *Islamic Values*, 88. *Tawhidi* was a term widely used in Iran under Khomeini to denote what accorded with Islamic values and principles.

37. Ibid., 89.

38. Does a state like Iran possess the authority to initiate the *jihad*? Opinions will differ. Khomeini was officially referred to in Iran as "the Imam" and made a statement to the effect that the authority of Iran's Islamic government should be considered "tantamount to a total vice-regency from God" bestowed upon the Prophet Muhammad. See the statement of January 7, 1988, in which Khomeini expressly corrected President Ali Khamene‘i's interpretation of the limits of Islamic government. The latter was said to have erred in saying that "the government has jurisdiction within the framework of divine injunctions." Instead, Khomeini argued,"The government, which is part of the total vice-regency of the prophet of God (PBUH), is one of the foremost injunctions of Islam and has priority over all the other secondary injunctions, even prayers, fasting, and the *hajj*." In accord with the "interests of Islam and the country," the government has "complete vice-regency." The broadcast of the statement is reported in FBIS-NES-88-004, January 7, 1988, 49–51. This could be taken to mean that Khomeini, as Iran's leader, would possess the authority to conduct a *jihad*.

39. Rajaee, *Islamic Values*, 82–83.

40. FBIS-NES-88-140, July 21, 1988, 44–45, 47.

41. Peters, *Islam and Colonialism*, 130–33.

42. Johannes J. G. Jansen, *The Neglected Duty: The Creed of Sadat's Assassins and Islamic Resurgence in the Middle East* (New York: Macmillan, 1986), 193.

43. Ibid., 195–96.

44. Ibid., 167–68.

45. Ibid., 193.

46. Useful review of the issues and debates in this area is presented in John Dugard, *Recognition and the United Nations* (Cambridge: Grotius, 1987); and Malcolm Shaw, "The International Status of National Liberation Movements," in *Third World Attitudes toward International Law*, 141–55.

47. This is noted in Antonio Cassese, "Return to Westphalia? Consideration of the Gradual Erosion of the Charter System," in *The Current Legal Regulation of the Use of Force*, 513; Shaw, "International Status of National Liberation Movements," 141–55; and Moinuddin, *Charter of the Islamic Conference*, 32–34.

48. Bert V. A. Roeling, "The 1974 U.N. Definition of Aggression," in *The Current Legal Regulation of the Use of Force*, 407.

49. Rosalyn Higgins, "The Attitude of Western States," in *The Current Legal Regulation of the Use of Force*, 448–50. The topic is also covered in two other chapters in the same edited collection: Antonio Tanca, "The Prohibition of Force in the U.N. Declaration of Friendly Relations of 1970," 407–12, and Roeling, "1974 U.N. Definition of Aggression," 418.

50. Cassese, "Return to Westphalia?" 511.

51. Roeling, "1974 U.N. Definition of Aggression," 418; Cassese, "Return to Westphalia?" 510.

52. Dugard, *Recognition and the United Nations*, 123–24; Shaw, "International Status of National Liberation Movements," 150–51.

53. Examples of such views are discussed in James Piscatori, *Islam in a World of Nation States* (Cambridge: Cambridge University Press, 1986), 106, 109, 113. A particularly striking example of the hostility of Muslim conservatives to the

nation-state can be seen in the strong opposition of Abul Ala Mawdudi, the influential Islamic fundamentalist from the subcontinent, and his allies to the foundation of Pakistan on the grounds that such a political entity violated Islamic precepts. See Masudul Hasan, *Sayyid Abul A'ala Maududi and His Thought*, vol. 1 (Lahore: Islamic Publications, 1984), 249.

54. For example, this is the position taken by the eminent scholar of Islamic law and professor of law at the University of Cairo, Muhammad Abu Zahra, in *Al-'Alaqat al-dawliya fi al-islam* (Cairo: Dar al-qawmiya li al-tiba'a wa al-nashr, 1964), 47; al-Ghunaimi, *Muslim Conception*, 61–70, 195; al-Zuhaili, *Al-'Alaqat*, 18.

55. See, for example, Abu Atlah, *Al-Islam*, 106–8.

56. Piscatori, *Islam in a World of Nation States*, 86.

57. Ibid., 87.

58. Yaqut, *Al-Shakhsiya*, 4 [English section].

59. Ibid., 7–9 [English section], 482–85 [Arabic section].

60. Ibid., 707–8 [Arabic section]. In fact, subsequent to the publication of Yaqut's book, the PLO has won considerable status and recognition under international law.

61. Moinuddin, *Charter of the Islamic Conference*, 90.

62. The relevant sections of the charter are published ibid., 186–87.

63. The opinion is set forth in Western Sahara Advisory Opinion, I.C.J. Reports 1975.

64. Western Sahara Advisory Opinion, I.C.J. Pleadings 1982, 4:489, 5:305.

65. Ibid., 5:304.

66. Ibid., 4:171–72.

67. Ibid., 4:171–76.

68. Ibid., 5:292–99, 368–70.

69. Ibid., 4:357, 368, 371–72.

70. Nels Johnson, *Islam and the Politics of Meaning in Palestinian Nationalism* (London: Kegan Paul, 1982), 27, 40–45, 54–56.

71. Ibid., 74–75.

72. Charnay, *L'Islam et la guerre*, 109. It is noteworthy that the conference did not call for a *jihad* against the Soviet forces in Afghanistan, but only for the withdrawal of foreign troops.

73. Nels Johnson, *Islam and the Politics of Meaning*, 57.

74. Ibid., 65.

75. Peters, *Islam and Colonialism*, 134.

76. One might see certain parallels here between the deconfessionalization of *jihad* and James Turner Johnson's observations of how in Western civilization "the ideological value base for just war ideas had shifted from the religious— the church's notion of 'divine law'—to a secular concept of natural law." This remark from Johnson's *Just War Tradition and the Restraint of War* (Princeton: Princeton University Press, 1981) is quoted in the introduction to Abedi and Legenhausen, *Jihad and Shahadat*, 6. It is worth noting that Johnson is quoted in the context of a section of a book on the Islamic treatment of *jihad* that includes interesting comparisons of aspects of the Christian and Islamic traditions on war as well as some discussion of just war.

77. DeLupis, *Law of War*, 21.

78. Ibid., 23.

79. Marshall Hodgson, *The Order of Assassins: The Struggle of the Early Nizari Isma'ilis against the Islamic World* (The Hague: Mouton, 1955).

80. Robin Wright, *Sacred Rage: The Wrath of Militant Islam* (New York: Simon and Schuster, 1986), 94–95.

Select Bibliography

Abbott, Walter M., ed. *The Documents of Vatican II*. New York: Guild Press/America Press/Association Press, 1966.

Abedi, Mehdi, and Gary Legenhausen, eds. *Jihad and Shahadat: Struggle and Martyrdom in Islam*. Houston: Institute for Research and Islamic Studies, 1986.

Abel, Armand. "Changements politiques et littérature eschatologique dans le monde musulman." *Studia Islamica* 2 (1954): 23–43.

Abu Atlah, Khadija Ahmad. *Al-Islam wa al-ʾalaqat al-dawliya fi al-silm wa al-harb*. Cairo: Dar al-maʿarif, 1983.

Abu Daʾud Sulayman ibn al-Ashʿath al-Sijistani al-Azdi. *Sunan Abi Daʾud*. Edited by Muhammad Muhyi al-Din ʿAbd al-Hamid. N.p. [Beirut?]: Dar al-Fikr, n.d.

Abu Zahra, Muhammad. *Al-ʾAlaqat al-dawliya fi al-islam*. Cairo: Dar al-qawmiya li al-tibaʾa wa al-nashr, 1964.

Adas, Michael. *Prophets of Rebellion: Millenarian Protest Movements against the European Colonial Order*. Chapel Hill: University of North Carolina Press, 1979.

Aho, James A. *Religious Mythology and the Art of War: Comparative Religious Symbolisms of Military Violence*. Contributions to the Study of Religion, no. 3. Westport, Conn.: Greenwood Press, 1981.

Alexander, Paul J. *The Byzantine Apocalyptic Tradition*. Berkeley: University of California Press, 1985.

———. "Medieval Apocalypses as Historical Sources." *American Historical Review* 73 (1968): 997–1018.

———. *The Oracle of Baalbek: The Tiburtine Sibyl in Greek Dress*. Washington, D.C.: Dumbarton Oaks, 1967.

———. *Religious and Political History and Thought in the Byzantine Empire*. London: Variorum, 1978.

ʿAli, Abdullah Yusuf, trans. *Holy Qurʾan: Text, Translation, and Commentary*. 3d ed. 2 vols. Cairo: Dar al-Kitab al-Masri; Beirut: Dar al-Kitab al-Lubnani, n.d.

Almagro, Martin, Luis Caballero, Juan Zozaya, and Antonio Almagro. *Qusayr 'Amra*. Madrid: Instituto Hispano-Arabe de Cultura, 1975.

Ambrose. *Of the Duties of the Clergy*. In *A Select Library of Nicene and Post-Nicene Fathers*, edited by Philip Schaff and Henry Wace, 2d ser., 10: 1–89. New York: Christian Literature Co.; Oxford and London: Parker and Co., 1896.

Ames, William. *Conscience, with the Power and Cases Thereof*. Amsterdam: Theatrum Orbis Terrarum; Norwood, N.J.: W. J. Johnson, 1975.

Al-Ansari al-Awsi, 'Umar ibn Ibrahim. *Tafrij al-kurub fi tadbir al-hurub: A Muslim Manual of War*. Edited and translated by George T. Scanlon. Cairo: American University at Cairo Press, 1961.

Aquinas, St. Thomas. *Aquinas: Selected Political Writings*. Edited by A. P. D'Entrèves. Translated by J. G. Dawson. Oxford: Blackwell, 1948.

Arazi, Albert, and 'Amikam El'ad. "«L'Épitre à l'armée.» Al-Ma'mun et la seconde da'wa." Part 1. *Studia Islamica* 66 (1987): 27–70.

Arberry, Arthur J. *The Koran Interpreted*. New York: Macmillan, 1955.

Ashcraft, Richard. *Revolutionary Politics and Locke's Two Treatises of Government*. Princeton: Princeton University Press, 1986.

Auerbach, Erich. *Mimesis: The Representation of Reality in Western Literature*. Translated by Willard R. Trask. Princeton: Princeton University Press, 1953.

Augustine. *The City of God*. Translated by M. Dods. New York: Modern Library, 1950.

———. *The Political Writings of St. Augustine*. Edited by Henry Paolucci. Chicago: Regnery Gateway, 1962.

Ayala, Balthasar. *De Jure et Officiis Bellicis et Disciplina Militari*. Duaci: Ioannes Bogardi, 1582.

Bainton, Roland H. *Christian Attitudes toward War and Peace: A Historical Survey and Critical Re-evaluation*. Nashville, Tenn.: Abingdon Press, 1960.

———. "Congregationalism and the Puritan Revolution from the Just War to the Crusade." In *Studies on the Reformation*. Boston: Beacon Press, 1963.

Balmer, Randall. *Mine Eyes Have Seen the Glory*. New York and Oxford: Oxford University Press, 1989.

Barber, Richard W. *The Knight and Chivalry*. New York: Charles Scribner's Sons, 1970.

Barkun, Michael. *Law without Sanctions: Order in Primitive Societies and the World Community*. New Haven: Yale University Press, 1968.

Beeston, A.F.L. *Warfare in Ancient South Arabia (2nd–3rd Centuries A.D.)*. Qahtan: Studies in Old South Arabian Epigraphy, no. 3. London: Luzac, 1976.

Berger, A. "Encyclopedic Dictionary of Roman Law." *Transactions of the American Philosophical Society* 43 (1953): 333–809.

Best, Geoffrey. *Humanity in Warfare*. New York: Columbia University Press, 1980.

Blichfeldt, Jan-Olaf. *Early Mahdism*. Leiden: E. J. Brill, 1985.

Blum, Wilhelm, translator and commentator. *Byzantinische Fürstenspiegel*. Stuttgart: Hiersemann, 1981.

Boisard, Marcel. "On the Probable Influences of Islam on Western Public and International Law." *International Journal of Middle Eastern Studies* 11 (1980): 429–50.

Bonet, Honoré. *The Tree of Battles of Honoré Bonet*. Cambridge, Mass.: Harvard University Press, 1949.

Born, Lester K. *The Education of a Christian Prince by Desiderius Erasmus*. New York: Octagon Books, 1965.

Bossuet, Jacques-Bénigne. *Discourse on Universal History*, trans. Elborg Forster and ed. Orest Ranum. Chicago: University of Chicago Press, 1976.

Boyce, Mary, trans. *The Letter of Tansar*. Rome: Istituto Italiano per il Medio ed Estremo Oriente, 1968.

Brandon, S.G.F. *Jesus and the Zealots: A Study of the Political Factor in Primitive Christianity*. New York: Charles Scribner's Sons, 1967.

Brierly, J. L. *The Law of Nations*. Ed. Sir Humphrey Waldcock. 5th ed. Oxford: Oxford University Press, 1955.

Brockelmann, Carl. *Geschichte der arabischen Litteratur*. Rev. ed. 3 vols. Leiden: E. J. Brill, 1943–49.

Bulliet, Richard W. *The Patricians of Nishapur: A Study in Medieval Islamic Social History*. Cambridge, Mass.: Harvard University Press, 1972.

Burton, John. *The Collection of the Qur'an*. Cambridge: Cambridge University Press, 1977.

Cadoux, C. John. *The Early Christian Attitude to War*. New York: Seabury Press, 1982.

Canard, Marius. "La guerre sainte dans le monde islamique et dans le monde chrétien." *Revue Africaine* 79 (1936): 605–23.

Casanova, Paul. *Mohammed et la fin du monde: Étude critique sur l'Islam primitif*. 2 vols. Paris: Paul Geuthner, 1911–24.

Cassese, Antonio. "Return to Westphalia? Consideration of the Gradual Erosion of the Charter System." In *The Current Legal Regulation of the Use of Force*, edited by A. Cassese. Dordrecht: Martinus Nijhoff, 1986.

Chadwick, Henry. *The Early Church*. Harmondsworth: Penguin, 1967.

Charles, R. H., trans. *The Book of Enoch*. London: SPCK, 1917.

Charnay, Jean-Paul. *L'Islam et la guerre*. Paris: Fayard, 1986.

Childress, James F. *Moral Responsibility in Conflicts*. Baton Rouge: Louisiana State University Press, 1982.

Clancy, Martin J. "Rules of Land Warfare during the War of the American Revolution." *World Polity* 2 (1960): 203–317.

Clement of Alexandria. *Paedagogus*. In *The Ante-Nicene Fathers*, edited by Alexander Roberts and James Donaldson, 2:207–298. Buffalo, N.Y.: Christian Literature Publishing Co., 1885.

———. *Stromata*. In *The Ante-Nicene Fathers*, edited by Alexander Roberts and James Donaldson, 2:199–568. Buffalo, N.Y.: Christian Literature Publishing Co., 1885.

Cohn, Norman. *The Pursuit of the Millennium: Revolutionary Millenarians and Mystical Anarchists of the Middle Ages*. Rev. ed. New York: Oxford University Press, 1970.

Conrad, Lawrence I. "The Plague in the Early Medieval Near East." Ph.D. diss., Princeton University, 1981.

———. "Portents of the Hour: History and Hadith in the First Century A.H." *Der Islam* (forthcoming).

Contamine, Philippe. *War in the Middle Ages*. Oxford: Basil Blackwell, 1984.

Craigie, Peter C. *The Problem of War in the Old Testament*. Grand Rapids, Mich.: Eerdmans, 1978.

Cromwell, Oliver. *The Writings and Speeches of Oliver Cromwell*. Edited by W. C. Abbott. 4 vols. Cambridge, Mass.: Harvard University Press, 1937–1947.

Crone, Patricia. *Slaves on Horses: The Evolution of the Islamic Polity*. Cambridge: Cambridge University Press, 1977.

Crone, Patricia, and Michael Cook. *Hagarism*. Cambridge: Cambridge University Press, 1977.

Curran, Charles E. *Politics, Medicine, and Christian Ethics: A Dialogue with Paul Ramsey*. Philadelphia, Pa.: Fortress Press, 1973.

Danish'pazhuh, Muhammad Taqi, ed. *Bahr al-fava'id*. Tehran: B.T.N.K., 1345 solar A.H./1966 C.E.

Deane, Herbert. *The Political and Social Ideas of St. Augustine*. New York: Columbia University Press, 1963.

Delbrück, Hans. *History of the Art of War within the Framework of Political History*. 4 vols. Westport, Conn.: Greenwood Press, 1975–85.

DeLupis, Ingrid. *The Law of War*. Cambridge: Cambridge University Press, 1987.

Dennis, George, trans. *Maurice's Strategikon*. Philadelphia: University of Pennsylvania Press, 1984.

————, ed. and trans. *Three Byzantine Military Treatises*. Washington, D.C.: Dumbarton Oaks, 1985.

Dessouki, Ali, ed. *The Iraq Iran War: Issues of Conflict and Prospects for Settlement*. [Princeton]: Center of International Studies, Woodrow Wilson School of Public and International Affairs, Princeton University, 1981.

Dietl, Wilhelm. *Holy War*. Translated by Martha Humphreys. New York: Macmillan, 1984.

Donner, Fred McGraw. *The Early Islamic Conquests*. Princeton: Princeton University Press, 1981.

Draper, G.I.A.D. "The Interaction of Christianity and Chivalry in the Historical Development of the Law of the War." *International Review of the Red Cross* 5 (1965): 18–19.

Dugard, John. *Recognition and the United Nations*. Cambridge: Grotius, 1987.

Eco, Umberto. *A Theory of Semiotics*. Bloomington: Indiana University Press, 1976.

Edwards, George R. *Jesus and the Politics of Violence*. New York: Harper and Row, 1972.

Encyclopaedia of Islam. 1st ed. Edited by M. T. Houtsma et al. Leiden: E. J. Brill, 1913–34. Supplement to the first ed. Leiden: E. J. Brill, 1938. 2d ed. Edited by H.A.R. Gibb et al. Leiden: E. J. Brill, 1960–.

Eppstein, John. *The Catholic Tradition of the Law of Nations*. Washington, D.C.: Carnegie Endowment for International Peace and The Catholic Association for International Peace, 1935.

Erasmus, Desiderius. *Julius exclusus*. Translated by Paul Pascal and edited by J. Kelley Sowards. Bloomington: Indiana University Press, 1968.

Fadlallah, Muhammad Husayn. *Al-Islam wa-mantiq al-quwwat*. Beirut: Dar al-Islamiya, 1981.

Ferguson, John. *War and Peace in the World's Religions*. New York: Oxford University Press, 1978.

Ferguson, R. Brian, and Leslie E. Farragher. *The Anthropology of War: A Bibliography*. New York: Harry Frank Guggenheim Foundation, 1988.

Fohrer, G. *Geschichte der israelitischen Religion*. Berlin: De Gruyter, 1969.

Ford, Gerald F. "Renunciation of Certain Uses in War of Chemical Herbicides and Riot Control Agents." *Federal Register* 40 (April 10, 1975): 16187.

Frankena, William. "Is Morality Logically Dependent on Religion?" In *Religion and Morality*, edited by Gene Outka and John P. Reeder, Jr. Garden City, N.Y.: Doubleday Anchor, 1973.

Freedman, David Noah. "The Flowering of Apocalyptic." *Journal for Theology and the Church* 6(1968): 166–74.

Fuller, J.F.C. *The Conduct of War, 1789–1961*. New Brunswick, N.J.: Rutgers University Press, 1961.

Gaube, Heinz. *Ein arabischer Palast in Südsyrien, Hirbet el-Baida*. Beirut: Orient-Institut der deutschen morgenländischen Gesellschaft, in Kommission bei Franz Steiner Verlag, Wiesbaden, 1974.

Geertz, Clifford. *Islam Observed: Religious Development in Morocco and Indonesia*. Chicago: University of Chicago Press, 1971.

———. "Religion as a Cultural System." In *Anthropological Approaches to the Study of Religion*, edited by Michael Banton. A.S.A. Monographs, 3. London: Tavistock Publications, 1966.

Gewirth, Alan. *Marsilius of Padua: The Defender of Peace*. Vol. 1, *Marsilius of Padua and Medieval Political Philosophy*, and vol. 2, *The Defensor Pacis*. New York: Columbia University Press, 1951–56.

Ghirshman, Roman. *Persian Art, Parthian and Sassanian Dynasties, 249 B.C.–A.D. 651*. New York: Golden Press, 1962.

al-Ghunaimi, Mohammed. *The Muslim Conception of International Law and the Western Approach*. The Hague: Nijhoff, 1968.

Gibb, Hamilton A. R. "The Social Significance of the Shuubiya." In *Studies on the Civilization of Islam*, edited by Stanford J. Shaw and William R. Polk. London: Routledge and Kegan Paul, 1962.

Gilsenan, Michael. *Recognizing Islam: Religion and Society in the Modern Arab World*. New York: Pantheon Books, 1982.

Girard, René. *Violence and the Sacred*. Translated by Patrick Gregory. Baltimore: Johns Hopkins University Press, 1977.

Goffman, Erving. *Frame Analysis: An Essay on the Organization of Experience*. Cambridge, Mass.: Harvard University Press, 1974.

Goldziher, Ignaz. *Muhammedanische Studien*. 2 vols. Halle: Max Niemeyer, 1889–90. English translation: *Muslim Studies*. Translated by S. M. Stern. London: George Allen and Unwin, 1967–71.

Good, Robert M. "The Just War in Ancient Israel." *Journal of Biblical Literature* 104 (1985): pp. 385–400.

Grabar, André. *L'Empereur dans l'art byzantin*. Publications de la Faculté des lettres de l'Université de Strasbourg, fascicule 75. Paris: Les Belles Lettres, 1936.

Graham, William A. *Beyond the Written Word: Oral Aspects of Scripture in the History of Religion*. Cambridge: Cambridge University Press, 1987.

Gratian. *Decretum*. In *Corpus Juris Canonici*. Vol. 1. Edited by A. Friedberg. Leipzig: Tauchnitz, 1879.

Greenspan, Morris. *The Modern Law of Land Warfare*. Berkeley: University of California Press, 1959.

Grohmann, Adolf. "Greek Papyri of the Early Islamic Period in the Collection of the Archduke Rainer." *Études de papyrologie* 8 (1957): 5–40.

Grotius, Hugo. *De Jure Belli ac Pacis Libri Tres*. Translated by Francis W. Kelsey. Oxford: Clarendon Press, 1925.

Hamerton-Kelly, R. G., ed. *Violent Origins: Walter Burkert, Rene Girard, and Jonathan Z. Smith on Ritual Killing and Cultural Formation*. Stanford, Calif.: Stanford University Press, 1987.

Hamidullah, Muhammad. *The Muslim Conduct of State*. 5th ed. Lahore: Sh. Muhammad Ashraf, 1968.

Harnack, Adolf von. *Militia Christi*. Philadelphia: Fortress Press, 1981.

Hartigan, Richard Shelly. "St. Augustine on War and Killing: The Problem of the Innocent." *Journal of the History of Ideas* 27 (1966): 195–204.

Hasan, Masudul. *Sayyid Abul A'ala Maududi and His Thought*. Vol. 1. Lahore: Islamic Publications, 1984.

Hauerwas, Stanley. *Against the Nations*. Minneapolis: Winston Press, 1985.

Haug, Martin, and E. W. West, trans. *The Book of Arda Viraf*. Bombay: Government Central Book Depot; London: Trübner, 1872.

Heffter, August Wilhelm. *Le Droit international de l'Europe*. Translated by Jules Bergson. 3d French rev. ed. Berlin: Schroeder Librairie, 1973.

Helgeland, John, Robert J. Daly, and J. Patout Burns. *Christians and the Military: The Early Experience*. Philadelphia: Fortress Press, 1985.

Higgins, Rosalyn. "The Attitude of Western States towards Legal Aspects of the Use of Force." In *The Current Legal Regulation of the Use of Force*, edited by A. Cassese. Dordrecht: Martinus Nijhoff, 1986.

Hodgson, Marshall. *The Order of Assassins: The Struggle of the Early Nizari Isma'ilis against the Islamic World*. The Hague: Mouton, 1955.

———. *The Venture of Islam: Conscience and History in a World Civilization*. 3 vols. Chicago: University of Chicago Press, 1974.

Hollenbach, J. David, S.J. "Ethics in Distress." In *The Nuclear Dilemma and the Just War Tradition*, edited by William V. O'Brien and John Langan, S.J. Lexington, Mass. and Toronto: Lexington Books, 1986.

Howard, Sir Michael. *War and the Liberal Conscience*. Oxford: Oxford University Press, 1978.

Ibn Manzur, Muhammad ibn Makram. *Lisan al-'Arab*. 15 vols. Beirut: Dar Sadir, n.d.

Inalcik, Halil. *The Ottoman Empire*. New York and Washington, D.C.: Praeger, 1973.

———. "Ottoman Methods of Conquest." *Studia Islamica* 2 (1954): 103–29.

Izutsu, Toshihiko. *Ethico-religious Concepts in the Qur'an*. Montreal: McGill University Press, 1966.

Jansen, Johannes J. G. *The Neglected Duty: The Creed of Sadat's Assassins and Islamic Resurgence in the Middle East*. New York: Macmillan, 1986.

Johnson, James Turner. *Can Modern War Be Just?* New Haven: Yale University Press, 1984.

———. *Ideology, Reason, and the Limitation of War: Religious and Secular Concepts, 1200–1740*. Princeton: Princeton University Press, 1975.

————. *Just War Tradition and the Restraint of War*. Princeton: Princeton University Press, 1981.

————. *The Quest for Peace*. Princeton: Princeton University Press, 1987.

Johnson, Nels. *Islam and the Politics of Meaning in Palestinian Nationalism*. London: Kegan Paul, 1982.

Jomier, Jacques. *The Bible and the Koran*. Translated by Edward P. Arbez. New York: Desclee, 1964.

Kaegi, Walter Emil, Jr. *Byzantium and the Decline of Rome*. Princeton: Princeton University Press, 1968.

————. *Byzantium and the Early Islamic Conquests*. Forthcoming.

————. "Initial Byzantine Reactions to the Arab Conquest." *Church History* 38 (1969): 139–49.

Keen, M. H. *The Laws of War in the Late Middle Ages*. London: Routledge and Kegan Paul; Toronto: University of Toronto Press, 1965.

Kelsay, John. "Religion, Morality, and the Governance of War: The Case of Classical Islam." *Journal of Religious Ethics* 18, no. 2 (Fall 1990): 123–39.

Kepel, Gilles. *Muslim Extremism in Egypt: The Prophet and Pharaoh*. Berkeley: University of California Press, 1985.

Khadduri, Majid. "International Law." In *Law in the Middle East*. Vol. 1. Edited by Majid Khadduri and Herbert J. Liebesny. Washington, D.C.: Middle East Institute, 1955.

————. *The Islamic Law of Nations: Shaybani's Siyar*. Baltimore: Johns Hopkins Press, 1966.

————. *War and Peace in the Law of Islam*. Baltimore: Johns Hopkins Press, 1955.

Kohlberg, Etan. "The Development of the Imami Shiʿi Doctrine of Jihad." *Zeitschrift der Deutschen Morgenlaendischen Gesellschaft* 126 (1976): 64–86.

Lambton, Ann K. S. "Islamic Mirrors for Princes." In *Atti del convegno internazionale sul tema: La Persia nel Medioevo*. Problemi attuali di scienza e di cultura, quaderno no. 160. Rome: Accademia nazionale dei Lincei, 1971.

Lammers, Stephen E. "Approaches to Limits on War in Western Just War Tradition." In *Cross, Crescent, and Sword: The Justification and Limitation of War in Western and Islamic Tradition*, edited by James Turner Johnson and John Kelsay. Westport, Conn.: Greenwood Press, 1990.

Landes, Richard. "Lest the Millennium Be Fulfilled: Apocalyptic Expectations and the Pattern of Western Chronography, 100–800 C.E.." In *The Use and Abuse of Eschatology in the Middle Ages*, edited by Werner Verbeke, Daniel Verhelst, and Andries Welkenhuysen. Leuven: Leuven University Press, 1988.

Langan, John. "Just War Theory and Decisionmaking in a Democracy." *Naval War College Review* 38 (1985): 67–79.

————. "Violence and Injustice in Society in Recent Catholic Teaching." *Theological Studies* 46 (1985): 685–99.

Lawrence, Bruce B. *Defenders of God: The Fundamentalist Revolt against the Modern Age*. San Francisco: Harper and Row, 1989.

Lewis, Bernard. *The Political Language of Islam*. Chicago: University of Chicago Press, 1988.

Lewy, Guenter. *America in Vietnam*. New York: Oxford University Press, 1978.

Little, David. "Some Justifications for Violence in the Puritan Revolution." *Harvard Theological Review* 65 (1972): 577–89.

Locke, John. *Two Treatises of Civil Government*. London: J. M. Dent and Sons; New York: E. P. Dutton and Co., 1924.

Loeffler, Reinhold. *Islam in Practice: Religious Beliefs in a Persian Village*. Albany: State University of New York Press, 1988.

Lowith, Karl. *Meaning in History*. Chicago: University of Chicago Press, 1950.

Lyall, Charles. *The Diwans of ʿAbid ibn al-Abras, of Asad, and ʿAmir ibn al-Tufail, of ʿAmir ibn Saʾsaʾa*. London: Luzac; Leiden: E. J. Brill, 1913.

———. *Translations of Ancient Arabian Poetry*. 2d ed. London: Williams and Norgate, 1930.

McCormick, Michael. *Eternal Victory: Triumphal Rulership in Late Antiquity, Byzantium, and the Early Medieval West*. Cambridge: Cambridge University Press; Paris: Editions de la Maison des sciences de l'homme, 1986.

McGinn, Bernard. *Visions of the End: Apocalyptic Traditions in the Middle Ages*. New York: Columbia University Press, 1979.

Mackenzie, Mary. *Plato on Punishment*. Berkeley: University of California Press, 1981.

Madelung, Wilferd. "Apocalyptic Prophecies in Hims in the Umayyad Age." *Journal of Semitic Studies* 31 (1986): 141–85.

———. *Religious Trends in Early Islamic Iran*. Columbia Lectures on Iranian Studies, no. 4. Albany, N.Y.: Bibliotheca Persica, 1988.

Mahmassani, Sobhi. "International Law in Light of Islamic Doctrine." *Academie de droit international, Recueil des cours* 117 (1966): 205–328.

Al-Mahmud, Ibrahim Mustafa. *Fi lʾharb ʾindal-ʿArab*. Damascus: Ministry of Culture and National Guidance, 1975.

Maimonides (Moses ben Maimon). *The Code of Maimonides* (*Mishneh Torah*). Book 14, *The Book of Judges*. New Haven: Yale University Press, 1949. Treatise 5, "The Laws of Kings and Their Wars."

Makdisi, George. *The Rise of Colleges: Institutions of Learning in Islam and the West*. Edinburgh: Edinburgh University Press, 1981.

Maricq, André. "Res Gestae Divi Saporis." *Syria* 35 (1958): 295–360.

Martin, Richard C. "Islamic Violence in Islam: Towards an Understanding of the Discourse on *Jihad* in Modern Egypt." In *Contemporary Research on Terrorism*, edited by Paul Wilkinson and A. M. Stewart. Aberdeen: Aberdeen University Press, 1987.

———. "Understanding the Qurʾan in Text and Context." *History of Religions* 21, no. 4 (1982): 361–84.

Martinez, Francisco Javier. "Eastern Christian Apocalyptic in the Early Muslim Period: Pseudo-Methodius and Pseudo-Athanasius." Ph.D. diss., Catholic University of America, 1985.

Mawqufati, Muhammad. *Sharh Multaqa al-abhur li-Ibrahim Halabi*. Istanbul, 1318 A.H. (1900–01 C.E.).

Millar, Fergus. "Government and Diplomacy in the Roman Empire during the First Three Centuries." *International History Review* 10 (1988): 345–77.

Moinuddin, Hasan. *The Charter of the Islamic Conference and Legal Framework of Economic Co-operation among its Member States*. Oxford: Clarendon Press, 1987.

Morrison, Cécile. *Catalogue des monnaies byzantines de la Bibliothèque nationale. 1. D'Anastase Ier à Justinien II (491–711).* Paris: Bibliothèque nationale, 1970.

Murray, John Courtney. *Morality and Modern War.* New York: Church Peace Union, 1959.

———. "Theology and Modern War." *Theological Studies* 20 (1959): 40–61.

———. *We Hold These Truths: Catholic Reflections on the American Proposition.* New York: Sheed and Ward, 1960.

Musil, Alois. *The Manners and Customs of the Rwala Bedouin.* New York: American Geographical Society, 1928.

Mutahhari, Murtaza. *Jihad: The Holy War of Islam and Its Legitimacy in the Quran.* Translated by Mohammad S. Tawheedi. Albany, Calif.: Moslem Student Association (Persian Speaking Group), n.d.

National Conference of Catholic Bishops. *The Challenge of Peace: God's Promise and Our Response: A Pastoral Letter on War and Peace.* Washington, D.C.: United States Catholic Conference, 1983.

Nelson, Kristina. *The Art of Reciting the Qur'an.* Austin: University of Texas Press, 1985.

Nizam al-Mulk. *The Book of Government; or, Rules for Kings: The Siyar al-muluk or Siyaset-nama of Nizam al-Mulk.* Translated by Hubert Darke. 2d ed. London: Henley, and Boston: Routledge and Kegan Paul, 1978.

Noth, Albrecht. "Heiliger Kampf (Gihad) gegen die 'Franken': Zur Position der Kreuzzüge im Rahmen der Islamgeschichte." *Saeculum* 37 (1986): 240–59.

———. *Heiliger Krieg und heiliger Kampf in Islam und Christentum.* Bonner historische Forschungen, Band 28. Bonn: Ludwig Röhrscheid, 1966.

O'Brien, William V. *The Conduct of Just and Limited War.* New York: Praeger, 1981.

———. "Legitimate Military Necessity in Nuclear War." *World Polity* 2 (1960): 35–120.

———. "The Meaning of 'Military Necessity' in International Law." *World Polity* 1 (1957): 109–76.

———. "Morality and War: The Contributions of Paul Ramsey." In *Love and Society: Essays in the Ethics of Paul Ramsey,* edited by James Johnson and David Smith. Missoula, Mont.: Scholars Press, 1974.

———. *Nuclear War, Deterrence, and Morality.* Westminster, Md.: Newman, 1967.

Ormsby, Eric L. *Theodicy in Islamic Thought: The Dispute over al-Ghazali's "Best of All Possible Worlds."* Princeton: Princeton University Press, 1984.

Osgood, Robert E. *Limited War.* Chicago: University of Chicago Press, 1957.

Overton, Richard. "An Appeal to the People." In *Puritanism and Liberty,* edited by A.S.P. Woodhouse. Chicago: University of Chicago Press, 1974.

Paret, Rudi, trans. *Der Koran.* 2 vols. Stuttgart: Kohlhammer, 1962–77.

———. "Die legendäre Futuh-Literatur, ein arabisches Volksepos?" In *Atti del convegno internazionale sul tema: La poesia epica e la sua formazione.* Problemi attuali di scienza e di cultura, quaderno no. 139. Rome: Accademia nazionale dei Lincei, 1970.

Paul, Robert S. *The Lord Protector: Religion and Politics in the Life of Oliver Cromwell.* Grand Rapids, Mich.: Eerdmans, 1964.

Peters, Rudolph. *Islam and Colonialism: The Doctrine of Jihad in Modern History.* The Hague: Mouton, 1979.

————. *Jihad in Mediaeval and Modern Islam*. Leiden: Brill, 1977.

Phillimore, Sir Robert Joseph. *Commentaries upon International Law*. 4 vols. 3d ed. London: Butterworth, 1879–86.

Phillips, Robert L. "Combatancy, Noncombatancy, and Noncombatant Immunity in Just War Theory." In *Cross, Crescent, and Sword: The Justification and Limitation of War in Western and Islamic Tradition*, edited by James Turner Johnson and John Kelsay. Westport, Conn.: Greenwood Press, 1990.

Pickthall, Mohammad Marmaduke, trans. *The Meaning of the Glorious Koran*. New York and Scarborough, Ontario: New American Library, n.d.

Pines, Shlomo. "A Note on an Early Meaning of the Term Mutakallim." *Israel Oriental Studies* 1 (1971): 224–40.

Pisan, Christine de. *The Book of Fayttes of Armes and of Chyvalrye*. London: Oxford University Press, 1932.

Piscatori, James. *Islam in a World of Nation States*. Cambridge: Cambridge University Press, 1986.

Planhol, Xavier de. *The World of Islam*. Translated by Cornell University Press. Ithaca, N.Y.: Cornell University Press, 1959.

Porch, Douglas. *The Conquest of Morocco*. New York: Alfred A. Knopf, 1983.

Rad, Gerhard von. *Der Heilige Krieg im Alten Israel*. Zurich: n.n., 1951.

Rahman, Fazlur. *Major Themes of the Qur'an*. Chicago and Minneapolis: Bibliotheca Islamica, 1980.

Rajaee, Farhang. *Islamic Values and World View: Khomeyni on Man, the State, and International Politics*. Lanham, Md.: University Press of America, 1983.

Ramsey, Paul. "The Just Revolution." *Worldview* 16, no. 10 (October 1973): 37.

————. *The Just War: Force and Political Responsibility*. New York: Charles Scribner's Sons, 1968.

————. *War and the Christian Conscience: How Shall Modern War Be Conducted Justly?* Durham, N.C.: Duke University Press, 1961.

Roeling, Bert V. A. "The 1974 U.N. Definition of Aggression." In *The Current Legal Regulation of the Use of Force*, edited by A. Cassese. Dordrecht: Martinus Nijhoff, 1986.

Rommen, Heinrich A. *The State in Catholic Thought*. St. Louis: Herder, 1945.

Rowley, H. H. *The Relevance of Apocalyptic*. Rev. ed. Greenwood, S.C.: Attic Press, 1980.

Russell, Frederick H. *The Just War in the Middle Ages*. Cambridge: Cambridge University Press, 1975.

Sachedina, Abdulaziz A. "The Development of *Jihad* in Islamic Revelation and History." In *Cross, Crescent, and Sword: The Justification and Limitation of War in Western and Islamic Tradition*, edited by James Turner Johnson and John Kelsay. Westport, Conn.: Greenwood Press, 1990.

Said, Edward W. "Opponents, Audiences, Constituencies, and Community." In *The Politics of Interpretation*, edited by W.J.T. Mitchell. Chicago: University of Chicago Press, 1983.

Al-Sanduq, ʿIzz al-Din. "Hajar Hafnat al-ʾUbayyid." *Sumer* 11 (1955): 213–17.

Sari Mehmed Pasha. *Ottoman Statecraft: The Book of Counsels for Vezirs and Governors (Nasaʾih ul-vüzera reʾl-ümera) of Sari Mehmed Pasha, the defterdar. of Sari Mehmed Pasha*. Tr. Walter Livingston Wright, Jr. London: H. Milford, Oxford University Press; Princeton: Princeton University Press, 1935.

Scharlemann, Robert P. "Theological Text." *Semeia* 39 (1987): 7.

Schindler, Dietrich, and Jiri Toman, eds. *The Laws of Armed Conflicts*. Leiden: A. W. Sijthoff; Geneva: Henry Dunant Institute, 1973.

Schmithals, Walter. *The Apocalyptic Movement*. Nashville, Tenn.: Abingdon Press, 1975.

Schwarzenberger, Georg. *A Manual of International Law*. 5th ed. London: Stevens and Sons, 1967.

Scott, James Brown. *The Spanish Origin of International Law*. Oxford: Clarendon Press; London: Humphrey Milford, 1934.

Shahid, Irfan. "The Kebra Nagast in the Light of Recent Research." *Le Muséon* 89 (1976): 133–78.

Shaw, Malcolm. "The International Status of National Liberation Movements." In *Third World Attitudes toward International Law: An Introduction*, edited by Frederick E. Snyder and Sirakiart Sathirathai. Dordrecht: Martinus Nijhoff, 1987.

Simocatta, Theophylact. *The History of Theophylact Simocatta*. Translated by Michael Whitby and Mary Whitby. Oxford: Clarendon Press, 1986.

Sivan, Emmanuel. "The Beginnings of the *Fada'il al-Quds* Literature." *Israel Oriental Studies* 1 (1971): 263–71.

———. *L'Islam et la croisade: Idéologie et propagande dans les réactions musulmans aux croisades*. Paris: Maisonneuve, 1968.

Smend, Rudolf. *Yahweh War and Tribal Confederation: Reflections upon Israel's Earliest History*. Translated by Max Gray Rogers. Nashville, Tenn.: Abingdon Press, 1970.

Smith, Jonathan Z. *Imagining Religion: From Babylon to Jonestown*. Chicago: University of Chicago Press, 1982.

Snyder, Frederick, and Surakiart Sathirathai, eds. *Third World Attitudes toward International Law: An Introduction*. Dordrecht: Martinus Nijhoff, 1987.

Sonn, Tamara. "Irregular Warfare and Terrorism in Islam." In *Cross, Crescent, and Sword: The Justification and Limitation of War in Western and Islamic Tradition*, edited by James Turner Johnson and John Kelsay. Westport, Conn.: Greenwood Press, 1990.

Stock, Brian. *The Implications of Literacy: Written Language and Models of Interpretation in the Eleventh and Twelfth Centuries*. Princeton: Princeton University Press, 1983.

Suarez, Francisco. *Selections from Three Works of Francisco Suarez, S.J.* Oxford: Clarendon Press; London: Humphrey Milford, 1944.

Sweet, Louise E. "Camel Raiding of North Arabian Bedouin: A Mechanism of Cultural Adaptation." *American Anthropologist* 67 (1965): 1132–50.

Al-Tabari, Muhammad ibn Jarir. *Ta'rikh al-rusul wal-muluk (Annales)*. Edited by M. J. de Goeje et al. 15 vols. Leiden: E. J. Brill, 1879–1901.

Tahir Bey, Bursali Mehmed. *Osmanli Müellifleri*. Istanbul: Meral, 1972.

Tanca, Antonio. "The Prohibition of Force in the U.N. Declaration of Friendly Relations of 1970." In *The Current Legal Regulation of the Use of Force*, edited by A. Cassese. Dordrecht: Martinus Nijhoff, 1986.

Thompson, Michael. *Rubbish Theory: The Creation and Destruction of Value*. Oxford: Oxford University Press, 1979.

U.S. Department of the Air Force. *International Law: The Conduct of Armed Conflict and Air Operations, 19 November 1976.* Air Force Pamphlet AFP 110–31. Washington, D.C.: Headquarters of the Air Force, 1976.

U.S. Department of the Army. *The Law of Land Warfare, July 1956.* FM 27-10. Washington, D.C.: Department of the Army, 1956.

Vanderpol, Alfred. *La Doctrine scolastique du droit de guerre.* Paris: Pedone, 1919.

Vattel, Emmerich de. *The Law of Nations; or, Principles of Natural Law.* Washington, D.C.: Carnegie Institution, 1916.

Verbeke, Werner, Daniel Verhelst, and Andries Welkenhuysen, eds. *The Use and Abuse of Eschatology in the Middle Ages.* Leuven: Leuven University Press, 1988.

Victoria, Franciscus de. *De Indis et De Jure Belli Relectiones.* Edited by Ernest Nys, and Translated by John Pawley Bate. Washington, D.C.: Carnegie Institution, 1917.

Volz, Paul. *Die Eschatologie der jüdischen Gemeinde im neutestamentlichen Zeitalter.* Tübingen: J.C.B. Mohr, 1934.

Waldman, Marilyn R. "The Popular Appeal of the Prophetic Paradigm in West Africa." *Contributions to Asian Studies* 17 (1982): 110–14.

———. *Toward a Theory of Historical Narrative: A Case Study in Perso-Islamicate Historiography.* Columbus: Ohio State University Press, 1980.

Walters, LeRoy Brandt, Jr. "Five Classic Just-War Theories: A Study in the Thought of Aquinas, Vitoria, Suarez, Gentili, and Grotius." Ph.D. diss., Yale University, 1971.

———. "The Just War and the Crusade: Antitheses or Analogies?" *Monist* 57, no. 4 (October 1973): 584–94.

Walzer, Michael. *Just and Unjust Wars.* New York: Basic Books, 1977.

———. *The Revolution of the Saints: A Study in the Origins of Radical Politics.* Cambridge, Mass.: Harvard University Press, 1965.

Wansbrough, John E. *Quranic Studies: Sources and Methods of Scriptural Interpretation.* Oxford: Oxford University Press, 1977.

Waugh, Earle H. *Peace as Seen in the Qur'an.* Ecumenical Institute, Occasional Papers 3. Tantur, Jerusalem: Ecumenical Institute, n.d.

Wensinck, Arent Jan. *A Handbook of Early Muhammadan Tradition.* Leiden: E. J. Brill, 1927.

Winch, Peter. "Understanding a Primitive Society." In *Rationality,* edited by Bryan Wilson. New York: Harper and Row, 1970.

Wright, Quincy. *A Study of War.* 2d ed. Chicago: University of Chicago Press, 1965.

———. "War. 1. The Study of War." In *International Encyclopedia of the Social Sciences,* 16:453–68. New York: Macmillan, 1968.

Wright, Robin. *Sacred Rage: The Wrath of Militant Islam.* New York: Simon and Schuster, 1986.

Yaqut, Muhammad Kamil. *Al-Shakhsiya al-dawliya fi al-qanun al-dawli al-'amm wa al-shari'a al-islamiya.* Cairo: 'Alam al-kutub, 1970–71.

Yoder, John Howard. *When War Is Unjust.* Minneapolis: Augsburg Publishing House, 1984.

Zampaglione, Gerardo. *The Idea of Peace in Antiquity.* Notre Dame, Ind.: University of Notre Dame Press, 1973.

Zuhaili, Wahba. *Al-'Alaqat al-dawliya fi al-islam muqarana bi al-qanun al-dawli al-hadith.* Beirut: Mu'assasat al-risala, 1981.

Index

About the Editors and Contributors

FRED M. DONNER is Associate Professor in the Oriental Institute and the Department of Near Eastern Languages and Civilizations at the University of Chicago. He is author of *The Early Islamic Conquests* (1981) and numerous articles on early Islamic history.

JAMES TURNER JOHNSON is Professor of Religious Studies and Director of International Programs at Rutgers University. His publications include *Just War Tradition and the Restraint of War* (1981) and *The Quest for Peace* (1987).

JOHN KELSAY is Associate Professor in the Department of Religion at Florida State University, where he teaches courses in ethics and Islamic Studies. He is coauthor of *Human Rights and the Conflict of Cultures* (1988), and author of several articles on Islamic approaches to war and peace.

JOHN LANGAN, S. J., is Joseph P. and Rose Kennedy Professor of Christian Ethics at Georgetown University, and is author of numerous articles on the ethics of war.

BRUCE LAWRENCE teaches Islamic Studies in the Department of Religion at Duke University, and is the author of *Defenders of God: The Fundamentalist Revolt Against the Modern Age* (1989).

DAVID LITTLE is Senior Scholar at the United States Institute for Peace in Washington, D.C. He is coauthor of *Human Rights and the Conflict of Cultures* (1988), and author of numerous articles in the field of religious ethics. He is currently working on a book dealing with the suspension of human rights in emergency conditions.

RICHARD C. MARTIN is Associate Professor in the Department of Religious Studies at Arizona State University. He is the author of *Islam: A Cultural Perspective* (1982), and editor for *Approaches to Islam in Religious Studies* (1985).

ANN ELIZABETH MAYER is Associate Professor in the Department of Legal Studies at the Wharton School, University of Pennsylvania. She has authored a number of articles and book chapters on topics in Islamic law, and is editor of *Property, Social Structure, and Law in the Modern Middle East* (1985). She is also the author of *Islam and Human Rights* (1991).

WILLIAM V. O'BRIEN is Professor in the Department of Government at Georgetown University and specializes in the areas of international law and international organizations. He is author of *The Conduct of Just and Limited War* (Praeger, 1981) and *Law and Morality in Israel's War with the PLO* (1991).